New Immigrants in New York

New Immigrants in New York

Edited by
Nancy Foner

COLUMBIA UNIVERSITY PRESS
New York

15366679

Library of Congress Cataloging-in-Publication Data

New immigrants in New York.

Includes bibliographies and index.
1. Immigrants—New York (N.Y.). 2. New York (N.Y.)—
Emigration and immigration. I. Foner, Nancy
F128.9.A1N38 1987   304.8'7471   87–6545
ISBN 0–231–06130–7

Columbia University Press
New York Guildford, Surrey
Copyright © 1987 Columbia University Press
All rights reserved

Printed in the United States of America

c 10 9 8 7 6 5 4 3 2

Clothbound editions of Columbia University Press
books are Smyth-sewn and printed on permanent
and durable acid-free paper.

Book design by Ken Venezio

Contents

Contributors

LINDA BASCH is a projects director with the United Nations Institute for Training and Research. She received her Ph.D. in anthropology from New York University. She has done extensive field work in Africa and the Caribbean and has also worked in Iran. Her research interests have included health care practices in Africa and Iran, race and ethnicity in the Caribbean, the implantation of transnational corporations in developing countries, and migration and development. More recently, she has explored and published on migrant women's organizations.

NANCY FONER, professor of anthropology at the State University of New York, Purchase, has done field research in rural Jamaica as well as among Jamaicans in New York and London. Her major publications include *Status and Power in Rural Jamaica: A Study of Educational and Political Change* (Teachers College Press, 1973), *Jamaica Farewell: Jamaican Migrants in London* (University of California Press, 1978), and *Ages in Conflict: A Cross-Cultural Perspective on Inequality Between Old and Young* (Columbia University Press, 1984).

ILLSOO KIM, an assistant professor of sociology at Drew University, received his Ph.D. from the Graduate Center of the City University of New York. He has done extensive field work among Koreans in New York and his publications include *The New Urban Immigrants: The Korean Community in New York* (Princeton University Press, 1981).

ELLEN PERCY KRALY is assistant professor of geography at Colgate University. Her Ph.D. in sociology from Fordham University was the beginning of her analysis of both federal and international statistics on immigration and emigration. A member of the National Academy of Sciences Panel on Immigration Statistics, her recent research and publications focus on systems of migration statistics as well as the relationship between immigration and population growth, trends in emigration from the United States, and the status of ethnic and racial minorities.

ADRIANA MARSHALL is professor of labor economics and senior researcher at the Facultad Latinoamericana de Ciencias Sociales (Latin American Faculty of Social Sciences) in Buenos Aires. She has done research on labor market and labor migration topics, including the social and economic impact of immigration in Western Europe, Latin America, and the United States. Her publications include *The Import of Labour* (Rotterdam University Press, 1973) and *The Labor Market in Peripheral Capitalism* (PISPAL—El Colegio de Mexico, 1981).

ANNELISE ORLECK is a Ph.D. candidate in history at New York University. She has been doing field work among Jewish immigrants in Brighton Beach since 1980 and is currently completing a book on the community, *Brighton Beach: A World Apart.* She also teaches history at the Elizabeth Seeger School in Manhattan.

PATRICIA R. PESSAR is research director of the Center for Immigration Policy and Refugee Assistance at Georgetown University. She received her Ph.D. in anthropology from the University of Chicago in 1976 and has done field work in Brazil, the Dominican Republic, and the United States. Her publications include numerous articles on Dominican migration to the United States. She is currently editing books on Dominican migration and international migration within the Americas.

SUSAN BUCHANAN STAFFORD, a program specialist with the Cuban/Haitian Resettlement Program, Department of Justice, Community Relations Service, received her Ph.D. in anthropology from New York University in 1980. She has conducted field research in Haiti and New York City and published numerous articles on Haitian immigrants in the United States.

BERNARD WONG, an associate professor of anthropology at San Francisco State University, has conducted field research in Manila, Lima (Peru), New York City, and Wisconsin. His publications include *A Chinese American Community* (Chopmen Publishers, Singapore, 1979), *Chinatown: Economic Adaptation and Ethnic Identity of the Chinese* (Holt, Rinehart and Winston, 1982), and *Patronage, Brokerage, Entrepreneurship and the Chinese Community of New York City* (AMS Press, 1984).

1. Introduction: New Immigrants and Changing Patterns in New York City

Nancy Foner

In the past two decades, more than a million immigrants have settled in New York City, most from the West Indies, Latin America, and Asia.[1] The collection of original essays in this volume examines and provides a new perspective on this recent massive immigration. It addresses two main questions: How have the new immigrants affected New York City? And, conversely, how has the move to New York influenced their lives?

The approach to the new immigration taken in this book is two-pronged: it combines "micro" and "macro" levels of analysis. Case studies explore the move to New York from the immigrants' viewpoint, analyzing the way New York has influenced their social and cultural worlds and the consequent emergence among them of new meanings and new patterns of behavior. The essays also demonstrate that the city itself has been deeply affected by the new immigrants. Their very presence in such large numbers has had a significant impact on a variety of social, economic, and cultural institutions in the city. In fact, there is a dialectical relationship or interplay between the two kinds of changes. As immigrants themselves change when they move to New York City, they affect the life of the city in special ways. And, as immigrants play a role in transforming New York City, this "new" New York, in turn, influences them.

The seven ethnographic essays in this collection deal with the experiences of a number of immigrant groups: Dominicans, Haitians, Jamaicans, Vincentians and Grenadians, Koreans, Chinese, and Soviet Jews. These groups were selected for several reasons. All of the case studies are based on in-depth research done in the last ten years, a type of research not yet available for many other new immigrant groups. The groups that are included illustrate the range and diversity of new immigrants in New York City and, with the exception of Vincentians and Grenadians, are among the most numerous new immigrant populations in the city. In fact, the Dominicans, Jamaicans, Chinese, and Haitians are, in order of size, the four largest groups of newcomers to New York City (New York City Department of City Planning n.d.).

Setting the stage for the ethnographic studies, a demographic essay by Ellen Kraly shows how immigration policy has influenced the number and types of new immigrants coming to New York and, in turn, how these immigrants have affected the demographic structure of the city. An essay by an economist, Adriana Marshall, examines the way newcomers have both influenced, and been influenced by, New York City's economy.

In this introductory essay, I set out a general framework for analyzing the interaction between new immigrants and the urban setting of New York. This allows us to place the material on particular immigrant groups in a wider perspective. It also points to certain common themes as well as differences among new immigrant populations and raises a number of theoretical issues that are important in immigration studies.

BACKGROUND ON THE NEW IMMIGRATION TO NEW YORK

New immigrants are usually considered to be those who have arrived since 1965, but it is not just their date of arrival that makes them different from "old" immigrants who came in record numbers at the turn of the century. "Old" immigrants were overwhelmingly European whereas today's new arrivals come mainly from the Third World, especially the West Indies, Latin America, and Asia. While immigrant males outnumbered females in every year but one between 1857 and 1929, more than half of the new legal immigrants are female (Houston et al. 1984). Unlike the "old" immigration, new arrivals include a significant proportion of illegal aliens as well as a higher percentage of professionals.

The most important factor ushering in the massive new immigration in recent years, as Ellen Kraly's essay makes clear, was the change in the United States immigration law in 1965 which abandoned the national origins quota system favoring northern and Western Europeans. Asians, who had been severely restricted from immigration, now had access to the 120,000 visas per year that were allocated to the Eastern Hemisphere, with a 20,000 per country limit. Natives of the English-speaking countries of the Caribbean, who had been subject to very small quotas for dependencies, were now included in the 120,000 ceiling for the Western Hemisphere (South and North America and the Caribbean), with a national limit of 20,000 added in 1976.[2] Spouses, children, and parents of U.S. citizens could enter without numerical limit. As the tables presented in Kraly's essay show, the New York metropolitan area witnessed a dramatic increase in immigration from Asia and the English-speaking Caribbean in the post-1965 years. According to the 1980 census, 80 percent of the Asian-born, 82 percent of the Jamaican-born, and 88 percent of the Trinidadian-born residents in the New York metropolitan area had arrived since 1965. The U.S. policy toward refugees in the past two decades has also permitted the large-scale admission of certain groups, the Soviet Jews and Cubans being especially prominent in the New York area.

Economic factors, of course, have also underpinned the large-scale immigration to New York in recent years: limited opportunities for the rapidly expanding population in Third World countries and the quest for steady employment, higher wages, and improved living standards in the United States (see Reimers 1985 for a recent analysis of the forces behind the new immigration to the United States).

Political factors in the sending countries are also important in many cases. Patricia Pessar in this volume notes that restrictive emigration policies in the Dominican Republic during the Trujillo era (1930–1960) made it extremely difficult for Dominicans to move to the United States; only after the dictator's death in 1961 did migration to this country become significant. Since 1961, economic motivation has propelled thousands to emigrate but, at various times, the experience or fear of political repression have also played a role. In the Haitian case, oppressive political as well as economic conditions under the regimes of François ("Papa Doc") and Jean-Claude ("Baby Doc") Duvalier underpinned the large movement to the United States in recent decades (see Stafford, this volume; Laguerre 1984). Political decisions in the Soviet Union have been crucial in the emigration of Soviet Jews, who were only allowed to emigrate in significant numbers after 1971; since 1981 the Soviet government has again curtailed emigration of Soviet Jews (see Orleck, this volume).

As in the past, New York City continues to be one of the major receiving centers for new immigrants in this country. (Los Angeles is now the other leading new immigrant city, with large numbers also settling in San Francisco, Chicago, Miami, and Houston.) New York City has a particular attraction for certain new immigrant groups, most notably those from the Caribbean and South America. Over half of the Barbadians, Trinidadians, Haitians, Jamaicans, and Guyanese; over three quarters of the Dominicans; and nearly half of the Ecuadorians and one third of the Colombians in the United States live in the New York metropolitan area (see Kraly, this volume). (Alternatively, less than 1 percent of the Mexicans in the United States—the largest immigrant group in the country—and less than 10 percent of the Japanese, Koreans, Filipinos, and Vietnamese live in the New York metropolitan area.)

→ The availability of employment opportunities in New York City, of course, draws new immigrants to the city. New York is also appealing because new immigrants do not stand out. The city has a tradition of immigration, with many different immigrant and racial groups living there. Some groups gravitate to New York in large numbers because of historical patterns of immigrant settlement. They feel a sense of security afforded by an established immigrant community and are attracted by the prospect of assistance from their fellow countrymen. Relatives who had already settled in New York sponsored, provided transportation, and arranged initial housing and jobs for many new immigrants. The emphasis on family reunification in recent U.S. immigration policy has reinforced and stimulated this kind of chain migration. Finally, the city itself has an image that draws certain immigrant groups. With large numbers of Caribbean immigrants in New York, the city has become, as Bryce-Laporte (1979:216) writes, the special object of the "dream, curiosity, sense of achievement, and drive for adventure" for many Caribbean people.

THE IMPACT OF NEW YORK CITY
ON NEW IMMIGRANTS

The move to New York City has a profound effect on the new immigrants, and their lives change in innumerable ways when they settle there. New York, as a major U.S. city, offers newcomers the economic opportunities of an advanced industrial society and exposes them to key values and institutions of "American" culture. But New York is special in many respects. That immigrants have settled there rather than, say, Los Angeles or Miami, influences them in particular ways. It is thus necessary to appreciate the role of New York as a specific urban context for the new immigrants in addition to considering the broader American setting. At the same time, their experience in New York is mediated by certain cultural beliefs and social practices the immigrants bring with them, as well as by other sociodemographic features of each immigrant group.

New York City as Context

In a symposium on "The City as Context" (*Urban Anthropology* 1975), several anthropologists stressed the importance of the unique features of particular cities in urban research. With regard to immigration, Jack Rollwagen (1975) criticized studies that implicitly assumed that the life of an immigrant group would be exactly the same regardless of the city in which they lived—what he called "the city is constant" argument. Rather, he suggested, there will be noticeable contrasts between immigrant groups from the same cultural background who settle in different American cities, if only because the size of the immigrant group and available opportunities in various cities diverge. In a specific comparison of recent Portuguese immigrants in two nearby New England cities, Estellie Smith (1975) argued that specific features in each city—including the history of Portuguese settlement and the contemporary ethnic structure—affected their experiences.

Ideally, to best understand the importance of the particular urban context for the immigrant experience we should compare similar immigrant populations in two or more cities. Yet even if we look at immigrant groups in only one city, as the essays in the present volume do, the "city as context" framework points to the way specific social and economic features of New York City affect the lives of new immigrants. A number of these features are, themselves, a product of the recent mass immigration.

New York stands out as the immigrant city par excellence in the United States. It served as the historic port of entry for several million immigrants early in the century and still attracts a major share of the nation's new arrivals. The census figures presented in Ellen Kraly's essay tell much of the story. Since 1900 more than 10 percent of the nation's foreign-born population has lived in New York City, with the figure at 12 percent in 1980. At the turn of the century, four out of ten New Yorkers were foreign-born. In 1980, after decades of steady decline, the proportion of immigrants stood at nearly a quarter of the city's population. Currently, few cities in the country have a comparable percentage of immigrants and only one, Miami, markedly surpasses New York in its share of foreign-born.

What is striking about New York City's immigrant population is not just the numbers but its extreme heterogeneity. New York is more ethnically diverse than other immigrant cities in the United States. Moreover, most of the different immigrant groups are represented in quite large numbers. Los Angeles's foreign-born population, for example, is overwhelmingly Mexican and Asian, with fewer Europeans and especially small proportions of West Indians and South Americans (see Kraly, this volume). In New York City, there are sizable numbers of nearly all European as well as most Asian, West Indian, and Latin American nationalities. New York's Hispanic residents— 20 percent of the population in 1980—include immigrants from the Caribbean and Central and South America as well as citizens from Puerto Rico. There is, moreover, an enormous native black population—altogether, in 1980, one out of every four New York City residents was black.

Ethnic diversity, as a result, is the expectation in New York—a fact of life, as it were. This is welcoming for many immigrants, although for some it can be confusing. Annelise Orleck recounts in her essay how Soviet Jewish teenagers in Brooklyn are confounded when they enter high school, wanting to know where the Americans are. In a telling quote, one teenager remarked: "It's hard to know what we are supposed to be becoming. Everybody here is from someplace else."

The large numbers of immigrants in so many groups, coupled with settlement patterns in the city, mean that New York neighborhoods provide a hospitable environment for most new arrivals. Immigrant settlements draw immigrants to the city in the first place, and they offer comfort and security to newcomers once they arrive—a kind of home away from home. Ethnic neighborhoods provide a basis for communal life. Formal associations are found in many immigrant neighborhoods, and shops, restaurants, and street corners are informal meeting places. Ethnic neighborhoods also provide economic opportunities in the form of clientele and, in some cases, workers for immigrant enterprises. Large immigrant concentrations have spawned small businesses that serve the needs of new arrivals, ranging from Soviet-style restaurants and pastry shops along Brighton Beach Avenue and Haitian and Jamaican bakeries and groceries in East Flatbush, to Korean beauty and barber shops in Flushing. In the case of Chinatown, the ethnic niche, as Bernard Wong terms it, not only provides consumption services but also the economic livelihood for most newcomers in Chinese-run restaurants, garment factories, and groceries (see his essay, this volume).

In general, the immigrant employment sector in New York City, consisting of enterprises organized and controlled by immigrants, has generated jobs for substantial numbers in certain groups. Responding to opportunities in the apparel industry, for example, many Dominicans, as well as the Chinese, have set up small garment factories that employ their compatriots (see Pessar's and Wong's essays, this volume; and Waldinger 1985). Small businesses established by recent Korean immigrants may well involve, either as owners or employees, nearly three quarters of employed Koreans in the New York metropolitan area. A high percentage of these small businesses cater to non-Koreans, and Illsoo Kim suggests that their proliferation in ghetto or transitional areas is due, in part, to a vacuum created by

the exodus of Jewish and Italian shopkeepers from these neighborhoods (see Kim, this volume).

These comments pertain to the larger question of how New York
City's economy shapes the employment possibilities open to new
immigrants. Despite high unemployment rates in recent years, New
York continues to be a city of opportunity for immigrants. Quite apart
from immigrant-owned firms, the low-wage manufacturing and service sectors in general have provided countless numbers of newcomers with jobs.

Manufacturing is particularly interesting since it has experienced
dramatic employment declines in the past few decades, with a 35
percent drop in manufacturing jobs during the 1970s alone (Sassen-
Koob 1985:300). While many plants have closed or relocated, there
has, at the same time, been an expansion of what Sassen-Koob
(1985:302) calls a "downgraded manufacturing sector" where sweatshops and industrial homework are common forms of production
(see also Waldinger 1985). In her essay in this volume, Adriana Marshall argues that the abundant supply of new immigrants actually
stimulated a demand for labor in certain manufacturing industries—
apparel and leather, for example. These relatively unprofitable and
low-wage industries had difficulty attracting native workers in the
1960s, when better jobs were emerging in the New York area. Immigrant workers filled the gap, willing to accept the poor wages and
working conditions offered. The continued and regular inflow of immigrants discouraged technological innovation. Instead, it encouraged labor-intensive techniques and the readoption of such forms of
production as sweatshops, home labor, and subcontracting as well
as the revival of small-sized, often immigrant-owned firms. These
developments, in turn, increased the dependence on immigrant
workers to meet labor demands. The end result: manufacturing became increasingly populated by new immigrant workers. By 1980,
according to the census, 44 percent of the manufacturing workers in
the New York area were foreign-born. Nearly three-quarters of these
foreign workers were new immigrants, with the participation of
Asian and Hispanic women especially pronounced.

It is the service sector, however, that provides jobs for most new
immigrants. This is hardly surprising given that New York is basically
a service economy, with services supplying almost one job in three

in the city in 1980 (Sassen-Koob 1985:303). Relatively few new immigrants are found in the highly paid and high-status professional, administrative, technical, and managerial positions in the service sector; rather, new immigrants are a significant source of labor for low-level service work. Low-skilled and low-paid jobs in service industries—ranging from cleaners, dishwashers, and stock clerks to hospital orderlies—are available to new arrivals. Many also find work catering to the needs of high-income New Yorkers—as building attendants, for example, or domestic workers (Sassen-Koob 1985:303–305). Indeed, Adriana Marshall's essay notes that in New York's relatively high-income areas there is an almost infinitely expanding demand for household workers. It should be noted, too, that New York offers opportunities for certain lower-level professionals in the health services, most notably as nurses.

A wide array of institutions and social services in New York City also influences recent arrivals. These range from the large number of city hospitals and social agencies to the educational system. To take one example, The City University of New York, with its network of seventeen colleges, continues to provide opportunities for the city's immigrants despite the imposition of tuition in the late 1970s. The world of New York City ethnic politics also affects newcomers; many organize along ethnic lines to press their political demands and aspiring immigrant politicians make alliances with other ethnic minorities in their bid for power.

Finally, a few words about the real estate market in Manhattan which has received so much media attention lately. As factories, tenements, and offices in many areas are transformed into luxury housing and offices—and as commercial and cultural enterprises become more oriented to high-income residents—the poor, including many new arrivals, are displaced. Haitians on the Upper West Side of Manhattan are a case in point (see Stafford, this volume). Washington Heights, the largest Dominican settlement in the city, is also undergoing change. Commercial rents have risen, threatening to wipe out many Dominican small businesses, and affordable housing is scarcer as more rental units are converted to high-income housing. Eugenia Georges (1985) speculates that if Dominicans are squeezed out of the area and dispersed, the political and organizational base that has developed among Dominicans in the community will be disrupted.

The Wider U.S. Society

Crucial as the New York City context is in shaping the experiences of new immigrants, we must also consider the effects of living in the United States generally.

In the United States, an advanced industrial society, job opportunities in urban centers are wider, wage levels are higher, and living standards are better than in the Third World countries from which most new arrivals come. Further, although new immigrants frequently end up in jobs of lower status than those they occupied in the home country, they can still afford more consumer goods and more amenities in the United States (see Pessar, this volume; and Foner 1983).

The broader scope for employment and higher wages in the United States affect the position of immigrant women and relations between the sexes. In many new immigrant groups, women have more autonomy in certain spheres. Jamaican women, for example, have greater independence in New York where jobs pay more than in Jamaica. Along with larger incomes comes more say in family affairs (Foner 1986). Patricia Pessar reports that in New York, Dominican women are more likely to be working outside the home than in the Dominican Republic, and wage work brings them greater household authority and self-esteem (see Morokvasic 1985 for a summary of the losses as well as gains that migration brings to women).

Immigrants in New York, as in other U.S. cities, feel the effects of broad American social and political institutions. Bernard Wong, for instance, describes how many new Chinese immigrants have become interested and involved in American political life, and he notes the impact of U.S. government "equal opportunity" programs in giving newcomers more scope to get ahead (see his essay, this volume). In general, civil rights legislation in the 1960s and affirmative action programs opened up employment and other new opportunities for many new immigrants. Various federal social welfare programs affect new arrivals as well. And the Bilingual Education Act of 1968, and subsequent federal, state, and local programs, have made language assistance available to children whose primary language is not English in urban public schools across the country.

Moving to the United States, not simply to New York City, has heightened new immigrants' awareness of their national or ethnic identity as they come into increased contact with groups and individuals they perceive as different from themselves. Ethnicity assumes a new symbolic meaning in the immigrant situation. It is encouraged in large U.S. urban centers where it may bring political and economic advantages. Ethnicity is also reinforced by immigrant social networks in the United States as well as continued ties to the home society.

Of crucial significance to many new immigrant groups is the structure of race relations in the United States. Whites and nonwhites have, throughout American history, "been 'differentially incorporated' into the polity," and the treatment of nonwhite citizens has led some to designate their relationship to the larger society as "colonial" (Sutton and Makiesky 1975:127). Prejudice against racial minorities in this country has long been, in Stephen Steinberg's (1981:42) words, virulent and pervasive: "The unspoken dictum was 'No matter how much like us you are, you will remain apart.'" Nonwhite, especially black, immigrants suffer numerous social and economic disadvantages because of their race, and a new racial consciousness develops among them when they settle in this country.

The three essays in this volume on black immigrants make clear that race is central in their everyday lives. Used to societies where blacks were a majority and where education, income, and culture partially "erased" one's blackness, West Indians find that their skin color now brands them as inferior by the white majority and that they face racial discrimination in housing, employment, and innumerable personal encounters. An important reason why West Indians emphasize their ethnicity in informal contexts—and as Linda Basch shows, in formal association settings as well—is that they are stigmatized as blacks and identified with black Americans in this country. Race and ethnicity are thus closely intertwined, with a sense of ethnic distinctiveness nurtured by racial exclusion.

Whatever their race, new immigrants in New York are influenced by dominant American cultural beliefs and values. These run the gamut from how and when one should marry and raise a family to notions about appropriate political behavior. The term influence includes cases where immigrants enthusiastically embrace certain American beliefs and values or tentatively begin to accept or even angrily reject them. Consider a few such beliefs and values mentioned or alluded to in the essays in this volume: the view that nuclear family "togetherness" and joint husband-wife activities are desirable; that it is appropriate for women to enter the work force and for teenagers to engage in a wide range of social activities outside the home; and that corporal punishment in school and severe beating of youngsters at home are wrong and abusive. The mass media, schools, and other institutions disseminate these and other dominant American beliefs and values, opening the door to changes in the behavior and orientations of the new arrivals.

CHARACTERISTICS OF IMMIGRANT GROUPS AND NEW PATTERNS IN NEW YORK

That new immigrants are influenced by the New York and broader American context does not mean that their former traditions and values are replaced by "American" customs and ideas or that they become homogenized in a so-called "melting pot" of New York. Immigrants have not wiped out the old nor are they fully ready to be assimilated or socialized into the new. The old and new blend in many ways in response to circumstances in their new home—a kind of New Yorkization process. The blend of meanings, perceptions, and patterns of behavior that emerge, needless to say, is different for each immigrant group, reflecting its specific cultural, social, and demographic characteristics.

Premigration Cultural and Social Patterns

New immigrants come to New York carrying with them a "memory of things past" that operates as a filter through which they view and experience life in the city. Some of their former beliefs and social institutions may persist intact, although usually they undergo change, if only subtly, in form and function in response to circumstances in New York. What needs stressing is that these premigration values, attitudes, and customs do not simply fade away; rather they shape, often in a complex fashion, the way individuals in each group adjust to and develop new cultural and social patterns in New York.

Linda Basch observes that although voluntary associations in New York assume a much more important role among Vincentians and Grenadians than in the home society, these organizations have a distinct West Indian orientation and flavor. Among Soviet Jews in Brighton Beach, fears rooted in the Soviet Union discourage formal communal organizations; instead, restaurants modeled on those patronized in the USSR are the most important public gathering places (see Orleck, this volume). Immigrants' cooking and cuisine, too, are molded by premigration habits. Newcomers may add hamburgers, hotdogs, and pizza to their diets in New York, and concoct new dishes that use ingredients available here, but they also still eat such traditional foods as plantain and rice and peas (Jamaicans) or pickled herring and shashlik (Soviet Jews). And, of course, there are immigrants' native languages which for non-English speakers limits patterns of association as well as the ability to obtain high-level jobs in the mainstream economy.

Premigration family and religious patterns also have an impact. True, they may fill new needs and acquire new meanings in New York or be transformed in significant ways. Patricia Pessar demonstrates that Dominican households become less patriarchal and more egalitarian in New York (see Pessar, this volume). Nonetheless, traditional family values continue to exert an influence, if only as a standard against which immigrants evaluate current arrangements. In the Korean case, Illsoo Kim argues that the legacy of Confucian familism is a factor in the proliferation and success of small businesses, inducing immigrants to work long hours in family concerns (see Kim, this volume). Premigration religious beliefs are what draws many to Protestant and Catholic churches in New York; they also explain the continuation of customs like Haitian voodoo ceremonies (see Stafford, this volume; and Laguerre 1984) and the use of folk healers (Harwood 1981).

Class Composition

The move to New York affects immigrant groups differently not only because of their particular cultural backgrounds but because of the class composition of each immigrant stream.

The relative importance of class versus cultural heritage is an issue that inevitably arises in discussions of why some immigrant groups are more successful occupationally and economically than others. On the "cultural heritage" side, many scholars emphasize various cultural characteristics immigrant groups bring with them from the homeland, most notably attitudes to education, family values (e.g., Petersen 1971; Sowell 1981), and imported cultural institutions like rotating credit associations (e.g., Light 1972). Class theories, by contrast, stress social class background in the home country which, it is argued, gives some groups an occupational head start in the United States and helps explain the presence of values that support social and economic advancement (e.g., Steinberg 1981). What is key in class theories is the relationship between immigrants' class background and the ability and motivation to "make it" in their new home. Relevant class-linked abilities include professional, business, and other occupational skills as well as educational training. Immigrants from well-off backgrounds may also bring with them substantial amounts of capital. Those who come with social class advantages are also more likely to set high goals and to have the confidence and motivation to work hard to achieve these goals than, say, immigrants from laboring or peasant backgrounds.

Injected into the culture versus class debate on immigrant achievement is the view, advanced by Portes and Bach (1985:339), that emphasizes the "social structures into which immigrants become inserted." Specifically, they have in mind the existence of a substantial ethnic enclave economy which, they argue, accounts for the greater economic and occupational success of Cubans compared to Mexicans in this country. Ultimately, however, class and cultural factors emerge as key in their analysis, explaining why such economic enclaves develop in the first place. In terms of class, they stress the presence of a significant proportion of immigrants with entrepreneurial backgrounds in the home country. They also point to the existence of traditional economic institutions in the immigrant community, such as rotating credit associations, that provide capital accumulation for businesses (Portes and Bach 1985:339, 47).

Although cultural factors certainly cannot be discounted, I would maintain that, on balance, the social class origins of immigrant groups are more important in their relative occupational and economic achievement in New York. Illsoo Kim's analysis, in this volume, of the Korean case is just one instance lending support to this view, as he highlights the decisive role of social class resources Koreans brought with them—advanced education, professional experience, high economic motivation, and money—in their success in small businesses.

Demographic Factors

The demographic composition of each immigrant group is still another factor having an impact on social patterns that develop in New York. The sheer size, as well as spatial concentration, of each group influences, among other things, whether it can support a significant enclave employment sector and is a potential effective political force in its own right. Sex and age ratios in each group affect marriage and family patterns. For example: A markedly unbalanced sex ratio will encourage marriage outside the group or consign many to singlehood or the search for spouses in the home country; and a sizable proportion of old people may, as among Soviet Jews in Brighton Beach, ease the child care burdens of working women.

Race and Ethnicity

Obviously, immigrants' race has crucial consequences for their experiences and reactions to New York City life. Because they are consigned to the bottom of the racial hierarchy, black immigrants develop new attitudes and new perceptions of themselves in New York. Racial discrimination also influences where they live, what jobs they can take, and the kinds of associations and political organizations they join. Other nonwhite immigrant groups confront racial discrimination as well although, on the whole, this is less virulent than that experienced by black immigrants. As for ethnicity, it can be a stigma in some contexts, the case of Hispanic immigrants being especially noteworthy in this respect.

Differentiation Within New Immigrant Groups

Immigrant groups are not homogeneous, and internal distinctions—too often ignored in migration studies—must be considered. I refer not to the unique personal history and special characteristics that contribute to individual variation. Rather, the focus here is on social distinctions that mark off groups within immigrant populations, namely, gender, class, race, culture, and age and generation.

Because of sex role patterns and inequalities in New York and the home society, the experiences and perceptions of male and female immigrants at home, work, and in the community are bound to differ in important respects. Men and women immigrants tend to cluster in different occupational spheres, for example, and their household roles are distinct. They may have different orientations to remaining permanently in New York. Patricia Pessar reports that Dominican women, who have experienced social and economic gains as a result of the move to New York, want to remain abroad while their husbands are struggling to return to the Dominican Republic (see Pessar, this volume; and Pessar 1986).

Social class distinctions within immigrant groups affect a broad range of behavior and attitudes, from style of life and consumption patterns to perceptions of discrimination and the American political process. With some immigrant populations from one country, moreover, there are religious, linguistic, and other cultural differences, derived from the homeland, that affect patterns of formal association and ethnic identity in New York (see Fisher 1980 on Indians and Wong 1982 on Chinese in New York). Racial divisions may also be present. Black Hispanic immigrants suffer disadvantages that their white counterparts do not experience, and some Haitians, according to Susan Buchanan Stafford, have gained benefits in New York by being able to "pass for white" (see Stafford, this volume).

Age and generation, too, are important bases of differentiation. Among adults in each group, the young, middle-aged, and elderly may vary in their relations in and reactions to New York partly because they are at different life stages and because they grew up and immigrated at different time periods (see Orleck, this volume, on age-related differences among Soviet Jews). The distinction between the immigrant generation and the second U.S.-born generation is of special interest. Immigrant parents and children, each born and raised in different countries and historical periods, have different, often conflicting, attitudes, aspirations, and patterns of behavior. These include their sense of ethnic identity and the extent to which they accept "traditional" values. The two generations are also likely to differ in their occupational, educational, and economic achievements, a crucial point in any consideration of prospects for the future.

THE IMPACT OF NEW IMMIGRANTS ON NEW YORK CITY

If new immigrants in New York undergo transformations as they come to terms with their new home so, too, the "new New Yorkers" have brought changes to the city. One journalist writes of new immigrants revitalizing New York and of the city drawing "its energy, its soul from the entire spectrum of immigrant life" (Freedman 1985:28, 95). The particular way each immigrant population affects New York varies, of course, depending on such factors as its size and residential concentration, class origins and occupational makeup, and race and cultural background. The very cultural and social patterns that emerge among each group in response to circumstances in the city are also important. There are, however, broad spheres and institutions where virtually all new immigrant groups have had an impact, and these are the focus of the pages that follow.

New York's Population Structure

Perhaps the most striking impact of the new immigration is on the population structure of the city. As many American-born New Yorkers and old immigrants died or left the city in the 1970s, newcomers came pouring in. In 1980, according to the census, over half of the city's foreign-born population—about 13 percent of the city's total population—had arrived since 1965. In actual numbers, this meant that close to a million immigrants had come between 1965 and 1980—and the figure could be as high as 1.5 million if we include the thousands of undocumented immigrants who were missed by the census. According to demographers at the Bureau of the Census, about 200,000 undocumented immigrants were included in the counts for the New York metropolitan area (see Kraly, this volume) but many—some estimate another 500,000—were left out.

The census reports that the largest group of newcomers to New

York City between 1965 and 1980 was the Dominicans. The next largest group was Jamaicans, followed by the Chinese, Haitians, and Italians. After that, in descending order, were immigrants from Trinidad and Tobago, Colombia, Ecuador, the Soviet Union, and Guyana (New York City Department of City Planning n.d.).

The newcomers are spread throughout the city but, as Ellen Kraly shows, there are particular patterns of concentration for each group. According to the 1980 census, which shows the distribution of the foreign-born among the five boroughs, almost half the Chinese immigrants in the city live in Manhattan and more than a quarter in Queens. Queens, in fact, is home to two out of five Asian immigrants in New York City, with more than half of the Indian and Korean populations. Nearly half of the South Americans live in Queens as well. West Indians from Haiti and the Commonwealth Caribbean are concentrated in Brooklyn as are immigrants from the Soviet Union. Over half of the Dominican immigrants live in Manhattan (see Kraly, this volume).

Local Communities and Neighborhoods

As immigrant groups cluster in particular communities within each borough, they have had a dramatic effect on these neighborhoods, especially where they have moved in large numbers.

Certain sections of the city have taken on a new "cultural" character. In Crown Heights and East Flatbush in Brooklyn, for example, West Indian barber shops, beauty parlors, restaurants, record stores, groceries, and bakeries dot the landscape, and sounds of Haitian Creole and West Indian accents are everywhere (see Stafford, Basch, and Kim, this volume).

Clusters of new immigrants in specific communities have affected the composition of local schools and churches. The new immigrant presence has also given rise in many instances to neighborhood-based immigrant institutions and organizations like community centers, voluntary associations, and political groups as well as churches and temples.

While many poor immigrants crowd into rented apartments in deteriorating buildings, newcomers who buy their own homes, in particular, sometimes upgrade local housing. In the case of Soviet Jews in Brighton Beach, the newcomers have revived a fading community. Annelise Orleck relates how Brighton was, by the mid-1970s, in decline: apartments stood empty and the main commercial avenue was a dying strip of old stores. The massive influx of Soviet Jews has filled apartments and turned the avenue into a thriving commercial center, replete with new "international-style" groceries, Russian restaurants, and The Black Sea Bookstore. Dubbed "Little Odessa" by journalists, Brighton now "smells and tastes increasingly Russian" (p. 302). Its "age character" has also changed, from an almost exclusively elderly community, to a home for Soviet Jews of all ages.

In Chinatown, the arrival of new immigrants has fortified the community with additional members and, as Bernard Wong tells us, led to many significant changes. Chinatown itself has expanded, spilling over into surrounding areas of Lower Manhattan, and, partly due to the recent inflow of capital from Hong Kong, real estate values have soared and there are growing pressures for gentrification. New businesses have emerged and the banking industry has grown markedly. At the same time, the new immigration is related to the rise of youth gangs and sometimes tense relations between old settlers and new arrivals in the community.

"Cultural" Influences

Within as well as beyond their own neighborhoods, the sounds and spices of recent immigrants have added to the "cultural" and culinary life of the city.

Restaurants and groceries run by newcomers have exposed New Yorkers to new cuisines and foods, perhaps most notably broadening their taste for Chinese cooking beyond Cantonese to regional dishes from Shanghai, Peking, Hunan, and Szechuan (Wong 1982). Musically, too, new immigrants have had an influence. Jamaicans, for instance, have helped popularize reggae in the city. Salsa, New York Afro-Latin dance music based on Cuban folk and popular traditions with Puerto Rican, Dominican, Panamanian, and Colombian influences, is an important feature of the New York popular music scene (Bilby 1985:208). There are new ethnic theaters, and new ethnic parades and festivals have emerged. Since 1969, for example, West Indian Carnival has been celebrated every Labor Day on Eastern

Parkway in Brooklyn and it attracts huge—over 800,000 in 1984—crowds (Hill and Abramson 1979; Kasinitz and Friedenberg-Herbstein 1987). Brooklyn's museums, libraries, and theaters reflect the increased West Indian presence in the borough by staging exhibits, events, and plays with West Indian themes. While these events draw heavily West Indian audiences, they also attract, and broaden the cultural horizons of, non-West Indians.

Race and Ethnic Relations

The nature of new immigrants' contact with people from different ethnic groups—and the implications of this contact for race and ethnic relations in the city—are of critical importance.

Relations with Old Minorities and Other Immigrant Groups. Outside their own group, the key relationships for most new immigrants are with other ethnic minorities—both "old" minorities and other new immigrants. Sometimes these relationships are amicable and cooperative, but sometimes they are tinged with conflict.

When ethnic conflicts in New York arise, ethnic group identity and belonging are rarely the major reasons. Rather, these conflicts are typically rooted in inequalities of status, power, and wealth among groups and competition for housing and economic, educational, and government resources. Cultural and linguistic differences play a role but often because they come to symbolize inequalities among ethnic groups and are manipulated in competitive struggles.

Tensions between new immigrants and Afro-Americans are a dominant issue for West Indians (see Stafford and Foner, this volume). In an attempt to distinguish themselves from native blacks and win preferential treatment from whites, West Indians often stress cultural, behavioral, and linguistic features thought to be superior to those of black Americans. They tend to have disdain for black Americans, stereotyping them as spendthrifts and irresponsible. In fact, English-speaking West Indians, as a group, appear to do better occupationally than black Americans for a variety of reasons, probably the most important being their social class background. On their side, black Americans frequently resent what they regard as West Indians' arrogant behavior. There is, as well, some competition for jobs and housing between them.

The frictions between Korean merchants and American blacks in many New York commercial districts involve classic problems that arise when immigrants assume the shopkeeping role in poor minority areas. As shopkeepers, Koreans sell goods at profits to economically deprived buyers, although they worry about stealing. A *New York Times* story on the picketing of Korean stores in Harlem notes that Harlem residents complained that some Korean proprietors were rude, overcharged or shortchanged customers, and resorted to force in dealing with suspected shoplifters. Koreans countered that problems were caused by customers who were drunk or had taken drugs (Douglas 1985).

Thus, although new immigrants often come to New York with negative images of "old minorities," it is because their social position and their views are also shaped by the new context that strains and conflicts with old minorities may develop. This dialectical process is also a factor in new immigrants' relations with each other: as New York changes the newcomers, so patterns of interaction with other new immigrant groups take shape.

Admittedly, "traditional" animosities affect relations among new immigrant groups, and distinctive cultural values and customs are distancing factors. Susan Buchanan Stafford writes that Haitians bring to New York a sense of distinctiveness from other Caribbean peoples, and their language isolates them from their English-speaking West Indian neighbors. But, she also notes, a new factor in New York—the ethnic structuring of the political system—indirectly fosters competition among immigrant groups by distributing community services and government programs along ethnic lines. Whether competition for these services and programs, or for jobs and housing, creates serious conflicts between Haitians and other West Indians—or among other new immigrant populations—is an open question.

Important, and dramatic, as conflict is, we must not forget that there is frequent cooperation and accommodation. For example, while relations between native blacks and West Indians are often strained, friendships arise among some West Indians and black Americans, and informal links develop through children. New patterns of cooperation among immigrant groups actually emerge in the

New York context, as among the several English-speaking West Indian groups where bonds develop in churches, schools, and on the job and a common West Indian identity becomes important (see Foner, this volume).

New immigrants from different groups, and new immigrants and old minorities, come together in temporary coalitions for political purposes (see Stafford, Basch, and Foner, this volume, on Afro-Americans and West Indians; Georges 1985 on links between Puerto Rican and Dominican activists). And trade unions unite the rank and file as well as organizers from different ethnic groups on bread-and-butter issues (e.g., Fox 1984:33).

New Immigrants and Dominant Whites. Most writings on race relations in the United States focus on the factors generating and maintaining white domination and the impact of political and economic subordination for nonwhite minorities. The main issue here is whether the presence of such large numbers of nonwhite newcomers has added to, or changed the nature of, racial conflict between whites and nonwhites in New York City.

In my essay I discuss the ways the influx of West Indians has fed into and occasionally intensified black-white strains and conflicts. The movement of many West Indians into "white" areas of the city has sometimes sparked resistance from working-class and lower-middle-class whites who, among other things, fear reduced property values and deteriorating neighborhoods and schools. Racial conflicts also arise over competition for employment. Highly trained West Indians frequently confront racial discrimination when they try to obtain "white" jobs and advance up the career ladder, and skilled tradesmen run a greater risk of being laid off than whites. In the political arena, the presence of so many thousands of West Indians is potentially an influential factor in racially based coalitions and struggles.

Alternatively, the new West Indian immigration has permitted, and encouraged, behavior among whites that serves, in a sense, to "divide and rule" (see Foner, this volume). White New Yorkers frequently compare West Indians favorably to American blacks, thus driving a further wedge between American and West Indian blacks and making black unity across ethnic boundaries more difficult. It has even been suggested that such invidious comparisons by whites may heighten discrimination against native blacks (Jackson 1983:332).

Old and New Immigrants. As the essays on Brighton Beach and Chinatown suggest, the influx of new immigrants has introduced divisions into some communities between "old" and "new" immigrants from the same ethnic group.

Strains and conflicts between old and new settlers may involve class, cultural, and cohort (or generation) factors. Bernard Wong, for example, notes that in Chinatown, old settlers, generally of peasant origin, are looked down on as "country bumpkins" by more educated, urban-bred newcomers. In Brighton Beach, Annelise Orleck emphasizes the cultural divide between Soviet Jews and earlier waves of Jewish immigrants—mainly their different sense of Jewish identity—that initially led to severe tensions, anger, and affronts. That old immigrants in Chinatown and Brighton are simply at a different life stage—old age—than most newcomers may play a role in strains. The fact of having arrived in America in different historical periods contributes to the clashing orientations of old Chinese settlers, who came in an era of intense anti-Chinese racism, and newer arrivals, who have benefited from the wider opportunities and lessened discrimination against Chinese in the post-1965 years.

Of course, conflicts and cleavages are only one side of the story, and Annelise Orleck argues that in Brighton Beach new understandings have developed as Soviet Jews and old-time immigrants socialize in neighborhood stores and as the Soviet Jews have become more comfortable with, and responsive to, Jewish customs in the community.

Labor Force Impact

Another crucial issue is the effects of the recent immigrant influx on the city's labor market.

There is a debate in the theoretical literature on the question of whether immigrants in the United States displace native-born workers from jobs. On one side, some argue that considerable displace-

ment has occurred because new immigrants, especially the undocumented, compete with native-born workers for low-skilled positions
(e.g., Briggs 1985; Fogel 1983) and make low-skilled jobs less desirable
for American workers by lowering wage rates. It has also been contended that native-born workers are excluded from certain jobs
through the processes of network recruiting (Martin 1986). Other
scholars argue, however, that there has been no massive displacement of native by immigrant workers in this country (e.g., Muller
1985; Piore 1979). Most immigrants, the argument goes, move into
jobs in the secondary sector—with low wages, harsh working conditions, and little or no opportunity for job mobility—jobs that relatively few native-born workers, cushioned by the welfare state, are
willing to take. While some immigrants are able to move into the
primary labor market—with relatively secure jobs, regular channels
for advancement, and wage levels set by collective bargaining or
other administrative arrangements—they often fill the less desirable
positions that have been vacated by native-born workers (Portes
1981). Moreover, large-scale immigration creates additional primary
sector jobs for native workers—teachers, for example, and workers
in state, county, and city agencies (Muller 1985). In addition, many
immigrants work in ethnic businesses in jobs created by immigrants
for immigrants. Native-born workers do not compete for these "ethnic" jobs which, in any case, pay low wages and offer undesirable
working conditions.

How do these perspectives apply to New York City? There has
been, to be sure, some competition between native-born and immigrant workers for jobs in the city (see Waldinger n.d. on the competition between immigrants and native blacks). Just how much
competition exists is unclear. Indeed, at present there is no definitive
evidence that the influx of new immigrants has led to significant
displacement of native-born workers in the city.

Adriana Marshall (this volume) shows that new immigrants supply
an increasingly large segment of manual labor in the New York metropolitan area; she estimates that by 1980 immigrants who arrived in
the 1970s made up about 35 percent of the area's manual work force.
The general trend in the early stage of the new immigration (1966–
1970), she argues, was for new immigrant workers to move into the

manual labor markets being deserted by American-born workers, who shifted into more attractive, often nonmanual, jobs. Later, she proposes, immigrant labor stimulated its own demand. As employers in labor-sensitive activities adjusted to, and came to depend on, the immigrant flow, a demand for labor arose that would not have emerged had immigrant workers been unavailable (Marshall 1984).

In general, many point out that immigrants in New York City often take jobs that native workers do not want in manufacturing and the expanding service economy. It has also been suggested that there would be far fewer manufacturing jobs in the city had low-wage immigrant labor not been available because many firms would have left the New York area altogether, for example, or introduced labor-saving production techniques (e.g., Marshall, this volume). And a detailed analysis of New York City's restaurant industry, where over half of all workers in 1980 were foreign-born, indicates that immigrant and native workers do not compete for jobs since they occupy and are preferred for different roles—with immigrants working in immigrant-owned establishments and in unskilled and semiskilled kitchen jobs in expensive restaurants (Bailey 1985).

Immigrants do appear, however, to have had an adverse effect on wage levels in certain sectors of New York City's economy. Adriana Marshall argues that, in manufacturing, the large supply of immigrant workers contributed to slow wage growth, especially in industries where new immigrants were overrepresented (see Waldinger 1985; compare Muller and Espenshade 1985 for Los Angeles). This adverse effect on wages, Marshall speculates, probably has also occurred in service-sector fields with heavy concentrations of new immigrant labor (see her essay, this volume).

Unionization and Working-Class Solidarity

The new immigration into the city may also affect working-class solidarity and unionization attempts. Labor immigration in advanced capitalist societies, according to one theoretical approach, divides the working class. In this view, native workers often blame deteriorating economic conditions on immigrants, and racial and ethnic divisions obscure common economic interests, preventing the emergence of a unified working class front. Employers may deliberately encourage these divisions through such practices as ethnic preferences in work assignments (summarized in Portes 1981:281).

What Patricia Pessar emphasizes (this volume) is the role of immigrant ideology in reducing the potential for collective sentiments and solidarity in the workplace. Despite their low-level jobs, most Dominican women garment workers she interviewed were satisfied with their employment and identified themselves as middle, rather than working, class. These views, Pessar notes, may hinder unionization attempts, especially if labor organizers stress working-class identification and values. Elsewhere, she observes that some Dominican workers rejected union organization drives because they feared the owners' threats to close down or relocate if the firm unionized (Pessar 1985).

In addition, some argue that undocumented workers are a particular obstacle to union organizing due to their vulnerable legal status. And structural arrangements in ethnic firms, Roger Waldinger (1985) points out, discourage unionization. He found that workers in Hispanic-owned garment firms in New York City were tied to owners through friendship and kinship bonds, and owners often helped workers with legal, social, and economic problems. As a result, workers were loyal to their employers, and unions found it difficult to organize these firms.

A one-dimensional view of immigrants as shying away from unions and inevitably divided from native workers is misleading, however. Patricia Pessar (1985), for example, cites several cases where Dominican workers called in a union when wages were drastically cut. A 1979 study of undocumented workers in New York City found that a large proportion belonged to unions, some actively seeking them out and engaging in strike actions (Badillo-Viega et al. 1979). Where unions are already established immigrants often take an active role in union struggles alongside native workers, as I found in interviewing Jamaican hospital workers. While new immigrants pose special problems and challenges to union organizers in the city, they are not inherently "unorganizable" or inevitably uninterested in the activities of unions they do join. Obstacles to organization and lack of union involvement have as much to do with policies and practices of unions and features of industries or firms in which immigrants are employed as they do with characteristics of the immigrants themselves.

Dominant Formal Institutions

Recent immigrants have had an impact on dominant formal institutions in the city outside the world of work. Briefly consider three: schools, churches, and hospitals.

A growing number of immigrant children populate the city's public school system, bringing with them a host of special needs, not the least being placement in proper grades when no transcripts or records are available (see Hendricks 1974:138–39). Once enrolled, there are, among other difficulties, students' culture shock and, in many cases, language problems to contend with (see Orleck, this volume). In one Elmhurst elementary school, to take an extreme example, English was not the native tongue of half the students, who among them spoke more than thirty languages (Andersen 1985). By 1985, 86,000 students were enrolled in bilingual programs in the New York City public schools, most instructed in their native language. The largest number (almost three-quarters) of the students in the city's bilingual programs were of Spanish-speaking background, followed by, in descending order, Chinese, Haitian Creole, and Korean (Maeroff 1985).

Roman Catholic schools have also experienced an influx of new immigrant, especially Hispanic, children. And while immigrants often form their own churches, large numbers are drawn to the Catholic church and to mainstream Protestant denominations. The Catholic church in New York has begun to adapt to the increasing numbers of Spanish-speaking members and a growing number of Catholic churches conduct French or Haitian Creole masses (see Stafford, this volume; and Buchanan 1979).

The composition of the staff and patients at New York City's hospitals has changed as well. Asian immigrants now make up a high percentage of the physicians at municipal and less prestigious voluntary hospitals (Kim 1981:154–158). The nurses, aides, and orderlies at hospitals throughout the city are often Asian or West Indian, while patients at municipal hospitals in particular are frequently non-English-speaking immigrants who bring with them their own set of cultural values regarding health and medical treatment.

FOR FUTURE RESEARCH

New immigrants, it is clear, not only are shaped by social and economic forces in New York City but they also act as agents of change in their new environment. The studies in this volume illuminate these processes, but much work needs to be done. Despite the enormous flood of new immigrants into the city, surprisingly little research has yet been carried out on them and I want to close by suggesting a few areas where further exploration would be valuable.

Certainly, additional ethnographic studies are required to chart the emergence of new cultural and social patterns among newcomers as traditional beliefs and practices change in the New York context. Careful comparisons are also in order. Only through comparative analysis can we sort out the role of class and cultural factors in immigrant economic and occupational attainment. An intriguing comparative question as well, touched on briefly in several essays, is why immigrant groups are concentrated in different occupational niches.

Because of critical policy implications, it is important for researchers to probe the labor force impact of the new immigration on the city—and the way legal and illegal immigrants affect public service revenues and expenditures. The essays in this book do not deal with the question of undocumented immigrants, although they have received considerable attention in the media. Clearly, undocumented immigrants in New York face special problems, and one of the few systematic studies comparing the undocumented and documented found that undocumented Dominicians in the city were more likely to work in the smallest—often off-the-books and nonunionized—firms (Grasmuck 1984; see Papademetriou and DiMarzio 1986 for a recent survey of undocumented aliens in the New York area). Further research should examine how the New York experience varies for undocumented and documented immigrants and whether their impact on the city's economy, communities, and formal institutions is significantly different.

Most ethnographic studies of new immigrants draw on interviews and participant observation in immigrant communities and a few include some research in the workplace. Another fruitful approach is to explore, at first hand, the immigrant presence in dominant institutions like hospitals, schools, and labor unions. Such investigations will not only deepen our understanding of the way new conceptions and behavior patterns develop among newcomers but will also allow us to examine relations among new immigrants, old minorities, and native whites in concrete social settings.

Indeed, the field of ethnic and race relations is a fertile ground for further analysis. Little has been written on the effects of the new immigration on racial conflicts and contacts in New York—perhaps because New Yorkers have long been accustomed to a racially diverse city, because so many nonwhite immigrants have limited contact with whites, or because research on the new arrivals is yet so sparse. For all nonwhite groups, we need research examining the bonds as well as divisions with whites; the contexts in which interaction with whites occurs; and the extent of racial discrimination new immigrants experience. And the focus should not be new immigrants alone. How, after all, has the new immigration influenced native whites' conceptions and categories? And how do these conceptions shape and exert an influence on relations with newcomers?

Ethnic relations among immigrant groups and with old minorities, too, have received scant attention, particularly in the case of Hispanics and Asians. Intensive studies of interaction situations, including those marked by conflict as well as cooperation, are essential to tease out the complex interplay of factors involved in particular cases. An issue that deserves attention is new immigrants' impact on political life and political mobilization in the city. As New York City becomes increasingly black and Hispanic (45 percent in 1980) and as the non-white immigrant citizen population grows, this is an especially pressing question. What kinds of immigrant political organizations arise to represent their interests? Under what circumstances, and for what purposes, do immigrants make alliances with other immigrants and old minorities to advance their causes?

The ethnographic essays in this volume focus on first-generation immigrants but obviously the problems and prospects of the second generation are also key. For some, the children of Korean and Soviet Jewish immigrants, for example, the occupational outlook is good because their parents came with social class advantages or aggressively moved into businesses here. The likelihood is that second-generation Hispanic and black immigrants will not do as well, mainly on account of discrimination and the more limited networks and resources of their parents. Our research agenda for the future must include comparisons of the school and work careers of the second generation to see how they fare compared to other immigrant children as well as in relation to their parents.

The essays that follow, then, are a challenge for further study. They provide insights and raise questions that will enrich our understanding of the new immigration in New York and, in the end, also broaden our perspective on immigration generally.

NOTES

1. The terms "West Indies" and "West Indian" are apt to be used in several different ways and the essays in this book are no exception. In some essays, for example, the terms refer only to the English-speaking Caribbean. In this introductory essay, "West Indies" refers to the French (or Creole)-speaking and English-speaking Caribbean, including Guyana and Belize; "West Indians," unless otherwise specified, are those with origins in these areas. As used in this essay, "Latin America" includes the Hispanic Caribbean as well as Mexico and Spanish-speaking and Portuguese-speaking countries of South and Central America.
2. The 1965 law, it should be noted, was more restrictive with regard to long-independent Western Hemisphere countries, imposing numerical limits on immigration from these nations for the first time.

REFERENCES

Andersen, Kurt. 1985. "New York: Final Destination." *Time,* July 8.

Badillo-Viega, Americo, Josh DeWind, and Julia Preston. 1979. "Undocumented Immigrant Workers in New York City." *NACLA Report on the Americas* 13:1–46.

Bailey, Thomas. 1985. "A Case Study of Immigrants in the Restaurant Industry." *Industrial Relations* 4:205–221.

Bilby, Kenneth M. 1985. "The Caribbean as a Musical Region." In Sidney Mintz and Sally Price, eds., *Caribbean Contours.* Baltimore: Johns Hopkins University Press.

Briggs, Vernon M., Jr. 1985. "Employment Trends and Contemporary Immigration Policy." In Nathan Glazer, ed., *Clamor at the Gates.* San Francisco: Institute for Contemporary Studies.

Bryce-Laporte, Roy S. 1979. "New York City and the New Caribbean Immigrant: A Contextual Statement." *International Migration Review* 13:214–234.

Buchanan, Susan. 1979. "Language and Identity: Haitians in New York City." *International Migration Review* 13:298–313.

Douglas, Carlyle. 1985. "Korean Merchants Are Targets of Black Anger." *New York Times*, January 19.

Fisher, Maxine P. 1980. *The Indians of New York City*. Columbia, Mo.: South Asia Books.

Fogel, Walter. 1983. "Immigrants and the Labor Market: Historical Perspectives and Current Issues." In Demetrios G. Papademetriou and Mark J. Miller, eds., *The Unavoidable Issue: U.S. Immigration Policy in the 1980s*. Philadelphia: Institute for the Study of Human Issues.

Foner, Nancy. 1983. "Jamaican Migrants: A Comparative Analysis of the New York and London Experience." *Occasional Paper No. 36*. New York Research Program in Inter-American Affairs, New York University.

—— 1986. "Sex Roles and Sensibilities: Jamaican Women in New York and London." In Rita Simon and Caroline Brettell, eds., *International Migration: The Female Experience*. Totowa, N.J.: Rowman and Allanheld.

Fox, Geoffrey. 1984. "Hispanic Organizers and Business Agents in the New York Apparel Industries." *Occasional Paper No. 43*. New York Research Program in Inter-American Affairs, New York University.

Freedman, Samuel G. 1985. "The New New Yorkers." *New York Times Magazine* (part 2), November 3.

Georges, Eugenia. 1984. "New Immigrants and the Political Process: Dominicans in New York." *Occasional Paper No. 45*. New York Research Program in Inter-American Affairs, New York University.

—— 1985. "Conflict and Cooperation: Dominican Immigrants and Their Neighbors." Paper presented to the American Anthropological Association, Washington, D.C., December.

Grasmuck, Sherri. 1984. "Immigration, Ethnic Stratification, and Native Working Class Discipline: Comparisons of Documented and Undocumented Dominicans." *International Migration Review* 18:692–713.

Harwood, Alan, ed. 1981. *Ethnicity and Medical Care*. Cambridge: Harvard University Press.

Hendricks, Glenn. 1974. *The Dominican Diaspora: From the Dominican Republic to New York City*. New York: Teachers College Press, Columbia University.

Hill, Donald and Robert Abramson. 1979. "West Indian Carnival in Brooklyn." *Natural History* 88:72–85.

Houston, Marion F., Roger G. Kramer, and Joan Mackin Barrett. 1984. "Female Predominance of Immigration to the United States Since 1930: A First Look." *International Migration Review* 18:908–963.

Jackson, Kennell A. 1983. "The Old Minorities and the New Immigrants: Understanding a New Cultural Idiom in U.S. History." in Mary M. Kritz, ed., *U.S. Immigration and Refugee Policy*. Lexington, Mass.: Lexington Books.

Kasinitz, Philip and Judy Friedenberg-Herbstein. 1987. "Caribbean Public Celebrations in New York City: The Puerto Rican Parade and The West Indian Carnival." In Constance Sutton and Elsa Chaney, eds. *Caribbean Life in New York City*. New York: Center for Migration Studies.

Kim, Illsoo. 1981. *New Urban Immigrants: The Korean Community in New York*. Princeton: Princeton University Press.

Laguerre, Michel S. 1984. *American Odyssey: Haitians in New York City*. Ithaca: Cornell University Press.

Light, Ivan. 1972. *Ethnic Enterprise in America*. Berkeley: University of California Press.

Maeroff, Gene I. 1985. "Quinones Counters Attack on Bilingual Instruction." *New York Times*, September 27.

Marshall, Adriana. 1984. "Immigration, Labor Demand, and the Working Class." *Politics and Society* 13:425–453.

Martin, Philip. 1986. "Illegal Immigration and the Colonization of the American Labor Market." *Center for Immigration Studies Paper 1*. Washington, D.C.: Center for Immigration Studies.

Morokvasic, Mirjana. 1984. "Birds of Passage Are also Women." *International Migration Review* 18:886–907.

Muller, Thomas. 1985. "Economic Effects of Immigration." In Nathan Glazer, ed., *Clamor at the Gates*. San Francisco: Institute for Contemporary Studies.

Muller, Thomas and Thomas J. Espenshade. 1985. *The Fourth Wave: California's Newest Immigrants*. Washington, D.C.: Urban Institute Press.

New York City Department of City Planning. N.d. "Foreign Born Who Arrived in U.S.A. 1965–80, New York City." Mimeo.

Papademetriou, Demetrios G. and Nicholas DiMarzio. 1986. *Undocumented Aliens in the New York Metropolitan Area*. New York: Center for Migration Studies.

Pessar, Patricia. 1985. "The American Pie and the Limited Good: Dominican Immigrants' Roles in Workplace Struggles." Paper presented to the American Anthropological Association, Washington, D.C., December.

—— 1986. "The Role of Gender in Dominican Settlement in the United States." In June Nash and Helen Safa, eds., *Women and Change in Latin America*. South Hadley, Mass.: Bergin and Garvey.

Petersen, William. 1971. *Japanese Americans*. New York: Random House.

Piore, Michael J. 1979. *Birds of Passage*. New York: Cambridge University Press.

Portes, Alejandro. 1981. "Modes of Structural Incorporation and Present Theories of Labor Immigration." In Mary M. Kritz, Charles B. Keely, and Silvano M. Tomasi, eds., *Global Trends in Migration*. New York: Center for Migration Studies.

Portes, Alejandro and Robert L. Bach. 1985. *Latin Journey: Cuban and Mexican Immigrants in the United States*. Berkeley: University of California Press.

Reimers, David. 1985. *Still the Golden Door*. New York: Columbia University Press.

Rollwagen, Jack. 1975. "The City as Context: The Puerto Ricans of Rochester, New York." *Urban Anthropology* 4:53–60.

Sassen-Koob, Saskia. 1985. "Changing Composition and Labor Market Location of Hispanic Immigrants in New York City, 1960–1980." In George Borjas and Marta Tienda, eds., *Hispanics in the U.S. Economy*. New York: Academic Press.

Smith, Estellie. 1975. "A Tale of Two Cities: The Reality of Historical Differences." *Urban Anthropology* 4:61–72.

Sowell, Thomas. 1981. *Ethnic America*. New York: Basic Books.

Steinberg, Stephen. 1981. *The Ethnic Myth*. New York: Atheneum.

Sutton, Constance and Susan Makiesky. 1975. "Migration and West Indian Racial and Ethnic Consciousness." In Helen Safa and Brian Du Toit, eds. *Migration and Development*. The Hague: Mouton.

Urban Anthropology. 1975. "The City as Context: A Symposium." (Special Issue) 4:1–72.

Waldinger, Roger. 1985. "Immigration and Industrial Change in the New York City Apparel Industry." In George Borjas and Marta Tienda, eds., *Hispanics in the U.S. Economy*. New York: Academic Press.

—— N.d. "Changing Ladders and Musical Chairs: Ethnicity and Opportunity in Post-Industrial New York." *Theory and Society*, forthcoming.

Wong, Bernard. 1982. *Chinatown: Economic Adaptation and Ethnic Identity of the Chinese*. New York: Holt, Rinehart and Winston.

2. U.S. Immigration Policy and the Immigrant Populations of New York

Ellen Percy Kraly

During the past decade, approximately half a million people have been admitted to the United States each year as permanent resident aliens. Between 15 and 20 percent of these aliens have indicated their intention to reside in New York City. According to the 1980 census of population, 12 percent of the total foreign-born population of the United States lives in New York City, and nearly one-sixth resides in the New York-New Jersey metropolitan area. Certainly, recent immigrants have had an impact on local communities and the labor market in New York City. At the same time, the city and its receiving communities have conditioned the processes of immigration settlement, adjustment, and mobility. An overview of the demography of immigration in the United States and New York helps us to understand these consequences of immigration and processes of immigrant settlement. It also provides a useful backdrop to the rich studies of specific immigrant communities which form the body of this volume.

This essay has two main objectives.[1] One is to examine the relationship between U.S. immigration policy and recent patterns of immigration to New York, considering the way U.S. policy has provided the legal and administrative context in which immigration has occurred. The other aim is to document how recent immigration trends have affected the population dynamics of New York City. The analysis of data from decennial population censuses, although not without problems, allows us to compare immigration patterns in New York with those in other regions and in the country as a whole. It also highlights changes in immigrant streams to the city as well as changes in the ethnic composition of New York City communities.

PROVIDING A CONTEXT: U.S. IMMIGRATION POLICY

The causes of historical and contemporary patterns of immigration to New York can be addressed on a variety of levels. At the most macroscopic level, there are, for example, economic, social, and political forces which result in the structured movement of labor and the displacement of populations. This level of analysis, well represented in the work of Portes (1983) (and for refugees, Suhrke 1983), draws attention to the changing structure of the demand for migration to the United States from areas throughout the developed and developing worlds. At the other end of the analytic spectrum is the unique combination of factors that motivate particular individuals to move to New York—and these individuals' perceptions of their reasons for migrating.

Whether the analysis of the causes of international migration to New York and the United States focuses on the international or individual level, immigration law and administration—the gatekeeping factor—must be considered. U.S. immigration policy plays a significant role in determining the size and composition of legal, as well as illegal, migration streams. Moreover, a meaningful aspect of the immigration process to the immigrants themselves is their interaction with U.S. legal and bureaucratic arrangements. Aliens migrating to the United States are required to appreciate the intricacies of federal immigration law and administration, if only to complete the correct application form. The New York District Office of the U.S. Immigration and Naturalization Service, located at Federal Plaza in lower Manhattan, may well be considered a landmark to most recent immigrants in the city, a landmark that contrasts sharply to Miss Liberty, standing just across the channel.

A few definitions of relevant legal concepts are in order before elaborating on U.S. immigration policy. *Immigrants* are aliens who are legally admitted with an immigrant visa to the United States for permanent resident status. These persons obtain the proverbial "green card" and are accorded those civil rights consistent with being a resident of the United States.[2] Permanent resident aliens have the opportunity to obtain U.S. citizenship through the process of *naturalization*, usually after approximately five years of residence in the United States. *Admission* as an immigrant is also a legal term referring to the date immigrant status is conferred, not necessarily date of entry to the country; currently, approximately one-fifth of annual immigrant admissions are aliens already in the United States who have adjusted to permanent resident status. *Nonimmigrants* are aliens admitted on temporary visas for specific purposes for a defined period of time. Tourists and businesspersons, the largest groups of nonimmigrants, are usually authorized to remain in the United States for six months before an extension of stay is required. Students and employees of foreign governments and international organizations are nonimmigrants who may be authorized to reside in the United States for a much longer period of time.

Refugees were narrowly defined under the 1965 immigration amendments as persons fleeing a Communist-dominated state or areas in the Middle East. The Refugee Act of 1980 broadened the definition to be consistent with the concept endorsed by the United Nations. Hence a refugee is

[e]very person who, owing to well-founded fear of being persecuted for reasons of race, religion, nationality, membership of a particular social group or political opinion, is outside the country of his nationality and is unable or owing to such fear, is unwilling to avail himself of the protection of that country. (United Nations Protocol of 1967, quoted in Keely 1981:6)

Refugees are screened by federal agencies and are then admitted for permanent resettlement in the United States. *Asylees* are aliens applying for refugee status while in the United States. Most recently, Haitians and Salvadorans have been migrating to the United States and requesting political asylum.

Policies Regarding Permanent Residence

Contemporary U.S. immigration policy has been evolving in punctuated steps over the past thirty years. The basic statute, the Immigration and Nationality Act, was codified in 1952. That act, known popularly as the McCarran-Walter Act, embodied the system of national origins quotas which had been set in place in the 1920s. The national origins quota system, as it stood in 1952, applied to Eastern Hemisphere nations. Visas for permanent residence were distributed on the basis of nativity and, in the case of Asians, race, within an annual limit for the Eastern Hemisphere of approximately 156,000. Annual quotas were figured on the basis of the ethnic composition of the U.S. population according to the 1920 census, and as with the quota laws of the 1920s, favored what has been termed the "old immigrant" groups, essentially northwest European populations.[3] Spouses and children of U.S. citizens, however, were exempt from quota restrictions. There was no numerical limitation on immigration from areas within the Western Hemisphere (South and North America and the Caribbean); the good neighbor policy was maintained by allowing unrestricted immigration from independent Western Hemisphere countries, although individuals could be denied entry on the basis of statutory grounds for inadmissibility.[4]

While the Immigration and Nationality Act of 1952 perpetuated a highly discriminatory system for granting immigrant visas, it did initiate certain important shifts in policy. The law created a preference system to distribute quota visas which reflected the evolving immigration policy goals concerning family reunification and occupational skills. Top priority was given to those with skills needed in the United States, then to close relatives of American citizens and permanent residents. Moreover, the act continued the piecemeal, though very minor, modifications of the laws barring Asian immigration. These bars, introduced in the 1880s to exclude the Chinese, had been extended to virtually all Asians in the first decades of this century. Japanese immigration was restricted by the "gentleman's agreement" of 1908 according to which the Japanese government agreed to no longer issue passports to persons seeking employment in the United States. The Asiatic Barred Zone was established by Congress in 1917 basically to prevent immigration from the remaining areas of Asia. The significant exception was the status of Filipinos. The Philippines became a U.S. territory as a result of the Spanish-American War of 1898. Filipinos were able to migrate to and from the U.S. freely; restrictions in the 1930s, however, resulted in the imposition of an annual quota of only 50 visas (Reimers 1985:6–7). A shift in immigra-

tion policy came with World War II with evolving diplomatic relations in Asia. The Chinese exclusion laws were repealed in 1943 and
an annual quota for Chinese nationals, only 105 visas, was authorized
(Cafferty et al. 1983:46–47); and in 1946, a small amount of immigration from India was permitted. The volume of total Asian immigration remained severely restricted, however. The 1952 act gave a quota
of 100 visas a year to each independent Asian country that had previously been denied a quota, but a limit of 2,000 persons annually
was applied to an "Asia-Pacific Triangle." Furthermore, visas for
Asians were awarded on the basis of race rather than country of birth
as for other immigrant groups. A person of Chinese ancestry, for
example, came under the quota restriction for China even if he or
she had been born in another part of the world.[5]

The McCarran-Walter Act and the injustices it legitimized served
as stimuli for immigration reform. During the 1950s public commis-
sions and private groups called for comprehensive change in immigration policy. Although few changes were made in the immigration
statute in that decade, interests were articulated and evidence was
amassed supporting policy revisions. The discriminatory structure of
the law raised difficult issues in foreign relations. Perhaps more important, the law was inconsistent with the nature of the demand for
immigration to the United States. Between 1953 and 1965, only 35
percent of all immigrants admitted were quota immigrants, the rest
being immediate relatives of U.S. citizens or emigrants from countries
in the Western Hemisphere; another 300,000 people were admitted
as refugees during the period, but outside the bounds of the immigrant provisions of the Immigration and Nationality Act. There were,
meanwhile, severe backlogs within certain preferences for low-quota
countries which often shut off the possibility of immigrating. All in
all, "during the 13-year period [1953–1965], only 61 percent of the
available quota numbers were used . . . yet thousands of qualified
persons were required to wait because they were born in the 'wrong'
country" (United States Select Commission on Immigration and Refugee Policy 1981:322).

The 1965 amendments to the Immigration and Nationality Act represented a dramatic shift in policy. The principle of national origins
as a basis for selecting immigrants was explicitly rejected. Instead,
immigrant visas were to be issued on a first come, first served basis

according to the visa preference system. The 1965 amendments applied this system to countries in the Eastern Hemisphere within an annual ceiling of 170,000 (preference) visas with a per country limit of 20,000 each year. Also, for the first time a numerical limitation on immigration from the Western Hemisphere was set in place. The 120,000 annual ceiling was not, however, distributed according to the preference system, nor was the 20,000 per country limit imposed upon Western Hemisphere nations.

In 1976, the Immigration and Nationality Act was again amended to apply the preference system and per country limit to the 120,000 ceiling for countries of the Western Hemisphere. The logical next step occurred in 1978 when specific hemispheric limits were abolished and an annual *worldwide* ceiling of 290,000 immigrant visas was introduced. The Refugee Act of 1980 reduced this level to 270,000 (separate allocations for refugees were made available at that time; see below). Thus, for the most part, the last statutory vestige of discrimination on the basis of nationality was eliminated.

The emphasis on family reunification in current immigration policy is clearly overriding. First, the law does not restrict the annual immigration of immediate relatives (spouses and unmarried minor children) of U.S. citizens; moreover, this category was expanded from the 1952 law to include parents of adult U.S. citizens. Similarly, the preference system was modified in 1965 to emphasize even further the goal of bringing together immigrant families. As shown in figure 2.1, the current system allocates at least 80 percent of immigrant visas on the basis of family relationships. The preference system also reflects the general concern for both protecting domestic labor as well as facilitating the immigration of persons with needed skills. The occupational preferences can be used by aliens who have obtained authorization through the U.S. Department of Labor that the job sought in the United States by the alien will not displace domestic workers or depress working conditions. It was this process of "labor certification" that was used to select among numerically limited visa applicants from countries in the Western Hemisphere until the preference system was universally applied in 1976.

Changes in U.S. immigration policy during the past two decades have had the effect of increasing the volume of annual immigration and altering the composition of immigrant streams by nationality,

Figure 2.1. Visa Preference System

First preference	Unmarried sons and daughters at least 21 years of age, of U.S. citizens (20%)
Second preference	Spouses and unmarried sons and daughters of permanent resident aliens (26%)[a]
Third preference	Members of the professions, scientists, and artists (10%)
Fourth preference	Married sons and daughters of U.S. citizens (10%)[a]
Fifth preference	Brothers and sisters at least 21 years of age, of U.S. citizens (24%)[a]
Sixth preference	Skilled or unskilled workers needed in the U.S. (10%)
Nonpreference	Other qualified immigrants as visa numbers are not required for applicants in the six preferences[a]

[a]Plus any unused numbers from higher preferences.

perhaps most notably, ushering in an enormous increase in the proportion of Asians admitted as immigrants. The 1965 amendments also led to an increase in immigration from English-speaking areas of the Caribbean. Those islands that had recently achieved independence were now no longer subject to the small quotas for dependencies but had access to immigration within the 120,000 ceiling for the Western Hemisphere. To a certain degree, the structure of the preference system set up in 1965 frustrated immigration from Western Europe by emphasizing family relationships which benefited more recent immigrants. But probably more important has been the decline in the demand for permanent migration to the United States from Western industrialized nations. In the case of Spanish-speaking countries of the Caribbean and Latin America, recent U.S. immigration policy has hardly stimulated immigration since it actually imposed numerical limits on these nations for the first time. Rather, economic conditions have been the major stimulus for the dramatic increase in migration to the United States from these areas since 1965. Finally, recent U.S. policy toward refugees has, as I consider below, permitted large movements of refugees from Cuba and Indochina. (For a detailed discussion of the effect of the 1965 act, see Keely 1975 and 1971 and

Table 2.1. U.S. Immigration by Area and Selected Country of Birth, 1881–1983 (numbers in thousands)

Area and Country of Birth	Immigrant Admissions[a]					
	1881–1890	1891–1900	1901–1910	1911–1920	1921–1930	1931–1940
			Numbers			
Total Immigration	5246.6	3687.6	8795.4	5735.8	4107.2	528.4
Europe	4735.5	3555.4	8056.0	4321.9	2463.2	347.6
Germany	1453.0	505.2	341.5	143.9	412.2	114.1
Ireland	655.5	388.4	339.1	146.2	210.0	11.0
Italy	307.3	651.9	2045.9	1109.5	455.3	68.0
Poland[b]	51.8	96.7	—	4.8	227.7	17.0
United Kingdom	807.4	271.5	526.0	341.4	340.8	31.6
USSR[c]	213.3	505.3	1597.3	921.2	61.7	1.4
Asia	69.9	74.9	323.5	247.2	112.1	16.1
China	61.7	14.8	20.6	21.3	29.9	4.9
India	0.3	0.1	4.7	2.1	1.9	0.5
Japan	2.3	25.9	129.8	83.8	33.5	1.9
America	427.0	39.0	361.9	1143.7	1516.7	160.0
Canada	393.3	3.3	179.2	742.2	924.5	108.5
Mexico	1.9	1.0	49.6	219.0	459.3	22.3
Caribbean	29.0	33.1	107.5	123.4	74.9	15.5
Central America	0.4	0.5	8.2	17.2	15.8	5.9
South America	2.3	1.1	17.3	41.9	42.2	7.8
Africa	0.9	0.4	7.4	8.4	6.3	1.8
Oceania and other areas	12.6	4.0	13.0	13.4	8.7	3.0
Country not specified	0.8	14.1	33.5	1.1	0.2	—

Table 2.1 (continued)

Area and Country of Birth	Immigrant Admissions[a]						
	1941–1950	1951–1960	1961–1970	1971–1980	1981	1982	1983
				Numbers			
Total Immigration	1035.5	2515.5	3321.7	4493.3	596.6	594.1	559.8
Europe	621.1	1325.6	1123.4	800.4	66.7	69.2	58.9
Germany	226.6	477.8	190.8	74.4	6.6	6.7	7.2
Ireland	19.8	48.4	33.0	11.5	0.9	0.9	1.1
Italy	57.7	185.5	214.1	129.4	4.7	3.6	3.2
Poland[b]	7.6	10.0	53.5	37.2	5.0	5.9	6.4
United Kingdom	139.3	204.5	214.5	137.4	15.0	14.5	14.8
USSR[c]	0.5	0.6	2.3	39.0	9.2	15.5	5.2
Asia	32.4	150.1	427.8	1588.2	264.3	313.3	277.7
China	16.7	9.7	34.8	124.3	25.8	37.0	42.5
India	1.8	2.0	27.2	164.1	21.5	21.7	25.5
Japan	1.6	46.3	40.0	49.8	3.9	3.9	4.1
America	354.8	996.9	1716.4	1982.5	246.3	193.5	204.6
Canada	171.7	378.0	413.3	169.9	11.2	10.8	11.4
Mexico	60.6	299.8	453.9	640.3	101.3	56.1	59.1
Caribbean	49.7	123.1	470.2	741.1	73.3	67.4	73.3
Central America	21.7	44.8	101.3	134.6	24.5	23.6	24.6
South America	21.8	91.6	258.0	295.7	35.9	35.4	36.1
Africa	7.4	14.1	29.0	80.8	15.0	14.3	15.1
Oceania and other areas	19.2	16.2	21.3	25.6	2.1	2.1	2.0
Country not specified	0.1	12.5	3.9	15.9	2.1	1.7	1.6

Table 2.1 (continued)

Area and Country of Birth	1881–1890	1891–1900	1901–1910	Immigrant Admissions[a] 1911–1920	1921–1930	1931–1940
				Percent		
Total Immigration	100.0	100.0	100.0	100.0	100.0	100.0
Europe	90.3	96.4	91.6	75.3	60.0	65.8
Germany	27.7	13.7	3.9	2.5	10.0	21.6
Ireland	12.5	10.5	3.9	2.5	5.1	2.1
Italy	5.9	17.7	23.3	19.3	11.1	12.9
Poland[b]	1.0	2.6	—	0.1	5.5	3.2
United Kingdom	15.4	7.4	6.0	6.0	8.3	6.0
USSR[c]	4.1	13.7	18.2	16.1	1.5	0.3
Asia	1.3	2.0	3.7	4.3	2.7	3.0
China	1.2	0.4	0.2	0.4	0.7	0.9
India	0.0	0.0	0.1	0.0	0.0	0.1
Japan	0.0	0.7	1.5	1.5	0.8	0.4
America	8.1	1.1	4.1	19.9	36.9	30.3
Canada	7.5	0.1	2.0	12.9	22.5	20.5
Mexico	0.0	0.0	0.6	3.8	11.2	4.2
Caribbean	5.5	0.9	1.2	2.2	1.8	2.9
Central America	0.0	0.0	0.1	0.3	0.4	2.9
South America	0.0	0.0	0.2	0.7	1.0	1.5
Africa	0.0	0.0	0.1	0.1	0.2	0.3
Oceania and other areas	0.2	0.1	0.1	0.2	0.2	0.6
Country not specified	0.0	0.4	0.4	0.0	0.0	—

Table 2.1 (continued)

Area and Country of Birth	Immigrant Admissions[a]						
	1941–1950	1951–1960	1961–1970	1971–1980	1981	1982	1983
				Percent			
Total Immigration	100.0	100.0	100.0	100.0	100.0	100.0	100.0
Europe	60.0	52.7	33.8	17.8	11.2	11.6	10.5
Germany	21.9	19.0	5.7	1.7	1.1	1.1	1.3
Ireland	0.2	1.9	1.0	0.3	0.2	0.2	0.2
Italy	5.6	7.4	6.4	2.9	0.8	0.6	0.6
Poland[b]	0.7	0.4	1.6	0.8	0.8	1.0	1.1
United Kingdom	13.5	8.1	6.5	3.1	2.5	2.4	2.6
USSR[c]	0.0	0.0	0.1	0.9	1.5	2.6	0.9
Asia	3.1	6.0	12.9	35.3	44.3	52.7	49.6
China	1.6	0.4	1.0	2.8	4.3	6.2	7.6
India	0.2	0.1	0.8	3.7	3.6	3.7	4.6
Japan	0.2	1.8	1.2	1.1	0.7	0.7	0.7
America	34.3	39.6	51.7	44.1	41.3	32.6	36.5
Canada	16.6	15.0	12.4	3.8	1.9	1.8	2.0
Mexico	5.9	11.9	13.7	14.3	17.0	9.4	10.6
Caribbean	4.8	4.9	14.2	16.5	12.3	11.3	13.1
Central America	2.1	1.8	3.0	3.0	4.1	4.0	4.4
South America	2.1	3.6	7.8	6.6	6.0	6.0	6.4
Africa	0.7	0.6	0.9	1.8	2.5	2.4	2.7
Oceania and other areas	1.9	0.6	0.6	0.6	0.4	0.4	0.4
Country not specified	0.0	0.5	0.1	0.4	0.4	0.3	0.3

Source: U.S. Department of Justice 1985, table IMM. 2.
[a]Numbers may not add to total due to rounding.
[b]Poland was recorded as a separate country between 1820–1898 and since 1920. From 1899–1919, Poland was included with Austria-Hungary, Germany, and USSR.
[c]From 1931–1963, USSR is broken down into European and Asian USSR. Since 1964 all USSR has been included in Europe.

the U.S. Select Commission on Immigration and Refugee Policy 1981:333–38.) Historical trends in immigration to the United States are summarized in table 2.1.

Refugee Policies and Programs

As with general immigration policy, the past few decades have witnessed dramatic changes in the national stance concerning the admission and settlement of refugees. There has been tension between the Executive Branch and Congress regarding the appropriate policy response to refugee crises. The Refugee Act of 1980 is the most recent attempt by Congress to maintain control over refugee policy by establishing a comprehensive program monitoring admissions, resettlement, and adjustment of refugees. More important, federal policy now views the refugee phenomenon as a recurring, often structured, product of contemporary international relations, and recognizes the role of the United States as a country of permanent resettlement.

The roots of current refugee policy are found in various responses by the federal government to persons and populations displaced by World War II.[6] Over half a million European refugees displaced by the war were admitted in the following decade through presidential directive and followed by a series of federal statutes. A new mechanism—the parole authority of the Attorney General—facilitated the admission of refugees from the 1956 Hungarian uprising, and during the next two decades refugees from the Cuban revolution. Since 1959 nearly three-quarters of a million Cubans have been paroled into the United States. As in the case of the Hungarians, congressional action has been required to regularize the status of the Cuban parolees. In 1966, Congress passed an act allowing Cuban refugees, if admissible under immigration provisions, to adjust to permanent resident status after two years in the United States. Between 1968 and 1978, the number of Cubans adjusting status was charged to the annual ceiling for immigrant visas for the Western Hemisphere (for this period the number of Cuban numerically limited admissions was 145,000). In 1976, the courts ruled in *Silva* vs. *Levi* that this policy was inconsistent with federal law, and thus additional visas were now available to certain applicants from the Western Hemisphere who had applied but not been issued immigrant visas.

The 1965 amendments to the Immigration and Nationality Act sought to incorporate the admission of refugees within general immigration policy. A seventh preference was applied to "conditional entrants," narrowly defined as persons fleeing a communist state or the Middle East, and 6 percent of preference visas were allotted to this category. Adjustment to permanent resident status could occur after two years' stay in the United States. The small number of visas for refugees under these provisions, however, and the fact that until 1976 those available were only allocated to Eastern Hemisphere countries meant that other measures had to be adopted in the 1970s to deal with such emergencies as the evacuation of Indochinese refugees and, more recently, the Mariel boatlift from Cuba. As before, the Attorney General's authority was used, and again, subsequent congressional action has been required to provide a legal basis for resettlement.

The Refugee Act of 1980 raised the annual ceiling for refugees to 50,000 and required the president to consult with and get final approval from Congress before admitting refugees in excess of that number. In 1981, for example, about 155,000 refugees were approved for admission, the overwhelming majority from Vietnam, Laos, and Cambodia. The Refugee Act of 1980 also institutionalized a policy of ongoing federal involvement in the process of resettlement and refugee adjustment to local communities.[7]

Naturalization

Although the acquisition of U.S. citizenship is considered to be an appropriate final stage in the process of permanent immigration to the United States, virtually no official policy, let alone federal program, exists to facilitate the process of naturalization. The opportunity is simply there for eligible aliens to apply for citizenship.

Nonimmigrants

The policies governing the admission of temporary migrants to the United States are rarely included in discussions of national immigration policy. By far, nonimmigrants constitute the majority of foreign travelers, and the majority of aliens entering the United States. These "travelers" vary in their impact upon national social institutions and economic sectors as well as on particular localities. In the case of New York, for example, there are large numbers of foreign government officials, students, international representatives, intracompany transferees and, certainly, tourists. For certain of these groups length of stay in New York may be significant, often several years.

Illegal Aliens

Last, but certainly not least, are illegal aliens. The elimination of unrestricted immigration from Western Hemisphere countries by the 1965 amendments, combined with an increasing demand for visas, resulted in illegal immigration from Mexico and other Latin American nations. The issue of the appropriate policy response to the illegal alien population in the United States has dominated recent debate on immigration reform. The empirical foundation for policy analysis in this area is porous, in spite of the pervasive images of both the size and growth of the illegal population and the consequences of the phenomenon for U.S. economy and society.[8] The official policy concerning undocumented immigration is to prevent entry into the United States by identification during the process of inspection at ports of entry, apprehension as soon as possible of persons entering surreptitiously between ports, and the identification of aliens violating the terms of their visas. Immigration policy initiatives during the past decade have included provisions both to regularize the status of illegals who have lived in the United States for a relatively extended period of time and to reduce illegal entry and visa overstay through better enforcement and identification.

After more than a decade of various reform packages, the Immigration Reform and Control Act passed Congress in October 1986. Like most of the proposals which preceded it, the recent bill includes employer sanctions. It also contains provisions for the legalization of illegal aliens who have lived in the United States since before January 1, 1982. Less expected was the significant representation of U.S. agricultural interests in the legislation, with the creation of what is essentially an agricultural guestworker program for alien laborers.

ISSUES IN IMMIGRATION RESEARCH

In analyzing the way recent immigration policy and immigration trends have affected the population dynamics of New York City a number of methodological issues arise. I want to take a little time to discuss these issues for, I believe, they are crucial in immigration research.

The obstacles to conducting research on U.S. immigration patterns and processes have been documented by demographers and social scientists (see Hutchinson 1958, 1965; Tomasi and Keely 1975; and Kraly 1979a, 1979b). The statistical basis for immigration policy analysis has been sharply criticized by Congress. The final report of the National Academy of Sciences Panel on Immigration Statistics takes to task key players in the federal statistical system for failing to provide a comprehensive and accurate national data base concerning the flow of international migration to and from the United States and the stock of immigrant populations in the country (Levine, Hill, and Warren 1985).

The initial focus of criticism is typically data from the U.S. Immigration and Naturalization Service (INS). Most of our flow data, that is, data on immigrants to the United States arriving over time, are generated through INS administrative and statistical programs. The annual *Statistical Yearbook* published by INS includes fairly basic tabulations concerning the social demographic characteristics of alien admissions by visa status as well as tables outlining the characteristics of aliens processed within various operational units within INS such as the U.S. Border Patrol, Investigations, Inspections and Naturalizations.

INS statistical resources, however, have been harshly criticized for, among other things, insufficient population coverage of international migrants, unreliable data, and lack of timeliness. What is pertinent here is whether INS data are available for metropolitan and local analysis. On this level, concern over data accuracy and timeliness is a luxury. INS statistics on categories of alien migrants in local communities are extremely scarce, either failing to exist or existing in an extremely inaccessible form. In fact, the statistics on city of intended destination cited in the introduction to this essay (coded from immigrant visas) are the only figures in the INS published tabulations available for analyzing the flow of legal immigrants to the New York City area.[9] The *Statistical Yearbook* includes some statistics on local operations in INS District Offices—for example, a table on the number of persons naturalized, by country of origin in selected cities, including New York and Yonkers. But most other statistics on aliens collected by the New York District Office are not published and remain fairly inaccessible to researchers.

Thus, the analyst interested in urban and community contexts turns rather quickly from INS statistics to U.S. census data as a foundation for the social demographic analysis of immigration. The decennial census is what is key for the analysis in this essay.[10] The foreign-born population has been identified in each census since 1850.

Census data sources are accessible and are available in published detail as well as in the form of public use tapes for interactive research. And they provide a basis for highly refined analyses of the social, economic, and demographic characteristics of immigrant populations according to a wide range of geographic units. The census schedule includes several items in addition to place of birth (nativity) which enhance the utility of census data for immigration research. For example, the 1980 census included questions on country of birth of the foreign-born, language and English proficiency, ancestry, citizenship, and year of immigration. Because a full range of census information is also available on household and family composition as well as social and economic characteristics, census resources have allowed researchers to compare patterns of status attainment and socioeconomic mobility among immigrant populations and between immigrants and the native-born population (see for example Borjas 1981; Chiswick 1978; and Hirschman and Wong 1981).

Census data are not without problems for immigration research, however. Since census data refer to population stock, that is, the characteristics of the population at one point in time, persons who immigrated in earlier years but who have died or emigrated from the United States are not included in the census enumeration. The item on year of immigration permits the identification of cohorts of immigrants by year of entry, but again, only for those persons who are present at the time of the census. Unfortunately, year of immigration is coded for five-year periods making comparison with flow statistics on immigration quite difficult.

This last example raises another difficulty. The question on year of immigration asked in the decennial census yields data which may not be comparable to data on the legal *admission* of immigrants. It is not clear whether response to the census item implies actual entry to the United States or legal admission as an immigrant. Nor does the census enable us to distinguish aliens (as opposed to naturalized citizens) according to legal or visa characteristics. The census category "alien" includes legal immigrants as well as groups of nonimmigrants such as students, exchange visitors, and temporary workers. Resident illegal aliens may also be included in the category. The extent to which these populations are covered in the census can not be determined directly and has resulted in some controversy concerning the accuracy of 1980 census data for selected metropolitan areas. Demographers at the Bureau of the Census have estimated that approximately 234,000 undocumented aliens were included in the 1980 counts for the State of New York, with the vast majority, 205,000, located in the New York metropolitan area.[11] The relevant point to be made here is that census data reflect fairly pure social demographic concepts concerning international migration and as a result are limited as a basis for addressing certain important issues concerning immigration policy and programs.

Another issue, especially relevant for immigration research in local contexts, is the geographic referent of census data. Although census data are available for a wide array of geographic units, the degree of tabular detail decreases with the size of the place. Thus, the Census Bureau publishes a series of detailed tables on the *national* foreign-born population in 1980 (classifying the foreign-born by country of birth and year of immigration for full range of social and economic variables)—but it publishes only percent of foreign born, without country of birth, for census tracts within metropolitan areas. The 1980 census summary tape files do contain relevant tabulations for immigrant populations in metropolitan areas, and while these computer data are not formally published they are fairly accessible to researchers. For example, ancestry and nativity by country of birth are tabulated for census tract populations. Also, the program of public use sample (PUS) tapes facilitates refined analyses of immigration. The smallest unit of analysis is the county, and only those counties with populations greater than 100,000. An issue that is particularly critical for immigration studies using PUS data is the reliability of sample estimates for very small population groups resulting from multivariate analyses.

Finally, the geographic units of the census change from one census to the next. For example, counties included in metropolitan statistical areas can change due to shifts in the characteristics of the counties, particularly patterns of commuting between counties. In 1970 nine counties were included in the New York Standard Metropolitan Statistical Area (SMSA): the five boroughs of the city, and Nassau, Suffolk, Westchester, and Rockland. In 1980, Nassau and Suffolk fulfilled the criteria for a metropolitan statistical area, and Putnam County in New York and Bergen County in New Jersey were added to the New York-New Jersey SMSA. Since social demographic data are often tabulated for metropolitan areas, lack of comparability poses problems, and certainly headaches, for the analyst.

In the analysis that follows, I rely on census data for various geographic units, depending on the issue at hand. I present census data for the New York metropolitan area, but where possible, the focus is on the city, that is, the five counties of New York City: New York (Manhattan), Bronx, Kings (Brooklyn), Queens, and Richmond (Staten Island). In order to make this analysis relevant for discussions of local immigrant communities, I draw on census material for individual counties where possible. When I consider patterns of "suburbanization" among immigrant populations, I adopt the census criteria for standard metropolitan statistical areas, including New Jersey's Bergen County, since it has such strong links to New York City.

IMMIGRATION TO THE UNITED STATES AND TO NEW YORK

Certainly during this century, the United States has been the major receiving country for permanent migrants throughout the world. Since 1900, over thirty-three million aliens have been admitted as immigrants. This figure of course does not reflect *net* additions to the U.S. population—perhaps as much as one-third of the foreign population has emigrated from the United States since 1900 (see Warren and Kraly 1985). But the magnitude of flow into the country has been dramatic and provides quite a contrast to the level of long-term immigration to the other major receiving countries.[12]

The volume of annual immigration to the United States has varied during the century as a result of international events such as wars and economic depression as well as shifts in U.S. immigration and refugee policy. As I outlined earlier, the 1965 immigration amendments increased the volume of annual immigration and altered the composition of immigration streams by nationality. It would be difficult to overstate the historical prominence of New York City in the U.S. immigration system. The righthand column of table 2.2 shows the percent of the U.S. foreign-born population residing in New York City, that is, the five boroughs, between 1900 and 1980. New York City's share of immigrants has been undeniably high, despite a slight decline in the past few decades. Since 1900, more than 10 percent of the foreign-born population in the United States has lived in New York City. High as this percentage is, immigration to New York mirrors immigration to the United States in many ways, and the remainder of this section examines national and regional trends.

The recent decline in the proportion of the total foreign-born population residing in New York undoubtedly reflects trends in population distribution occurring throughout the United States. During this past decade urban areas in the Northeast and North Central regions of the country have experienced relative economic decline and absolute loss of population. The same economic and social magnets that attract native workers and their families to southern and western areas in the United States are likely to influence immigrants' residential choices. Between 1970 and 1980 the proportion of the total population living in the Northeast declined from 24 percent to 22 percent; in the North Central region, the proportion of the total population declined from 28 percent in 1970 to 26 percent; the West gained its share from 17 percent to 19 percent, and the South, 31 percent to 33 percent. The shifts among the immigrant population are relatively more dramatic: the proportion of the total foreign-born population living in the Northeast declined from 43 percent in 1970 to 32 percent in 1980 and in the North Central region from 19 percent

Table 2.2. U.S. and New York City Population by Nativity, 1900–1980 (numbers in thousands)

Year	United States			New York City			Percent U.S. Foreign-Born in New York City
	Total	Foreign-Born	Percent Foreign-Born	Total	Foreign-Born	Percent Foreign-Born	
1980	226545.8	14079.9	6.2	7071.6	1670.2	23.6	11.9
1970	203210.2	9619.3	4.7	7894.9	1437.1	18.2	14.9
1960	179325.7	9738.1	5.4	7783.3	1558.7	20.0	16.0
1950	150844.5	10431.1	6.9	7892.0	1860.9	23.6	17.8
1940	132165.1	11656.6	8.8	7455.0	2138.7	28.7	18.3
1930	123202.7	14283.3	11.6	6930.4	2358.7	34.0	16.5
1920	106021.6	14020.2	13.2	5620.0	2028.2	36.1	14.5
1910	92228.5	13630.1	14.8	4766.9	1944.4	40.8	14.3
1900	76212.2	10444.7	13.7	3437.2	1270.1	37.0	12.2

Source: Rosenwaike 1972, table 69; U.S. Bureau of the Census 1963, table 96; U.S. Bureau of the Census 1972, table 138; U.S. Bureau of the Census 1981, tables 77, 78, and 79; U.S. Bureau of the Census 1983a, table 172.

to 15 percent; the proportion increased in the West from 24 percent to 32 percent and in the South from 14 percent to 21 percent.

The geographic and cultural origins of the immigrants figure prominently in these figures. Approximately one-fifth of the foreign-born population living in the western states in 1970 were born in Mexico; in 1980 this proportion had increased to nearly one-third. Another quarter of the foreign-born population in the West is Asian. In contrast, the trend in composition of the foreign-born in the Northeast has been toward greater heterogeneity. Between 1970 and 1980 the Asian population in the Northeast increased from 5 percent to 12 percent of the foreign population; most Asian countries are represented in this population. Similarly, the population of immigrants from both Europe and North and Central America residing in the Northeast in 1980 draws from the full range of countries (U.S. Bureau of the Census 1983c: tables 77, 79).

The heterogeneity of the Northeast's population is in large part due to the attraction of immigrants to New York: nearly half of the foreign-born population in the region resides in the New York-New Jersey SMSA. In fact, relative to the total U.S. population, New York attracts an extremely diverse range of ethnic groups. This comparison is made in table 2.3 which shows that earlier immigrant groups such as the Irish and Italians are concentrated in the New York SMSA, as are Russians, Israelis, and Chinese. Certain of the newer immigrant groups are heavily represented in New York. West Indian and South American populations are the outstanding cases: over half of the Jamaicans, Barbadians, Trinidadians, Guyanese, and Haitians; over three-quarters of the Dominicans; nearly half of the Ecuadorians; and one-third of the total Colombians in the United States were residing in New York in 1980. When we narrow our focus, and look only at immigrants who have arrived since 1970, it is interesting that recent immigrants from countries of earlier immigration continue to concentrate in the New York area (see table 2.3). Many immigrants from China and India since 1970 also select New York.

Changes in the immigrant composition of New York have been consistent in many ways with shifts in the composition of the national foreign-born population. Table 2.4 compares this geographic distribution of the foreign-born population in the United States and in the

Table 2.3. U.S. and New York–New Jersey SMSA Total Foreign-Born Population and Foreign Born Immigrating Since 1970 by Country of Birth, 1980 (numbers in thousands)

Country of Birth	Total Foreign-Born Population			Foreign-Born Population Immigrating Since 1970		
	United States	New York–New Jersey SMSA		United States	New York–New Jersey SMSA	
	Number	Number	Percent of U.S.	Number	Number	Percent of U.S.
Total	14079.9	1946.8	13.8	5560.4	754.0	13.6
Europe	4743.5	734.6	15.5	741.6	116.5	15.7
Germany	849.4	83.7	9.9	90.1	4.6	5.1
Ireland	197.8	52.5	26.5	14.5	3.3	22.8
Italy	831.9	204.6	24.6	100.5	29.4	29.3
Poland	418.1	90.3	21.6	45.9	8.7	19.0
United Kingdom	669.1	48.6	7.3	131.8	12.3	9.3
USSR	406.0	95.5	23.5	98.5	34.9	35.4
Asia	2539.8	254.9	10.0	1763.1	168.0	9.5
China	286.1	64.0	22.4	136.0	31.9	23.5
Hong Kong	80.4	17.6	21.9	50.2	10.7	21.4
India	206.1	27.4	13.3	158.3	23.2	14.7
Israel	67.0	18.7	27.9	35.5	9.3	26.2
Japan	221.8	17.4	7.8	100.3	13.8	13.8
Korea	289.9	22.6	7.8	243.3	19.6	8.1
Philippines	501.4	25.3	5.0	319.0	17.8	5.6
Vietnam	231.1	4.0	1.7	225.6	3.8	1.7

North and Central America	4664.9	532.5	11.4	2153.3	267.6	12.4
Canada	842.9	22.9	2.7	127.9	4.6	3.6
El Salvador	94.4	7.4	7.8	72.9	5.5	7.5
Guatemala	63.1	6.3	10.0	43.7	4.1	9.4
Mexico	2199.2	8.7	0.4	1270.2	5.1	0.4
West Indies	1258.4	440.0	35.0	537.2	227.2	42.3
Barbados	26.8	18.7	69.8	15.0	10.3	68.7
Cuba	607.8	54.3	8.9	163.2	10.6	6.5
Dominican Republic	169.1	127.7	75.5	96.0	73.0	76.0
Haiti	92.4	52.6	56.9	59.7	31.3	52.4
Jamaica	196.8	98.8	50.2	115.5	55.0	47.6
Trinidad and Tobago	65.9	39.6	60.1	40.8	24.4	59.8
South America	561.0	172.2	30.7	315.6	100.6	31.9
Argentina	68.9	14.0	20.3	29.8	6.2	20.8
Brazil	40.9	6.5	15.9	19.7	3.3	16.8
Colombia	143.5	47.2	32.9	78.9	25.8	32.7
Ecuador	86.1	41.9	48.7	45.9	23.0	50.1
Guyana	48.6	31.7	65.2	35.2	24.0	68.2
Peru	55.5	12.0	21.6	33.0	7.5	22.7
Africa	199.7	27.2	13.6	129.9	16.0	12.3
Egypt	43.4	8.3	19.2	24.5	3.9	15.9
All other countries	78.9	3.1	3.9	41.3	1.6	3.9
Country not reported	886.0	126.8	14.3	317.1	48.6	15.3

Source: U.S. Bureau of the Census 1983b, table 195; U.S. Bureau of the Census 1984, table 254.

Table 2.4. U.S. and New York–New Jersey SMSA Foreign-Born Population by Area of Birth, 1960–1980 (numbers in thousands)

Area of Birth	United States			New York–New Jersey SMSA[a]		
	1960	1970	1980	1960	1970	1980
Total foreign-born population	9738.1	9619.3	14079.9	1858.9	1756.9	1946.8
Percent[b]	100.0	100.0	100.0	100.0	100.0	100.0
Europe	67.2	54.6	33.7	73.5	59.4	37.7
USSR	7.1	4.8	2.9	12.0	7.5	4.9
Asia	5.1	8.6	18.0	3.7	6.7	13.1
North and Central America	18.1	24.5	33.1	8.4	21.9	27.4
South America	0.9	2.7	4.0	1.5		8.8
Africa	0.2	0.6	1.4	0.2	1.2	1.4
All other countries	0.7	0.9	0.6	0.2		0.2
Country not reported	0.6	3.3	6.3	0.5	3.3	6.5

Source: U.S. Bureau of the Census 1963, table 99; U.S. Bureau of the Census 1973a, tables 81, 144; U.S. Bureau of the Census 1975, series A 105–118, series C 228–295; U.S. Bureau of the Census 1983b, table 195; U.S. Bureau of the Census 1984, table 254.
[a]Figures for the SMSA in 1960 and 1970 conform to the counties included in the New York metropolitan area at the time of the respective census. Accordingly, Bergen County, New Jersey, and Putnam County are not included in the SMSA in 1960 and 1970; Nassau and Suffolk are not included in 1980.
[b]Numbers may not add to total due to rounding.

New York SMSA in 1960, 1970, and 1980. Between 1960 and 1980 the proportion of the immigrant population born in Europe has declined significantly both in the nation and in New York, although the New York metropolitan area continues to maintain a slightly larger European population relative to the total foreign-born population. Similarly, the proportion of immigrants from Asia has increased, nationwide and in New York, although the proportion of Asians among New York's foreign-born population is below that for the total foreign-born. The data presented in table 2.5 indicate the changes in the geographic origins of immigrants resident in the United States and in the New York area in 1980 by period of immigration. Again, for New York as well as from a national perspective, one can appreciate the sharp shift in immigrant characteristics according to year of entry. The proportion of immigrants from Europe began to significantly decline in the 1960s while Asian immigration has steadily increased during the past two decades. However, the composition of recent immigrants to New York differs slightly from the distribution of the total immigrant population by place of birth. In comparison to the total foreign-born population table 2.5 shows that recent immigrants to New York have included a higher proportion of persons from Europe, South America (nearly half of whom were from Colombia and Ecuador), and the USSR.

In sum, although patterns of immigration to New York in the past two decades generally mirror national trends, the composition of New York's immigrant population reveals a high degree of selectivity compared to the characteristics of the total foreign-born population in the United States. New York clearly represents the residential choice for certain groups among contemporary immigrant populations, reflecting a special interaction between immigrants and the New York community. Recent waves of immigrants from areas in the Caribbean basin, Central and South America, and Asia represent a new era of immigration to the New York metropolitan area. The concept of the "new" immigration of the late nineteenth century needs rethinking in light of these contemporary trends.

THE IMMIGRANT POPULATIONS OF NEW YORK

Not only is the historical importance of New York as a place of settlement clear, but the significance of immigration for the makeup of

Table 2.5. U.S. and New York–New Jersey SMSA Foreign-Born Population by Area of Birth and Year of Immigration, 1980 (numbers in thousands)

Area of Birth	Total	Year of Immigration					
		1975–1980	1970–1974	1965–1969	1960–1964	1950–1959	Before 1950
		United States					
Total foreign-born	14079.9	3335.0	2225.3	1807.8	1327.1	1911.4	3473.3
Percent[a]	100.0	100.0	100.0	100.0	100.0	100.0	100.0
Europe	33.7	11.5	16.1	26.0	33.0	53.2	59.8
USSR	2.9	2.6	0.6	0.5	0.9	2.7	6.8
Asia	18.0	35.8	25.6	16.9	11.5	8.5	4.5
North and Central America	33.1	35.3	43.8	42.4	41.5	26.2	20.0
South America	4.0	5.5	6.0	6.3	5.3	1.9	0.7
Africa	1.4	2.6	1.9	1.3	1.1	0.8	0.5
All other countries	0.6	0.8	0.6	0.5	0.4	0.4	0.4
Country not reported	6.3	5.8	5.5	6.0	6.2	6.4	7.4
		New York–New Jersey SMSA					
Total foreign-born	1946.8	398.9	355.1	305.8	173.9	219.7	493.3
Percent[a]	100.0	100.0	100.0	100.0	100.0	100.0	100.0
Europe	37.7	12.7	18.5	24.0	36.3	62.0	70.0
USSR	4.9	7.7	1.2	0.6	1.3	2.8	10.2
Asia	13.1	24.9	19.4	12.0	10.1	6.7	3.7
North and Central America	27.4	32.5	38.9	42.2	33.6	17.2	8.0
South America	8.8	13.3	13.4	13.0	10.5	3.7	1.1
Africa	1.4	2.2	2.0	1.3	1.6	1.0	0.4
All other countries	0.2	0.3	0.1	0.1	0.1	0.1	0.1
Country not reported	6.5	6.4	6.5	6.8	6.6	6.4	6.5

Source: U.S. Bureau of the Census 1983b, table 195; U.S. Bureau of the Census 1984, table 254.
[a]Numbers may not add to total due to rounding.

the city is also remarkable. Referring back to table 2.2, New York, as one would expect, has always had a larger proportion of foreign-born than the national population, but the factor of difference is on the order of three or four times that of the national level in each censal year. Early in this century, New York's population was over one-third foreign-born; the proportion declined until 1980, when immigrants constituted nearly a quarter of the city's population, and 21 percent of the population of the New York SMSA (data not shown in table 2.2). If we compare the proportion of foreign-born in New York and in other metropolitan areas New York still stands out. In the Northeast, New York's status as a city of immigrants is matched only by Jersey City; moreover, Jersey City is classified within the New York-New Jersey-Connecticut Standard Consolidated Statistical Area (SCSA). Other cities in the Northeast pale in comparison: Buffalo, 6 percent; Washington, D.C., 8 percent; Philadelphia, 5 percent. Even Boston, the ethnic city, was only 10 percent foreign-born in 1980 and Chicago, 11 percent. It is only the cities in the Sun Belt, and along the southwest corridor of the United States, which are comparable to New York in the relative level of immigration. At the time of the 1980 census, the Los Angeles-Long Beach metropolitan area was 22 percent foreign-born; Brownsville, Texas, 19 percent, and Laredo, 21 percent. Miami, Florida appears to be in a class by itself with 36 percent of its population foreign-born in 1980 (U.S. Bureau of the Census 1983c: table 246).

But as shown earlier using regional comparisons, these changes in the size of the foreign-born population fail to reveal the extent of ethnic diversity. Thus, as a useful illustration, the foreign-born population of the Los Angeles metropolitan area is composed primarily of Mexicans (41 percent) and Asians (20 percent) with relatively small proportions of Europeans (14 percent for total Europeans), West Indians (2 percent) and South Americans (3 percent) (U.S. Bureau of the Census 1984: table 342). In contrast, New York's foreign-born population is composed of a wide variety of nationality groups. While over one-third of the foreign-born population in the New York metropolitan area is composed of Europeans, nearly all European nationalities are represented in sizable numbers. Similarly, the Asian population is 13 percent of the total foreign-born and includes in significant numbers all Asian nationalities except perhaps Vietnamese. The North and Central American immigrant population is composed primarily of West Indians, but within that category the diversity is striking: 3 percent of New York's foreign-born population is Cuban and Haitian, respectively; 5 percent is Jamaican; and 7 percent Dominican. The representation of South American nationalities also adds to the diversity of New York: between 2 and 3 percent of the foreign-born population is composed of Colombians, Ecuadorians, and Guyanese, respectively.

New York's flair as an immigrant city may be unsurpassed in the United States, a distinction that takes on even greater demographic significance when an additional regional contrast is made: most urban areas in the South and West are experiencing general population growth, that is, growth in the native-born population due to migration from other areas in the United States; the recent population dynamics in New York, on the other hand, have included an absolute loss of population in both the city and the metropolitan area between 1970 and 1980 (see table 2.6). A focus on New York City shows that between 1960 and 1970 the total population of the city grew slightly, with an absolute decline (113,000) in the total number of immigrants residing in the central city. In fact, the foreign-born population in New York City has been declining since 1930, when the population was its largest (2.4 million persons of foreign birth; see table 2.2). The loss of population has most likely resulted from mortality among the older immigrant populations. Between 1970 and 1980, New York City, like most other cities in the Northeast and North Central regions in the country, lost in total population, over 800,000 persons. The immigrant population, however, increased during the decade, by 46 percent in the United States, and by 16 percent in New York. As alluded to above, this turnaround in trends reflects dramatic shifts in the volume and composition of recent immigrant streams and the relationship of these trends to New York as a residential location.

These patterns of population change are far from being distributed equally among local communities within the New York area. Table 2.7 shows that each of the boroughs except Richmond has lost in total population during the past decade, the Bronx population declining by 21 percent or 300,000 persons. In contrast, the foreign population of the city increased by nearly a quarter of a million between 1970 and 1980, with large increases in the two largest bor-

Table 2.6. U.S., New York Metropolitan Area, and New York City Population and Population Change by Nativity, 1960–1980 (numbers in thousands)

Area of Residence and Nativity	Population			Percent Change	
	1960	1970	1980	1960–70	1970–80
United States					
Total	179325.7	203210.2	226545.8	13.3	11.5
Foreign-born	9738.1	9619.3	14079.9	– 1.2	46.4
New York–New Jersey SMSA[a]					
Total	10696.0	11751.8	9120.3(10803.6)	9.9	–22.4(8.1)
Foreign-born	1858.9	1756.9	1946.8(2056.8)	– 5.5	10.8(17.1)
New York City					
Total	7783.3	7894.9	7071.6	1.4	–10.4
Foreign-born	1558.7	1437.1	1670.2	– 7.8	16.2

Source: U.S. Bureau of the Census 1963, tables 96, 99; U.S. Bureau of the Census 1973a, tables, 81, 141, 144; U.S. Bureau of the Census 1981, table 77; U.S. Bureau of the Census 1983a, tables 116, 172; U.S. Bureau of the Census 1983b, table 195.
[a]Figures in parentheses refer to the population of the New York metropolitan area in 1980 using the boundaries (counties) of the New York SMSA for 1960 and 1970.

Table 2.7. Population Change in New York Metropolitan Counties by Nativity, 1960–1980 (numbers in thousands)

County of Residence and Nativity	Population			Percent Change	
	1960	*1970*	*1980*	*1960–70*	*1970–80*
	Total Population				
New York City	7782.0	7894.9	7071.6	1.4	− 10.4
Bronx	1424.8	1471.7	1169.0	3.3	− 20.6
Kings	2628.2	2602.0	2230.9	− 1.0	− 14.3
New York	1698.3	1539.2	1428.3	− 9.4	− 7.2
Queens	1810.0	1986.5	1891.3	9.8	− 4.8
Richmond	222.0	295.4	352.1	33.1	19.2
Remainder of metropolitan area					
Nassau	1300.2	1428.1	1321.6	9.8	− 7.5
Suffolk	666.8	1124.9	1284.2	68.7	14.2
Putnam	31.7	56.7	77.2	78.9	36.2
Rockland	136.8	229.9	259.5	68.1	12.9
Westchester	808.9	894.1	866.6	10.5	− 3.1
Bergen, N.J.	780.3	898.0	845.4	15.1	5.9
	Foreign-Born Population[a]				
New York City	1558.7	1437.1	1670.2	− 7.8	16.2
Bronx	293.3	229.2	215.3	−21.9	− 6.1
Kings	486.2	456.6	531.0	− 6.1	16.3
New York	335.6	307.6	348.6	− 8.3	13.3
Queens	323.8	419.9	540.8	29.7	28.8
Richmond	24.9	26.7	34.5	7.2	29.2
Remainder of metropolitan area					
Nassau	119.3	118.0	135.9	− 1.1	15.2
Suffolk	59.9	74.8	94.6	24.9	26.5
Putnam	—[b]	4.8	6.2	—	29.2
Rockland	13.4	20.4	29.2	52.2	43.1
Westchester	101.5	106.6	126.9	5.0	19.0
Bergen, N.J.	87.7	95.4	114.3	8.8	19.8

Source: Rosenwaike 1972, tables 64, 65; U.S. Bureau of the Census 1963, tables 96, 99; U.S. Bureau of the Census 1973a, table 119; U.S. Bureau of the Census, 1983a, table 172.
[a]The figures for 1960 refer to white foreign-born only.
[b]Data are not available.

oughs, Kings and Queens, of 16 and 29 percent respectively. While the suburban counties experienced varied patterns of total population change, patterns of growth among the respective foreign-born populations were similar, though the large percentage increases in the foreign-born in these counties are, for the most part, based on absolute changes in small numbers.

Changing population dynamics at the metropolitan level and national patterns of immigration have significant consequences for the social demographic and ethnic composition of both the New York metropolis as well as local metropolitan communities. Just as specific immigrant groups selectively migrate to New York, there exist focused patterns of residential choice for ethnic groups *within* the city. These trends in residential location are consistent with patterns of congregation and segregation for earlier waves of immigrants and are revealed in both ethnic heterogeneity among local communities and ethnic homogeneity within communities. The composition of the immigrant populations within New York City counties is shown in table 2.8. Of course, reliance on the county as the unit of analysis captures only in broad strokes the extent of ethnic variation among local communities in New York. Yet the degree of detail in the classification of country of birth of the foreign-born does result in the identification of each case study population included in this volume except for Haitians, Vincentians and Grenadians, and Soviet Jews.

Table 2.8 reveals the variations in ethnic composition among New York City counties and suggests the different ethnic flavors offered throughout the city. Queens has the largest population of foreign-born which is also the most ethnically diverse. The population of Queens includes large numbers of Italians, Chinese, Koreans, West Indians and, clearly, South Americans. Brooklyn contains West Indians—likely many Haitians as well as Dominicans, Jamaicans, and other English-speaking West Indians—and a relatively large proportion of Russians. The population of the Bronx is composed of both old and new immigrant populations with large proportions of Italians, Irish, and West Indians. Manhattan is the home of many Chinese and Dominicans. Staten Island (Richmond County) includes the smallest number of foreign-born among New York counties but is also the residential choice for a mixture of both early and recent immigrant groups. The foreign-born population is primarily Italian

Table 2.8. New York City and Counties Foreign-Born Population by Area of Birth, 1980 (numbers in thousands)

Area and Country of Birth	New York City	County				
		New York	Kings	Queens	Bronx	Richmond
Foreign-Born Population	1670.2	348.6	531.0	540.8	215.3	34.5
Percent[a]	100.0	100.0	100.0	100.0	100.0	100.0
Europe	34.6	28.8	32.2	38.1	37.5	58.2
Germany	3.6	5.2	1.6	4.8	3.0	4.8
Ireland	2.1	2.1	1.2	2.5	5.9	3.9
Italy	9.4	2.5	11.7	9.1	12.4	27.3
Poland	4.7	3.0	6.8	3.7	4.9	3.0
United Kingdom	2.0	3.0	1.5	1.7	1.9	4.6
USSR	5.3	3.6	7.6	4.3	5.5	1.5
Asia	12.9	18.0	8.6	16.3	5.6	17.3
China	3.6	8.2	2.3	3.2	1.0	2.1
India	1.3	1.0	0.7	2.3	0.8	2.6
Japan	0.6	0.1	0.7	0.8	0.5	0.5
Korea	1.1	0.7	0.4	2.2	0.8	3.3
Philippines	1.2	1.4	0.7	1.7	0.6	4.5
Vietnam	0.2	0.2	0.2	0.2	0.1	0.1
North and Central America	29.6	32.6	36.5	20.6	33.5	10.2
Canada	3.7	1.5	0.8	0.8	0.7	2.1
West Indies	24.8	28.2	30.3	17.0	28.3	5.3
Cuba	2.8	4.6	1.4	3.3	2.4	1.3
Dominican Republic	7.4	18.4	3.7	4.3	7.8	0.6
Jamaica	5.4	1.6	7.7	3.6	11.5	0.8
South America	9.2	7.1	7.0	13.9	6.7	5.3
Africa	1.4	1.8	1.4	1.2	1.2	2.6
All other countries	0.1	0.4	0.1	0.1	0.0	0.3
Country not reported	6.9	7.8	6.6	5.6	10.0	4.6

Source: U.S. Bureau of the Census 1983a, table 172.
[a]Numbers may not add to total due to rounding.

but also contains relatively high proportions of the new Asian groups, particularly Koreans and Filipinos.

The striking ethnic variation among New York City counties is complemented by data presented in table 2.9 which show the patterns of urban residence among migrant groups. The attention here is to population characteristics rather than place characteristics. Table 2.9 reveals dramatic patterns of residential variation for nearly all immigrant groups except for persons born in the United Kingdom. Germans and Poles are among the more residentially selective Europeans; similarly, 46 percent of immigrants from the USSR are located in the one borough of Brooklyn. Patterns of residence among recent immigrants are extremely distinctive. Asian immigrants are residentially concentrated: nearly half of the Chinese population was living in Manhattan in 1980, and another sizable proportion, 29 percent, in Queens; Koreans are highly concentrated in Queens as are immigrants from the Philippines and India. Over half of the Dominican population was residing in Manhattan in 1980 while Jamaicans were concentrated in Brooklyn and almost half of the South Americans were living in Queens. Unfortunately, census data are not published by country of birth below the county level; thus indicators of local patterns of congregation and segregation have not been developed here.

The patterns of residential selection presented in table 2.9 for local urban communities should also be considered on the metropolitan level. Table 2.10 shows the distribution of immigrant populations between New York City and the remainder of the SMSA in 1980 (the New York counties of Westchester, Putnam, and Rockland, and the New Jersey county of Bergen). Patterns of residence vary sharply between earlier and more recent immigrant streams with the latter being much more concentrated in the central city. Only 6 percent of West Indian immigrants live outside of the central city with the Dominicans being even more centralized than the Jamaicans and Cubans. Only 7 percent of Russians reside in suburban counties. Chinese, too, are highly concentrated in the city counties. The suburban pattern among the Japanese is an interesting exception.

The results shown in tables 2.11 and 2.12 complement those just presented for metropolitan communities and populations by illustrating the impact of patterns of immigration over time for urban

Table 2.9. New York City Foreign-Born Population by Area of Birth and County of Residence, 1980 (numbers in thousands)

Area and Country of Birth	New York City (Number)	(Percent)[a]	County New York	Kings	Queens	Bronx	Richmond
Total population	7071.6	100.0	20.2	31.5	26.7	16.5	5.0
Foreign-born population	1670.2	100.0	20.9	31.8	32.4	12.9	2.1
Europe	578.0	100.0	17.4	29.6	35.6	14.0	3.5
Germany	60.7	100.0	29.6	14.1	42.8	10.7	2.7
Ireland	41.4	100.0	17.6	15.9	32.9	30.5	3.2
Italy	156.4	100.0	5.5	39.7	31.6	17.1	6.0
Poland	78.1	100.0	13.6	46.2	25.4	13.5	1.3
United Kingdom	33.5	100.0	30.9	24.5	27.6	12.2	4.7
USSR	88.4	100.0	14.1	45.8	26.1	13.4	0.6
Asia	214.7	100.0	29.3	21.4	41.0	5.6	2.8
China	60.8	100.0	47.1	19.8	28.6	3.4	1.2
India	21.9	100.0	15.3	16.3	56.8	7.5	4.0
Japan	9.5	100.0	3.1	39.6	44.2	11.2	1.8
Korea	18.4	100.0	13.2	11.3	59.6	9.8	6.1
Philippines	20.2	100.0	23.5	17.5	44.7	6.5	7.8
Vietnam	3.4	100.0	24.6	27.9	36.8	9.5	1.2
North and Central America	494.6	100.0	23.0	39.2	22.5	14.6	0.7
Canada	15.9	100.0	32.0	27.2	27.1	9.1	4.6
West Indies	414.0	100.0	23.8	38.9	22.2	14.7	0.4
Cuba	46.9	100.0	34.1	15.8	38.3	10.9	0.9
Dominican Republic	124.1	100.0	51.6	16.0	18.8	13.4	0.2
Jamaica	90.8	100.0	6.2	44.9	21.3	27.3	0.3
South America	153.7	100.0	16.2	24.2	49.0	9.4	1.2
Africa	23.6	100.0	26.0	30.9	28.3	11.1	3.8
All other countries	2.2	100.0	57.3	14.3	18.6	4.5	5.2
Country not reported	115.0	100.0	23.5	30.3	26.1	18.7	1.4

Source: U.S. Bureau of the Census 1983a, table 172.
[a]Numbers may not add to total due to rounding.

Table 2.10. New York–New Jersey SMSA Foreign-Born Population by Area of Birth and Metropolitan Residence, 1980 (numbers in thousands)

Area and Country of Birth	N.Y.–N.J. SMSA	New York City (Number)	Remainder of SMSA	N.Y.–N.J. SMSA	New York City (Percent)[a]	Remainder of SMSA
Total population	9120.3	7071.6	2048.7	100	78	22
Foreign-born population	1946.8	1670.2	276.6	100	86	14
Europe	734.6	578.0	156.6	100	79	21
Germany	83.8	60.7	23.0	100	73	27
Ireland	52.5	41.4	11.1	100	79	21
Italy	204.6	156.4	48.2	100	76	24
Poland	90.4	78.1	12.2	100	87	13
United Kingdom	48.6	33.5	15.1	100	69	31
USSR	95.5	88.4	7.1	100	93	7
Asia	254.9	214.7	40.3	100	84	16
China	64.0	60.8	3.2	100	95	5
India	27.4	21.9	5.5	100	80	20
Japan	17.4	9.5	7.8	100	55	45
Korea	22.6	18.4	4.2	100	81	19
Philippines	25.2	20.2	5.0	100	80	20
Vietnam	4.0	3.4	0.6	100	85	15
North and Central America	532.5	494.6	37.9	100	93	7
Canada	22.9	15.9	7.0	100	69	31
West Indies	440.0	414.0	25.9	100	94	6
Cuba	54.3	46.9	7.4	100	86	14
Dominican Republic	127.7	124.1	3.6	100	97	3
Jamaica	98.8	90.8	8.0	100	92	8
South America	172.2	153.7	18.5	100	89	11
Africa	27.2	23.6	3.6	100	87	13
All other countries	3.1	2.2	0.9	100	71	29
Country not reported	126.8	115.0	11.8	100	91	9

Source: U.S. Bureau of the Census 1983a, table 172; U.S. Bureau of the Census 1983b, table 195.
[a]Numbers may not add to total due to rounding.

communities. Table 2.11 provides the distribution of the foreign-born population by period of immigration for counties and illustrates how communities within the city vary according to the pace of population change due to immigration. The patterns of variation dovetail with the ethnic characteristics of areas shown in the previous two tables. Brooklyn, Manhattan, and Queens are each composed of a high proportion, nearly a quarter, of recent immigrants to New York City. The populations of Richmond, the Bronx, and suburban counties include relatively fewer recent immigrants and are composed of a high proportion of earlier immigrant stock.

Finally, the timing of immigration is distinctive for nationality groups. Table 2.12 presents the distribution of selected immigrant populations in the New York metropolitan area in 1980 by period of immigration. For the most part European residents in New York in 1980 entered the United States before 1960 while Asians, Central and South Americans, and West Indians have immigrated since 1965. These patterns reflect changes in immigration policy as well as changes in the demand for immigration and refuge. Certain groups have dramatically stepped up their immigration since 1975. The influx of the Vietnamese is a clear response to the end of the Vietnam War, and there are also the recent Soviet refugees. Nearly two-thirds of the Japanese and over half of the Koreans in New York have immigrated since 1975. Similarly, the pace of immigration from Guyana to New York has accelerated in recent years.

CONCLUSION

The role played by international migration in the population dynamics of New York has been historically significant—and continues to be. Patterns of immigration to New York sharply contrast with other areas in the country; the recent immigrant streams of West Indians and South Americans are virtually unique to New York. Concurrently, the composition of immigrants residing in New York has changed as a result of the changing international structure of the demand for immigration to the United States, shifts in U.S. immigration policy, and the striking selectivity among certain of the new immigrant groups for the New York area. These patterns of selective

Table 2.11. New York Metropolitan Counties Foreign-Born Population by Year of Immigration, 1980 (numbers in thousands)

Place and County of Residence	Total Foreign-Born Population (Number)	Year of Immigration (Percent)[a]						
		All Years	1975–1980	1970–1974	1965–1969	1960–1964	1950–1959	Before 1950
New York–New Jersey SMSA	1946.8	100.0	20.5	18.2	15.7	8.9	11.3	25.3
New York City	1670.2	100.0	21.2	18.9	16.1	8.9	10.6	24.3
County								
New York	348.6	100.0	23.6	18.2	15.8	9.4	10.2	22.8
Kings	531.0	100.0	22.8	20.2	16.1	7.8	9.8	23.4
Queens	540.8	100.0	20.5	18.8	16.9	9.8	11.5	22.4
Bronx	215.3	100.0	16.8	17.5	15.2	8.1	10.6	31.8
Richmond	34.5	100.0	11.4	15.3	12.3	9.6	13.7	37.7
Remainder of metropolitan area								
Nassau	135.9	100.0	11.6	11.8	13.0	9.8	16.2	37.5
Suffolk	94.6	100.0	8.9	9.9	11.1	9.7	19.4	40.9
Putnam	6.2	100.0	4.7	5.2	9.7	11.7	23.2	45.5
Rockland	29.2	100.0	15.0	14.4	13.0	9.0	17.2	31.5
Westchester	126.9	100.0	17.0	15.1	13.6	9.3	14.6	30.4
Bergen, N.J.	114.3	100.0	16.0	13.9	13.3	9.5	15.6	31.7

Source: U.S. Bureau of the Census 1983a, table 172; U.S. Bureau of the Census 1983b, table 195.
[a]Numbers may not add to total due to rounding.

Table 2.12. New York–New Jersey SMSA Foreign-Born Population by Area of Birth and Year of Immigration, 1980 (numbers in thousands)

Country of Birth	Total Foreign-Born Population (Number)	All Years	Year of Immigration (Percent)[a]					
			1975–1980	1970–1974	1965–1969	1960–1964	1950–1959	Before 1950
New York–New Jersey SMSA	1946.8	100.0	20.5	18.2	15.7	8.9	11.3	25.3
Europe	734.6	100.0	6.9	8.9	10.0	8.6	18.6	47.0
Germany	83.8	100.0	3.4	2.1	3.3	6.6	23.5	61.2
Ireland	52.5	100.0	2.5	3.8	4.5	9.9	19.9	59.4
Italy	204.6	100.0	4.1	10.3	12.2	10.1	19.1	44.3
Poland	90.4	100.0	5.6	4.0	5.3	7.3	16.6	61.3
United Kingdom	48.6	100.0	15.6	9.7	9.5	9.8	15.3	40.0
USSR	95.5	100.0	32.1	4.4	2.0	2.3	6.5	52.7
Asia	254.9	100.0	38.9	27.0	14.4	6.9	5.8	7.1
China	64.0	100.0	26.7	23.1	17.9	11.1	8.6	12.5
Hong Kong	17.6	100.0	31.8	29.2	25.4	8.6	3.0	1.9
India	27.4	100.0	48.1	36.5	10.3	2.6	1.6	0.8
Israel	18.7	100.0	28.5	21.4	14.6	11.7	15.5	8.3
Japan	17.4	100.0	64.4	15.0	8.3	5.3	5.2	1.8
Korea	22.6	100.0	54.9	32.0	7.5	3.3	1.9	0.4
Philippines	25.2	100.0	31.1	39.5	19.3	4.2	2.1	3.7
Vietnam	4.0	100.0	87.4	8.4	2.6	0.6	0.8	0.3

North and Central America	532.5	100.0	24.3	25.9	24.2	11.0	7.1	7.4
Canada	22.9	100.0	12.5	7.4	9.3	10.0	15.9	45.0
El Salvador	7.4	100.0	43.3	31.8	19.2	2.4	2.0	1.3
Guatemala	6.3	100.0	28.9	35.8	25.7	3.9	2.5	3.1
Mexico	8.7	100.0	35.5	23.3	14.8	8.0	8.0	10.4
West Indies	440.0	100.0	24.5	27.1	25.7	10.8	6.2	5.7
Barbados	18.7	100.0	28.0	27.1	18.9	6.5	5.7	13.8
Cuba	54.3	100.0	3.9	15.7	27.9	26.1	18.6	7.9
Dominican Republic	127.7	100.0	30.9	26.3	25.4	12.3	3.6	1.6
Haiti	52.6	100.0	26.7	32.8	27.8	8.3	3.4	1.0
Jamaica	98.8	100.0	25.8	29.8	26.8	5.8	4.9	6.9
Trinidad and Tobago	39.6	100.0	26.7	35.0	26.1	5.1	3.1	4.0
South America	172.2	100.0	30.8	27.7	23.1	10.6	4.7	3.2
Argentina	14.0	100.0	22.2	22.2	19.7	18.9	9.9	7.2
Brazil	6.5	100.0	26.8	23.4	20.0	13.3	6.7	9.8
Colombia	47.2	100.0	27.6	27.2	26.8	12.0	4.6	1.7
Ecuador	41.8	100.0	25.7	29.4	28.9	11.0	3.8	1.3
Guyana	31.7	100.0	48.5	27.1	17.1	2.2	2.3	2.8
Peru	12.0	100.0	28.8	33.9	17.6	12.7	4.7	2.2
Africa	27.2	100.0	32.6	26.4	14.6	10.3	8.3	7.7
Egypt	8.3	100.0	21.5	25.9	19.6	15.3	12.2	5.6

Source: U.S. Bureau of the Census 1983b, table 195.
aNumbers may not add to total due to rounding.

migration are having a dramatic impact on the social demography of local communities throughout the city and larger metropolitan area.

These observations are based on the analysis of population data available from recent censuses. Detailed tables have been included here both to illustrate specific trends and issues as well as to serve as a resource for future reference. In pointing to the interaction between immigration policy and changes in the demography of international migration to New York, this analysis provides a backdrop for studies that examine the specific effects of immigration on local communities and on the immigrants themselves. The demographic evidence presented here will, I hope, serve as a stimulus for future research into the causes and consequences of immigration to New York.

NOTES

1. Support for this research was provided by the Colgate Research Council. The author wishes to thank Nancy Foner, Lisa S. Roney, Mary G. Powers, Joseph Salvo, and Frank Vardy for extremely helpful comments and suggestions on early drafts, and Edgar and Marjorie Percy for logistical support.
2. For an excellent review of the rights of aliens and immigrants see Hull (1983).
3. Garis (1927) is an interesting primary source on the methods used to calculate visa quotas. See also U.S. Select Commission on Immigration and Refugee Policy (1981:296–322).
4. Grounds for inadmissibility for individual aliens, first introduced in the 1870s, were extended rapidly during the late nineteenth and early twentieth century. The list now includes over thirty separate criteria on the basis of which admission as either an immigrant or nonimmigrant may be denied. Among the criteria are mental retardation, alcoholism, insanity, likelihood of becoming public charges, vagrancy, illiteracy, espionage, and criminal history.
5. In spite of the Chinese Exclusion Acts of the 1880s, a small stream of immigration was maintained from China during this century (see table 2.1). These Chinese immigrants came under "exempt" classes of immigration, including spouses and unmarried minor children of U.S. citizens, expatriated citizens, students, teachers, returning laborers and merchants, and travelers for pleasure or curiosity.
6. U.S. immigration and refugee policy certainly reached its lowest level of international responsibility during the 1930s when Germans seeking asylum from the Nazi regime were denied admission to the United States

due to insufficient immigrant quotas for Germany; bills to admit Germans as refugees were introduced but then defeated by Congress.

7. A detailed review of the refugee programs of the 1970s is presented in Taft et al. (1979).

8. For a thorough review of estimates of the size and characteristics of the illegal alien population in the United States see Levine, Hill, and Warren (1985).

9. Zip code of intended residence is available in the annual public use sample for immigrant admission and can be used to develop a social demographic profile of immigrants intending to reside initially in areas in New York.

10. Other census data sources, also available in published detail and public use tapes, provide additional bases for immigrant research. The Current Population Survey (CPS), a national survey of households conducted since the 1940s, generates detailed data on selected social demographic topics such as fertility and geographic mobility. In recent years, ethnicity and immigration have been included as special topics. The Survey of Income and Education, an expanded form of the CPS, was conducted in 1976 to collect highly detailed information on children living in disadvantaged households. This survey has been a particularly important source of data on the characteristics of immigrant households (see, for example, Wolpin 1980 and Bean et al. 1980).

11. The estimate for New York State was derived by Passel and Woodrow (1985). Researchers at the Bureau of the Census have made preliminary estimates for metropolitan areas in the United States. The methodology on which these estimates are based was originally described in Warren and Passel (1983).

12. At this point in time there are only five countries which can be considered as major countries of permanent settlement: the United States, Canada, Australia, New Zealand, and South Africa. There is striking variation among these countries in terms of the numbers and characteristics of immigrants admitted (see Zolberg 1983).

REFERENCES

Bean, Frank et al. 1980. "Patterns of Fertility Variation Among Mexican Immigrants to the United States." Paper prepared for the U.S. Commission on Immigration and Refugee Policy. Austin: University of Texas.

Borjas, G. J. 1981. "Hispanic Immigrants in the U.S. Labor Market: An Empirical Analysis." In M. Tienda, ed., Hispanic Origin Workers in the U.S. Labor Market: Comparative Analyses, pp. 200–225. Final report to the U.S. Department of Labor, Employment and Training Administration, Washington, D.C.

Cafferty, P. et al. 1983. The Dilemma of American Immigration. New Brunswick, N.J.: Transaction Books.

Chiswick, B. R. 1978. "The Effect of Americanization on the Earnings of Foreign-Born Men." *Journal of Political Economy* 86:897–921.

Garis, Roy L. 1927. *Immigration Restriction.* New York: Macmillan.

Hirschman, C. and M. G. Wong. 1981. "Trends in Socioeconomic Achievement Among Immigrant and Native-Born Americans." *The Sociological Quarterly* 22:495–513.

Hull, Elizabeth. 1983. "The Rights of Aliens: National and International Issues." In D. Papademetriou and M. Miller, eds., *The Unavoidable Issue: U.S. Immigration Policy in the 1980s,* pp. 215–249. Philadelphia: Institute for the Study of Human Issues.

Hutchinson, E. P. 1958. "Notes on Immigration Statistics of the United States." *Journal of the American Statistical Association* 55:963–1025.

—— 1965. "Our Statistics of International Migration: Comparability and Completeness for Demographic Use." Mimeo.

Keely, Charles B. 1971. "Effects of the Immigration Act of 1965 on Selected Population Characteristics of Immigrants to the United States." *Demography* 8:157–169.

—— 1975. "Effects of U.S. Immigration Law on Manpower Characteristics of Immigrants." *Demography* 12:179–191.

—— 1981. *Global Refugee Policy: A Case for a Development-Oriented Strategy.* New York: The Population Council.

Kraly, Ellen Percy. 1979a. "Systems of International Migration Statistics: The United States as a National Case Study." Doctoral dissertation, Fordham University.

—— 1979b. "Sources of Data for the Study of U.S. Immigration." In S. R. Couch and R. S. Bryce-LaPorte, eds., *Quantitative Data and Immigration Research,* pp. 34–54. RIIES Research Note No. 2. Washington, D.C.: Smithsonian Institution.

Levine, Daniel, Kenneth Hill, and Robert Warren, eds. 1985. *Immigration Statistics, A Story of Neglect.* Washington, D.C.: National Academy Press.

Passel, Jeffrey and Karen Woodrow. 1985. "Geographic Distribution of Undocumented Immigrants: Estimates of Undocumented Aliens Counted in the 1980 Census, by State." *International Migration Review* 18:642–671.

Portes, Alejandro. 1983. "International Labor Migration and National Development." In M. M. Kritz, ed., *U.S. Immigration and Refugee Policy,* pp. 71–91. Lexington, Mass.: D. C. Heath.

Reimers, David. 1985. *Still the Golden Door.* New York: Columbia University Press.

Rosenwaike, Ira. 1972. *Population History of New York City.* Syracuse: Syracuse University Press.

Suhrke, Astri. 1983. "Global Refugee Movements and Strategies of Response." In M. M. Kritz, ed., *U.S. Immigration and Refugee Policy,* pp. 157–173. Lexington, Mass.: D. C. Heath.

Taft, Julia V., et al. 1979. *Refugee Resettlement in the U.S.: Time for a New Focus.* Washington, D.C.: New TransCentury Foundation.

Tomasi, S. M. and Charles B. Keely. 1975. *Whom Have We Welcomed?* New York: Center for Migration Studies.

U.S. Bureau of the Census. 1963. *1960 Census of Population.* Vol. 1, *Characteristics of the Population.* Part 32, New Jersey; part 34, New York. Washington, D.C.: U.S. Government Printing Office.

—— 1972. *1970 Census of Population.* Vol. 1, "Detailed Characteristics," part 34, New York. Washington, D.C.: U.S. Government Printing Office.

—— 1973a. *1970 Census of Population.* Vol. 1, *Characteristics of the Population.* Part 34, New York (section 2). Washington, D.C.: U.S. Government Printing Office.

—— 1973b. *1970 Census of Population.* Vol. 1, *Characteristics of the Population.* Part 1, United States Summary (section 1). Washington, D.C.: U.S. Government Printing Office.

—— 1975. *Historical Statistics of the United States, Colonial Times to 1970.* Bicentennial Edition, part 1. Washington, D.C.: U.S. Government Printing Office.

—— 1981. *1980 Census of Population.* Vol. 1, *Characteristics of the Population,* ch. C, "General Social and Economic Characteristics," part 1, United States Summary. Washington, D.C.: U.S. Government Printing Office.

—— 1983a. *1980 Census of Population.* Vol. 1, *Characteristics of the Population,* ch. C, "General Social and Economic Characteristics," part 32, New Jersey; part 34, New York (section 2). Washington, D.C.: U.S. Government Printing Office.

—— 1983b. *1980 Census of Population.* Vol. 1, *Characteristics of the Population,* ch. D, "Detailed Population Characteristics," part 34, New York (section 1). Washington, D.C.: U.S. Government Printing Office.

—— 1983c. *1980 Census of Population.* Vol. 1, *Characteristics of Population,* ch. A, "General Social Economic Statistics," part 1, U.S. Summary. Washington, D.C.: U.S. Government Printing Office.

—— 1984. *1980 Census of Population.* Vol. 1, *Characteristics of the Population,* ch. D, "Detailed Population Characteristics," part 1, United States Summary (section A): United States. Washington, D.C.: U.S. Government Printing Office.

U.S. Department of Justice. 1985. *1983 Statistical Yearbook of the Immigration and Naturalization Service.* Washington, D.C.: U.S. Government Printing Office.

U.S. Select Commission on Immigration and Refugee Policy. 1981. *U.S. Immigration Policy and the National Interest. Staff Report.* Washington, D.C.: U.S. Government Printing Office.

Warren, Robert and Ellen Percy Kraly. 1985. "The Elusive Exodus: Emigration from the United States." *Population Trends and Public Policy* 8. Washington, D.C.: Population Reference Bureau.

Warren, Robert and Jeffrey Passel. 1983. "Estimates of Illegal Aliens from Mexico Counted in the 1980 United States Census." Paper presented at the Annual Meeting of the Population Association of America. Pittsburgh, Pa.

Wolpin, Kenneth. 1980. "The Household Structure of Immigrants and Natives." Paper prepared for the U.S. Commission on Immigration and Refugee Policy. New Haven: Yale University.

Zolberg, Aristide R. 1983. "Contemporary Transnational Migrations in Historical Perspective: Patterns and Dilemmas." In M. M. Kritz, ed., *U.S. Immigration and Refugee Policy*, pp. 15–51. Lexington, Mass.: D.C. Heath.

3. New Immigrants in New York's Economy

Adriana Marshall

As is well known, one consequence of the change in the United States immigration law in 1965 was a dramatic increase in the volume of immigration. This new immigration wave has been dominated by migrants from Latin America, Asia, and the non-Hispanic Caribbean, while the share of Europeans in the total immigration flow declined.

New-wave immigrants are overwhelmingly concentrated in large metropolitan areas, and, as in the past, New York City is one of the most important receiving areas. In 1980, New York rivaled Los Angeles in the proportion of foreign-born in the population; of the major metropolitan areas, only Miami had a larger share of immigrants. Throughout the 1970s, large numbers of immigrants settled in New York despite the fact that there were already too many native-born workers in the region relative to the number of available jobs.

This essay focuses on the way the "new" immigrant workers fit into the New York labor market and on some implications for the city's economy and labor force.[1] I am particularly concerned here with Latin American, Asian, and non-Hispanic Caribbean immigrants who arrived since 1965 and it is these immigrants I have in mind when I use the term "new" or "new-wave" immigrants.[2] During the period examined in this chapter, the 1970s, New York was characterized by high unemployment levels and a negligible growth in labor demand. Given these circumstances, new immigrants faced a restricted range of employment options. How the new immigrant groups were distributed in New York's employment structure in the 1970s was a result of two main influences: the alternatives available to immigrants in the city's economy and the sociodemographic composition of different migration streams. The fact that, due to the excess labor supply conditions, employment for new immigrants tended to be concentrated in certain economic activities—manufacturing, for example—had important consequences for New York City's economy and for the labor force in general.

THE EMPLOYMENT DISTRIBUTION OF
NEW-WAVE IMMIGRANTS IN NEW YORK

In 1980 over two million immigrants—including an estimated 750,000 undocumented immigrants—were living in the New York metropolitan area.[3] As more and more new immigrants arrived in the city during the 1970s, large numbers of the U.S.-born population—whites as well as blacks—moved out. In addition, there was a marked decline in new Puerto Rican in-migration in the 1970s, a trend that had already begun in the 1960s. In fact, in the 1970s, there was a net return movement to Puerto Rico (see McClelland and Magdovitz 1981; and Jaffe et al. 1980:190).

The rapid growth of foreign in-migration during the 1970s, combined with the continuous exodus of American-born people out of New York City, meant that by 1980 the foreign-born (legal as well as illegal immigrants) might have represented as much as 27 percent of the New York metropolitan area's population.[4] Most of the immigrants who arrived in the 1970s were from Latin America, Asia, and the non-Hispanic Caribbean. Data from the Immigration and Naturalization Service (INS) show that between 1971 and 1980 these three geographic regions accounted for 70 percent of the total legal inflow into the city.

Even more crucial than the purely demographic effects of the new immigration, I would argue, is the impact of the newcomers on New York's labor force. The new immigrants have especially high rates of labor force participation. A large proportion of recent immigrants are young adults, that is, those most likely to be active in the labor force in the first place. Besides, all immigrant adults (sixteen years and over) have higher rates of labor force participation than the American-born (Marshall 1983:9). The impact of the new immigration is particularly felt on the manual labor force—manual work referring here to all blue-collar occupations, including factory and "service" work. I estimate that in 1980, foreign workers who arrived in the 1970s, including illegal and legal immigrants, constituted about 35 percent of the New York metropolitan area's manual labor force (Marshall 1983:7–13)—although they did not exceed 16 percent of the area's population. Post-1970 immigrants from Latin America, Asia, and the non-Hispanic Caribbean specifically probably accounted for about a quarter of New York's manual labor force.

Large-scale immigration from Latin America, Asia, and the non-Hispanic Caribbean thus continued to increase during the 1970s despite unfavorable labor market conditions in the New York area in these years. Overall manufacturing employment decreased even more drastically in the 1970s than during the previous decade. In 1980, for example, manufacturing payroll employment was 30 percent lower than in 1970, following a 16 percent decline between 1960 and 1970. The negligible growth of employment outside of manufacturing did not compensate for this loss. Unemployment reached a peak in 1975 (11.5 percent of New York City's labor force) and remained at high levels for the rest of the decade. Total nonagricultural employment in the New York metropolitan area, which had risen in the 1960s, was below the 1960 level by 1980 (unpublished data from the New York State Department of Labor).[5]

Despite the dramatic worsening of the labor market situation in the 1970s, the employment distribution of the new-wave immigrant labor force shows a remarkable stability over time. Indeed, the differences in the location of immigrant and native workers in New York's employment structure that were found in 1970, a year preceded by a period with relatively low unemployment rates,[6] were still the same in 1980, after a decade of persistently high unemployment levels.

The more stable traits of the employment distributions of new-wave immigrant workers, in terms of employment status, occupation, and industry, and the minor changes in these distributions between 1970 and 1980 are discussed in the following pages.

Employment Status

In 1980, as ten years earlier, new-wave immigrants in the New York metropolitan area were first and foremost wage workers in the private sector (as opposed to public sector employees, the self-employed, and unpaid family workers). Wage employment in the private sector was more common among immigrants, both women and men, than among the American-born and Puerto Ricans (see table 3.1).[7] Moreover, the most recent immigrants (who arrived between 1975 and 1980) had higher rates of wage employment in the private sector than earlier immigrant cohorts (table 3.1). The higher level of wage employment, and lower rates of self-employment, among recent immigrants as compared to earlier cohorts, are probably due to their shorter residence in New York as well as to the higher proportion of young adults in the twenty to thirty-five age group in their numbers (see Marshall 1983:18). Recent immigrants have had less time than earlier immigrants to gather the capital required to set up their own enterprises, and, in general, young adults are less likely to be self-employed than the middle-aged, for similar reasons.

Table 3.1. Employment Status: Percent of Native and Foreign Employed Labor Force in Private Sector Wage Employment, New York SMSA, 1970–80

				Born in:		
	New York State	*Rest U.S.*	*Puerto Rico*	*Latin America*	*Non-Hispanic Caribbean*	*Asia*
Males						
1970	69.5	73.8	84.3	88.9[a]	84.2	73.6
1980	70.4	69.7	78.4	87.2	83.1	79.9
Arrival:						
Before 1970				84.6	77.9	73.0
1970–74				88.4	82.9	79.1
1975–80				92.7	94.6	86.8
Females						
1970	77.8	73.1	85.3	88.1[a]	85.4	77.7
1980	77.1	77.5	71.8	86.8	82.5	82.7
Arrival:						
Before 1970				86.4	80.5	81.1
1970–74				86.3	84.5	83.3
1975–80				89.1	84.1	84.2

Source: Unpublished data from the Census of Population and Housing 1970, Public Use Sample and from the Census of Population and Housing 1980, Public Use Microdata Sample.

[a]Does not include Cubans. The fact that Cubans are included in 1980 and not 1970 has little effect on the comparisons since the Cubans are very similar to other Latin Americans in their employment distributions (Marshall 1983:15).

It should be noted, however, that the proportion of immigrants with wage employment in the private sector was somewhat smaller in 1980 than in 1970, except for Asians (see table 3.1). The slight decline in the share of wage workers in the private sector among Latin Americans and non-Hispanic Caribbeans was, in the case of men, the result of a small movement into self-employment and, in the case of women, some access to employment in the government sector, often as cleaners in public buildings and nursing aides in public hospitals. Among Puerto Rican migrants, the decrease in the rate of wage employment in the private sector is particularly noticeable, and was due to a visible move into government employment. As for Asians, in 1970, the rate of wage employment in the private sector was considerably lower than for other immigrant groups—and close to that of native workers—because they were more oriented to self-employment. Private sector wage employment for Asians, however, had increased by 1980, paralleled by a decline in their employment in government, nonincorporated self-employment, and as "unpaid family workers" (Unpublished data from the Census of Population 1970 and 1980).

Occupational Structure

The 1980 census shows that new immigrants were concentrated in manual occupations (table 3.2). With the exception of Asian males, new-wave immigrant workers were, as compared to native labor, overrepresented in nearly all manual positions, particularly as operatives and in certain service worker jobs. It is interesting that immigrant men were not overrepresented as laborers, one of the least skilled manual jobs. Asians had a considerably lower proportion in manual occupations than other new immigrants, undoubtedly because, as INS reports indicate, admitted Asians included a much higher percentage of nonmanual workers than other nationalities.

Although census data show that the comparative occupational distribution of native and immigrant labor did not alter much during the 1970s (table 3.2), certain trends are worth mentioning. One of these trends has to do with the representation of American-born workers in manual jobs. The figures in table 3.2 for 1970 reflect the outcome of the occupational shift that had been underway in New York during the 1960s. The participation of the American-born in the

Table 3.2. Occupational Structure: Percent of Native and Foreign Employed Labor Force in Manual Occupations, New York, SMSA, 1970–80

| | Born in: | | | | | |
	New York State	Rest U.S.	Puerto Rico	Latin America	Non-Hispanic Caribbean	Asia
Males						
1970	44.5	43.7	76.7	63.6[a]	57.9	43.1
1980	47.2	54.6	70.1	68.7	61.7	40.2
Arrival:						
Before 1970				62.5	58.0	35.2
1970–74				73.7	63.5	43.1
1975–80				77.6	66.9	44.4
Females						
1970	19.0	31.1	60.6	60.2[a]	48.1	44.2
1980	14.4	17.6	48.8	59.5	48.5	39.8
Arrival:						
Before 1970				55.5	44.3	36.6
1970–74				59.8	49.6	34.5
1975–80				73.4	56.1	49.4

Source: Unpublished data from the Census of Population and Housing 1970, Public Use Sample and from the Census of Population and Housing 1980, Public Use Microdata Sample.

Note: Manual occupations includes service, farming, fishing and forestry, precision production, craft and repair occupations, operators, fabricators, and laborers.

[a]Does not include Cubans.

manual labor market had declined sharply in this decade, when non-manual employment was still growing (Bahl et al. 1974; Bureau of Labor Statistics 1973) and New Yorkers and other United States natives (including descendants of earlier immigrants and ethnic minorities) were appropriating white-collar jobs.[8] Meanwhile, foreign workers were taking the place of native labor in many manual occupations. While the shift of the American-born toward nonmanual jobs continued during the 1970s in the case of females, this was not so for native men. Native men seem to have "returned," albeit on a small scale, to manual positions, possibly as a result of the slowing down of the rate of growth of nonmanual employment during the 1970s. As for new-wave immigrant workers, Latin American and non-Hispanic Caribbean men increased their participation in the manual labor market in 1980 as compared with 1970, while women in these groups continued to be as overrepresented in manual occupations in 1980 as they had been ten years earlier. The proportion of Asian men and women in manual occupations, however, declined slightly between 1970 and 1980, although the overrepresentation of Asian women in these jobs was still very marked. And while Puerto Rican men were still considerably overrepresented in manual jobs, they seem to be gradually moving out of the manual labor market (table 3.2).

A look at different cohorts of new-wave immigrants in 1980—those who arrived before 1970, in the early 1970s, and between 1975 and 1980—reveals another trend. Recent cohorts of all three new-wave immigrant groups, including Asians, have more workers employed in manual occupations than earlier cohorts (table 3.2), due both to the employment options available to new immigrants in the New York area and to the "manualization" of the new inflows. Immigration and Naturalization Service data on the occupational composition of immigrant flows at the time of entering the United States document this process of "manualization": with the exception of European immigrants, the proportion of manual workers in the inflows tended to increase during the 1970s. For instance, excluding nonlabor force participants, the proportion of manual workers went from 30 percent among Asians admitted in 1967 to 43.5 percent among Asians admitted in 1979; from 51 percent among South Americans admitted in 1967 to 60 percent among South Americans admitted in 1979; and from 61 percent among North Americans (a category including the rest of the Latin Americans and the non-Hispanic Caribbeans) admitted in 1967 to 68 percent among North Americans admitted in 1979 (Immigration and Naturalization Service 1967, 1979).

Industrial Distribution

New-wave immigrants are concentrated in a number of sectors in New York's economy, and manufacturing is one of the most important. In fact, the substitution of native by foreign workers in the manual labor market in recent years has been quite remarkable in New York's manufacturing industry.

First consider the relation of new immigrants to the manufacturing industry in the early phase of the new-wave immigration: 1970. From the late 1960s on, new immigrants were increasingly drawn to manufacturing jobs (Marshall 1983:19–21). At the same time as new-wave immigrants were moving in ever-growing numbers into manufacturing, native New Yorkers and those born in the rest of the country were leaving manufacturing for employment in other sectors of the economy. It is doubtful, however, that the outward movement of native labor from factory jobs would have created a substantial labor scarcity in manufacturing if new immigrants had not appeared on the scene. Native workers were abandoning an industry that was losing jobs and, at least in the early years of the new immigration, the impact of new immigrants on the labor supply in manufacturing was still relatively small.

In 1970, then, new-wave immigration was in its initial stages, and so was the substitution of native by foreign labor. At this time, immigrants who arrived after 1965 provided a small additional labor supply in New York. Even assuming that the 1970 census failed to include some illegal immigrants, the number of Latin American, Asian, and non-Hispanic Caribbean workers in the labor force was not striking. Altogether, according to the 1970 census, immigrants from these three regions—those who arrived before as well as after 1965—constituted only about 7 percent of the manual labor force in the New York area (see Marshall 1983:24). As for new immigrants' role in manufacturing, according to 1970 census counts, all immigrant workers from Latin America, the non-Hispanic Caribbean, and Asia, including pre- as well as post-1965 immigrants, represented no more than 10 percent of manufacturing employment, although there were heavier concentrations in certain industries. Puerto Rican workers, who had been coming to New York in massive numbers since the end of World War II, made up almost 12 percent of the manufacturing work force. The main source of labor for manufacturing in the New York area was still U.S.-born workers, and in some industries European immigrants who came earlier in the century were dominant. These European immigrants were older, however, and soon the European-immigrant component of the manufacturing sector would be depleted.

Ten years later, in 1980, new immigrants were much more of a presence in New York's labor force and in the manufacturing sector in particular. According to the population census, by 1980 foreign-

born workers—about 70 percent of them new-wave immigrants—
held as much as 44 percent of total manual manufacturing employment in the New York area (while the foreign-born represented only
21 percent of the area's population) (DeFreitas and Marshall 1984).
Thus, manufacturing witnessed increases of immigrant employment
in the 1970s despite the fact that employment levels in this economic
sector were declining drastically.

Workers in nearly all the new immigrant groups were much more
heavily represented than native workers in manufacturing, and this
partly reflects their differential access to the nonmanual labor market
(see table 3.3). However, within the manual labor market as well, the
same pattern of overrepresentation of new immigrants as compared
to native workers is found. As table 3.3 indicates, native-born manual
workers were less likely to be employed in manufacturing in 1980
than manual workers in all new immigrant groups (except non-His-

Table 3.3. Industrial Structure: Percent of Native and Foreign Employed Labor Force in Manufacturing, New York SMSA, 1970–80

		Born in:				
	New York State	Rest U.S.	Puerto Rico	Latin America	Non-Hispanic Caribbean	Asia
Males						
1970	19.5(21.5)	19.6(21.4)	34.4(40.1)	33.2(39.2)ᵃ	20.4(23.7)	12.3 (8.4)
1980	15.3(17.9)	18.0(18.4)	27.9(33.2)	30.0(37.0)	22.9(26.8)	13.7(19.1)
Arrival:						
Before 1970				25.2	21.4	13.3
1970–74				30.0	18.0	19.5
1975–80				41.4	34.6	11.9
Females						
1970	16.6(32.3)	15.4(23.2)	49.1(72.5)	43.2(64.5)ᵃ	12.8(14.4)	36.2(68.8)
1980	12.7(21.2)	15.3(23.0)	35.6(63.6)	43.7(62.5)	12.5(17.8)	34.1(72.8)
Arrival:						
Before 1970				41.3	7.3	35.6
1970–74				38.7	18.6	31.0
1975–80				57.6	16.5	36.2

Source: Unpublished data from the Census of Population and Housing 1970, Public Use Sample and
from the Census of Population and Housing 1980, Public Use Microdata Sample.

Note: Percentages within parentheses indicate the proportion of the total *manual* labor force of each
nationality in manufacturing.

ᵃDoes not include Cubans.

panic Caribbean women). The case of Latin American and Asian women is especially striking, with well over half of the manual workers in these two groups employed in manufacturing, both in 1970 and 1980. In fact, the proportion of new-wave immigrant manual workers in manufacturing did not change much between 1970 and 1980. While the participation of native manual labor in this sector continued to shrink (except for American women born outside the New York area)—a trend shared by Puerto Rican migrants—Latin American manual workers, who had been noticeably overrepresented in manufacturing in 1970, had only very slightly reduced their participation in this sector by 1980. The proportion of immigrant manual workers from Asia and the non-Hispanic Caribbean in manufacturing in 1980 was higher than it had been in 1970 (table 3.3). Furthermore, several of the recent immigrant cohorts were more oriented to production jobs than earlier cohorts (table 3.3), suggesting that factory work is one of the opportunities readily available to newcomers.

While I have emphasized new immigrants' role in the manufacturing industry, they are also employed outside of this economic sector. It is only natural that in a "service economy" such as New York's, the service or tertiary sector[9] was the major employer of both native and immigrant labor in 1980. Immigrant workers from Latin America, Asia and the non-Hispanic Caribbean were overrepresented in several economic activities in the service sector: in the case of men, in eating and drinking places (Latin Americans and Asians), wholesale trade (Asians), and, to a minor extent, business and repair services (non-Hispanic Caribbeans); in the case of women, in eating and drinking places (Asians), personal and household services (Latin American and non-Hispanic Caribbeans, the latter particularly in private households), and professional services, including a wide range of nonprofessional jobs, in hospitals, for instance (non-Hispanic Caribbeans) (Unpublished data from the Census of Population 1980). Most of the above overrepresentations were already visible ten years before, in 1970, and in some economic activities, for example, eating and drinking places, immigrants were more overrepresented in 1980 than in 1970 (Unpublished data from the Census of Population 1970 and 1980).

ECONOMIC, SOCIAL, AND CULTURAL
FACTORS IN EMPLOYMENT DISTRIBUTION

A number of factors determined the employment distribution of new immigrants in New York. That immigrants of diverse national origins were overrepresented or increasing their participation in manufacturing in the 1970s, while the American-born were not, points to the importance of the economic options available in the New York area. Yet immigrant groups also had divergent employment patterns, and social and cultural factors help to explain these differences.

Clearly, New York's economy determined the occupational alternatives open to foreign manual workers, whatever their nationality. Although New York's economy was marked by a labor surplus in the 1970s, manufacturing and other sectors offered job opportunities for new immigrants, often in "labor-sensitive" activities where, as I argued elsewhere, the regular inflow of foreign labor actually stimulated a demand for foreign workers.[10] While these activities became increasingly dependent on foreign workers, other fields were harder for new immigrants to enter: native labor had preferential access to the "better" job opportunities, partly because they were best adapted in terms of training to the requirements of new, more attractive employment possibilities.

Within the range of economic alternatives available to new immigrants, however, each ethnic group shows a distinct pattern of labor market location. Surely, one factor responsible for such "ethnic-specific" employment patterns is that new immigrants often followed the occupational path of their ethnic or national predecessors. Earlier immigrants of the same or similar ethnic identity opened up "occupational frontiers" and thus created channels that were frequently followed by recent immigrants, who learned about and obtained jobs through relatives and friends in their ethnic group. That certain groups clustered in particular occupations also fostered prejudices among employers about desirable or undesirable ethnic traits. Indeed, employers often preferred to hire immigrants in certain groups, who they believed made better workers for their industries, while they rejected others.

But it is not just a question of new immigrants moving into economic spheres pioneered by their compatriots who came before. The composition of immigrant streams also plays a role in determining their labor market location. Obviously, the class background and skill levels of different immigrant groups influence how they will be distributed in the receiving economy, and I have noted that the increasing proportion of manual workers in the new inflows helps account for their considerable presence in New York's manual labor force. Here I wish to discuss how the proportion of women with spouses present in different immigrant groups has affected their participation in domestic service or "private household" employment. This discussion of one specific example highlights how differences in the sociodemographic composition of the immigrant streams may influence employment distributions.

An analysis of both 1970 and 1980 census data reveals that women from the non-Hispanic Caribbean were more likely than Hispanic immigrants from Latin America and Puerto Rico to be employed in private household service work (see table 3.4). At first glance, it might appear that non-Hispanic Caribbean women, who are mostly black, were so heavily represented in domestic service simply be-

Table 3.4. Household Services: Percent of Native and Foreign Employed Female Labor Force in Household Services, New York SMSA, 1970–80

| | Born in: | | | | | |
	New York State	Rest U.S.	Puerto Rico	Latin America	Non-Hispanic Caribbean	Asia
1970	1.1(5.4)	5.4(17.1)	0.8(1.3)	4.7(7.8)[a]	13.3(26.6)	0.7(1.6)
1980	0.6(3.4)	1.1(6.3)	0.7(1.5)	4.5(7.5)	9.1(18.3)	1.0(2.5)
Arrival:						
Before 1970				2.7	5.7	0.0
1970–74				5.5	7.1	1.7
1975–80				8.7	20.1	1.3

Source: Unpublished data from the Census of Population and Housing 1970, Public Use Sample and from the Census of Population and Housing 1980, Public Use Microdata Sample.

Note: Household services are defined according to the industrial classification (private household services).

Numbers in parentheses refer to the proportion of the employed female *manual* labor force in household services.

[a]Does not include Cubans.

cause they followed the occupational path created by American-born black females, while Latin American and Puerto Rican immigrant women were more reluctant to look for employment in private households because this was not their established ethnic occupational niche. But the domestic service sector is a typical absorber of internal and cross-national female migrants in urban centers throughout underdeveloped countries. Indeed, within Latin America, domestic service is still the overwhelming occupation of migrant women so that one might have expected Latin American women who moved to the United States to find employment as domestics as often as women from the non-Hispanic Caribbean. It is true that, compared to intra-Latin America migration streams, Latin American immigration to New York includes a much higher percentage of white-collar labor. Yet non-Hispanic Caribbean inflows to this country also include substantial proportions of white-collar, lower-middle-class labor. Available studies suggest that these non-Hispanic Caribbean white-collar women were more likely than white-collar Latin American female immigrants to take up employment in private households in New York, even though this represented considerable downward mobility.[11]

An important reason why women from the non-Hispanic Caribbean were more often employed in private households in New York, I would argue, is that they often migrated on their own, without spouses, while Latin American and Puerto Rican women were more likely to come with their husbands. When an immigrant woman's spouse is present in the household, her income usually supplements his wage. Because many Latin American and Puerto Rican women came to New York with their husbands, they often looked for manufacturing jobs, which were more attractive (in social and sometimes in economic terms) than domestic service, even though they were not always stable. Non-Hispanic Caribbean women who migrated alone needed incomes on a regular basis, which they often found in private household employment. And women on their own were less averse to live-in domestic service than those who came with their spouses, partly because such jobs assured them a place to live.[12] Figures from the 1970 census, in fact, show that the proportion of "married women with spouse present" in an immigrant group is inversely related to employment in domestic service. Thus, among new immigrant groups in New York in 1970, working non-Hispanic Caribbean female immigrants had the lowest proportion of "married women with spouse present" (39 percent) and the highest proportion in domestic service (13 percent). The husband's presence also seems relevant for explaining the differential participation in domestic service among specific nationalities of Latin American women in New York. Working Puerto Rican and Cuban females had significantly higher proportions of "married women with spouse present" (51 and 56 percent, respectively) and substantially lower participation in domestic service (about 1 percent for both groups) than the rest of the Latin American women (among whom 42 percent of working married women had a spouse present and 5 percent were in domestic service) (Marshall 1983:23).

In concluding this discussion, it should be mentioned that domestic service seems to be an employment option readily available to the most recent female immigrant cohorts (see table 3.4), if only as a temporary job on the way to obtaining more attractive and better positions. This is especially marked in the case of non-Hispanic Caribbean working women, among whom 20 percent of the most recent arrivals (in contrast to less than 8 percent of those who came earlier) worked in private households. Domestic service is a viable possibility since in New York's relatively high-income environment there is an almost infinitely expanding demand for household employees.

THE IMPACT OF LABOR IMMIGRATION: THE MANUFACTURING INDUSTRY

So far I have examined the employment structure of the immigrant labor force in 1970 and 1980 and I have discussed certain factors that influenced the employment allocation of new-wave immigrant workers. A final question remains: What have been the consequences of large-scale manual labor immigration for New York City's economy and labor force? The focus here is on the impact of new-wave immigration on the manufacturing industry, considering in particular the issue of wage growth.

First, it is necessary to say a few words about the employment distribution of new-wave immigrants within the manufacturing sector. The location of native and new immigrant workers in this sector is quite dissimilar, even if we consider only production workers. In 1970, during the first stage of the new immigration, new-wave immigrant men, except Asians (who were seldom in manufacturing), were overrepresented in six manufacturing industries: apparel, textiles, plastics, footwear and other leather goods, nonspecified nondurable goods, and the "miscellaneous" industries. These six industries—what I call "immigrant industries"—employed almost half of the Puerto Rican, Latin American, and non-Hispanic Caribbean manual workers in the New York area in manufacturing, but only about a quarter of the male American-born manual workers in this sector. New-wave immigrant women were concentrated in even fewer industries; apparel, leather, and the miscellaneous industries. Seventy-one percent of the Puerto Rican and Latin American women in manufacturing, in contrast to about a half of the native-born females, worked in these three branches (Marshall 1983:26–27).[13]

The six immigrant industries had, in 1970, the lowest wage levels and were among the most labor-intensive in New York's manufacturing industry. The immigrant industries were also less profitable than other manufacturing branches (Marshall 1983:28). Moreover, nonskilled—generally, semiskilled—labor predominated in these six industries, the most extreme case being the garment industry where about 80 percent of factory employment was semiskilled (New York State Department of Labor 1978, 1982).

In 1970, then, the disproportionate reliance on the use of immigrant labor seems to have been a response to real objective limitations encountered by the immigrant industries. Because they had relatively low profit margins, firms in these industries faced constraints both for investing in modern technology and equipment and for raising wages and improving working conditions. That left them less able to attract new generations of native workers who had better employment alternatives; however, employers in these industries had no difficulties in recruiting foreign workers, who were willing to accept the prevailing wage levels and working conditions and who were suitable in terms of their skills for these "traditional" manufacturing industries. The growing supply of new-wave immigrants in the New York area made this feasible.

As long as better job opportunities were emerging in New York, as they were in the 1960s, native labor moved away from less attractive industries, creating vacuums that were filled by immigrants. But by accepting low wages and unsatisfactory working conditions, new-wave immigrants reinforced and helped to maintain the very characteristics that made these industries so unattractive to natives.

By 1980, immigrant workers, including Puerto Ricans, were still overrepresented in most of the same industries as in 1970 (see table 3.5 for apparel and leather). Practically all of them were remarkably overrepresented in the garment industry where, for instance, 90 percent of the Asian women factory workers were employed. By 1980, moreover, new immigrants probably were providing a very significant proportion of the labor force in several of the immigrant industries.

Indeed, during the 1970s, new-wave immigration had some impact on the productive structure in manufacturing, particularly through its effect in fostering labor demand in immigrant industries—and this impact was visible by 1980 (see Marshall 1983, 1984 for a more detailed discussion of these topics). The regular inflow of legal and illegal immigrants throughout the 1970s discouraged technological innovation. Rather, it encouraged the use of labor-intensive techniques and the readoption of older forms of production organization. This, in turn, increased the dependence of some industries upon the influx of immigrant workers to meet their labor demands. The abundant supply of immigrants, in short, actually stimulated a demand

Table 3.5. Manufacturing Industry: Percent of Native and Foreign Manufacturing Labor Force in Selected Immigrant Industries, New York SMSA, 1980

	New York State	*Rest U.S.*	*Puerto Rico*	*Latin America*	*Non-Hispanic Caribbean*	*Asia*
Males	12.8(12.0)	7.9(5.6)[a]	23.4(21.6)	20.6(21.8)	12.0(9.9)	31.4(44.7)[a]
Females	15.9(31.0)	19.0(37.1)	53.5(69.2)	51.6(58.0)	34.8(45.4)	80.6(91.7)

Apparel and Leather

Born in:

Source: Unpublished data from the Census of Population and Housing 1980, Public Use Microdata Sample.

Note: The figures between parentheses refer to the proportion of the manufacturing *manual* labor force in apparel and leather.

[a]The small number of cases restricts the reliability of this figure.

for labor in immigrant industries. Several developments in these industries seem to have been a response to the abundance of foreign labor: a revival of small-sized firms and reversions toward anachronistic forms of employment such as subcontracting, sweat-shops, home labor, and piece-rate work. Wage levels and productivity in immigrant industries tended to lag behind those in other branches of manufacturing. Moreover, by holding down wage costs foreign labor helped to raise considerably the competitive advantage and profitability of immigrant industries. This process probably contributed to the continued specialization of New York's manufacturing sector in traditional labor-intensive industries (see Marshall 1983:43–46).

This brings us to the important question of how new-wave immigration affected wage growth in the 1970s. Because recent immigrants are prepared to work at the existing wage rate—which is obviously higher than in the home country—the continued influx of immigrants may well have been one factor responsible for the fact that manufacturing wages in New York grew at a slower pace than in the United States as a whole during the 1970s. A comparison of the evolution of wages of manufacturing production workers across large metropolitan centers in the country supports this argument. Manufacturing wages in New York and other cities with high proportions of immigrant workers in manufacturing employment increased more slowly than manufacturing wages in metropolitan areas with fewer foreign workers. The effect of immigration on wage growth was visible after controlling for the influence of unemployment, unionization, productivity, inflation, and other relevant factors (DeFreitas and Marshall 1984).[14] And when we compare manufacturing wages in New York with those in Philadelphia, a city with an industrial structure more like New York's than any other large U.S. metropolitan area but with far fewer immigrant workers, we find that between 1970 and 1977 wages of production workers increased faster in Philadelphia than in New York (Marshall 1983:47–48). This occurred despite the fact that in those years Philadelphia and New York had a labor surplus of comparable size.[15]

If new-wave immigration contributed to slowing down the pace of wage increases in New York's manufacturing sector as a whole, what about the effect of foreign labor on immigrant industries in particular?

Did foreign labor have an "additional" impact on wage growth in these industries?

The evidence, again from a comparison of New York and Philadelphia, suggests that it did. Between 1970 and 1977, manufacturing wages in New York worsened in relation to those of Philadelphia in eight out of fifteen industries. Admittedly, the differences between wage increases are small—but a definite pattern emerges. Of these eight New York industries, four were "immigrant industries" and two had substantial numbers of foreign workers. The relative deterioration in wages was most marked in the apparel industry, which in New York has particularly high concentrations of immigrants. In contrast, of the seven industries where wages grew at a faster rate in New York, only one was an immigrant industry.

That the large supply of new immigrant workers adversely affected wages in immigrant industries had two major consequences. On the one hand, as I noted earlier, it helped to make these industries more competitive and profitable—particularly those with heavier concentrations of immigrant workers. On the other hand, slower wage growth in immigrant industries meant that the levels of living of native as well as foreign production workers in these industries did not keep up with those of workers in other manufacturing branches.

I suspect that much of this analysis of the effects of new-wave immigration on manufacturing wages can be extended to other sectors of New York's economy with significant concentrations of immigrant labor. The service sector, of course, immediately comes to mind. Just what the consequences of labor immigration are for those service-sector activities in New York that employ large numbers of new immigrant workers is a subject that demands further research.

CONCLUSION

In the first phase of new-wave immigration to New York, in 1970, the relatively small number of new immigrant workers were already concentrated in a few economic activities. Many, for example, became industrial operatives, generally in semiskilled positions, and they were overconcentrated in certain manufacturing industries and service-sector activities. The general trend was for new immigrant workers to move into the manual labor markets being deserted by

American-born workers, who shifted toward more attractive, non-manual, tertiary-sector jobs.

Even at this initial stage, the employment structures of native and foreign labor were quite distinct. Later, in 1980, after more than ten years of immigration in the context of an increasing labor surplus in the New York area, the earlier employment patterns had not changed substantially, either in terms of the manual/nonmanual cleavage or in terms of economic activities. By 1980, new immigrant workers supplied a very considerable segment of manual labor in the New York area. With regard to manufacturing, despite large employment losses, increasing numbers of new immigrants of diverse ethnic origin were incorporated into manufacturing industries.

In examining the impact of the new large-scale manual labor immigration on the New York economy, this chapter has focused on the manufacturing industry. The abundance of foreign labor helped to make immigrant industries more competitive and profitable; at the same time, it fostered a deterioration of working conditions and employment practices (evidenced, for instance, by the surge of sweatshops) and contributed to slow wage growth. This adverse effect of immigration on wages seems to have extended beyond immigrant industries to other sectors of the manual manufacturing labor market that still attracted native workers.

If this essay has examined some detrimental effects of labor immigration on wages and working conditions in New York's manufacturing industry, it should be emphasized that reducing immigrant flows would not necessarily be beneficial for native labor. Without a continued influx of foreign workers, manufacturing firms might, for example, leave the New York area altogether or introduce labor-saving production techniques, both alternatives that would lead to serious losses of manufacturing jobs and to a rise in the numbers of unemployed workers. All this, of course, is speculative: at least in the near future, large-scale immigration is likely to persist. However, its negative effects for both native and new immigrant workers could indeed be reduced if trade unions press for the enforcement of labor laws in connection with wages and working conditions of new immigrant workers and if large numbers of new immigrants join the labor unions.

NOTES

1. Part of this article is based on a larger project carried out at New York

University's Center for Latin American and Caribbean Studies, supported by a grant from New York University's New York Research Program in Inter-American Affairs, and fully reported in Marshall (1983). The analysis of the data from the Census of Population and Housing of 1980 was conducted specifically for the present work. I wish to thank G. DeFreitas and Columbia University Center for the Social Sciences for facilitating use of the 1980 Population Census files.

2. New-wave or new immigrants refer to the streams from Latin America, Asia, and the non-Hispanic Caribbean. They are thus distinguished from earlier immigration waves, particularly those from Europe. The 1970 and 1980 census data for these three new immigrant groups that I draw on throughout this paper basically reflect the characteristics of post-1965 immigrants, although these census data include a small proportion of pre-1965 immigrants. Eighty percent of the Asians, 82 percent of the South Americans, and 74 percent of the Central and North Americans (including the rest of Latin Americans and the non-Hispanic Caribbeans) living in the New York metropolitan area in 1980 had arrived after 1965 (U.S. Bureau of the Census 1981).

3. According to the 1980 census, there were 1,946,800 foreign-born in the New York metropolitan area (U.S. Bureau of the Census 1981). Moreover, for New York City there is some consensus on a figure of 750,000–800,000 illegal residents (including non-labor force participants) by 1980, presumably only very partially registered by the census (see Marshall 1983). Some more illegal immigrants were settled in the rest of the New York metropolitan area as well. The 750,000–800,000 figure for New York City should be considered a maximum estimate. Larger, and ungrounded, estimates on undocumented residents in New York City tacitly assume that illegal immigration is a cumulative phenomenon, which it is not. There is a rate of transformation from illegal into legal status. It is too often ignored that while new illegal immigrants arrive, earlier illegal residents regularize their status, whatever the conversion mechanism is (see Perez 1981 and Waldinger 1980 for proportions of illegal residents among specific immigrant groups; and Hendricks 1974 and Portes 1979 for forms of status regularization).

4. For details as to how this percentage was arrived at, see Marshall (1983:11). According to the definition of the Population Census of 1980, the New York Standard Metropolitan Statistical Area (SMSA) includes the five boroughs of New York City as well as Westchester, Rockland, Putnam, and Bergen (New Jersey) Counties. Throughout this paper this is the New York metropolitan area definition that I use for 1980. In 1970, the New York SMSA also included Nassau and Suffolk, and did not include Bergen County.

5. There is a vast literature describing employment trends in the New York

area during the last two decades. See, for example, Armstrong (1980); Bahl et al. (1974); Bureau of Labor Statistics (1973); Chinitz (1978); Ehrenhalt (1981); Hughes and Sternlieb (1978); Klebaner (1981); and McClelland and Magdovitz (1981).

6. The late 1960s was a period of abnormally favorable labor market conditions in New York City, in that unemployment rates were quite low (under 5 percent) compared to those in other metropolitan areas in the country and compared to unemployment rates in the city in earlier time periods.

7. In this paper, the category "Latin Americans," unless otherwise noted, refers to those from Spanish- and Portuguese-speaking countries of South America and Central America as well as from the Spanish-speaking Caribbean. It does not, however, include Puerto Ricans, who were classified separately in my analysis of census data because they have a different status as U.S. citizens and because, as I pointed out above, their in-migration was declining. Puerto Rican migrants refer to those born on the island. Puerto Ricans born in the U.S. mainland were included in the category of "native labor" in general. In addition, in my analysis of census data for 1970, "Asians" include only the most numerous nationalities (the Chinese, Pakistanis, Koreans, Japanese, Indians, and Filipinos).

8. Of course, within the nonmanual labor market, there were important differences in the location of native workers according to their ethnic origin. Workers from certain ethnic minorities tended to be confined to the "bottom" of the nonmanual labor market.

9. The "service" or "tertiary" sector includes transportation, communications, and other public utilities; retail and wholesale trades; finance, banking, insurance, and real estate; business and repair services; private household and other personal services; entertainment and recreation services; professional services; and public administration.

10. "Labor-sensitive" activities are those where the availability of labor may have an impact on labor demand by influencing production techniques and production organization (see the discussions in Marshall 1983 and 1984). One important example of labor-sensitive activities are the technologically flexible industries.

11. For the social composition of Jamaican female immigration flows at origin and in New York see Foner (1983). For Colombian women see Urrea (1982).

12. Foner (1983:7) notes that in her small sample of twenty women "there were very few married women." She attributes this partly to the fact that many came to New York to take "live-in jobs as private household workers," but it might be the other way round. In other words, they might have taken live-in domestic service jobs because they were alone (only 15 percent of the sample were married and living with their husbands

at the time of the interviews). Steinberg (1981) also emphasizes the importance of the presence, or absence, of spouses in accounting for the different participation of Irish, Jewish, and Italian immigrant women in domestic service at the beginning of the century.

13. Of course, in 1970 "new-wave" immigrant groups included many pre-1965 immigrants (for detailed data, see Marshall 1983:8, 20, and Appendix).

14. The impact of immigration on wages is relatively modest, however, and is significant only in SMSAs in which 20 percent or more of the manual workers are immigrants (DeFreitas and Marshall 1984:155).

15. Philadelphia is a large industrial center, with 24.4 percent of its work force in manufacturing. The industrial structure of Philadelphia is quite close to New York's (the proportion of manufacturing employment in nondurable industries is 62 percent in New York and 46 percent in Philadelphia). Like New York, Philadelphia has a relatively important female-dominated garment industry (Marshall 1983:47). In 1980, unemployment levels were slightly higher in Philadelphia (8.6 percent) than in New York (7 percent) (Marshall 1983:47). According to data from the Bureau of Labor Statistics, in 1970–78, unemployment levels averaged 6.9 percent in Philadelphia and 7.7 percent in New York—indeed a small difference. But, according to the 1980 census, only 5.7 percent of the population of Philadelphia was foreign-born, in contrast to 20.8 percent in New York. (All the data used in the comparison between New York and Philadelphia here and in the text refer to New York and Philadelphia metropolitan areas.)

REFERENCES

Armstrong, Regina B. 1980. *Regional Account, Structure and Performance of the New York Region's Economy in the Seventies*. RPA (Regional Plan Association) Bulletin 129. Bloomington: Indiana University Press.

Bahl, Roy W., A. K. Campbell, and D. Greytack. 1974. *Taxes, Expenditures, and the Economic Base: Case Study of New York City*. New York: Praeger.

Bureau of Labor Statistics. Middle Atlantic Regional Office. 1973. "New York City in Transition: Population, Jobs, Prices and Pay in a Decade of Change." *Regional Report* 34.

Chinitz, Benjamin, ed. 1978. *The Declining Northeast*. New York: Praeger.

DeFreitas, G. and A. Marshall. 1984. "Immigration and Wage Growth in U.S. Manufacturing in the 1970s." *IRRA* (Industrial Relations Research Association) *36th Annual Proceeding*, pp. 148–156.

Ehrenhalt, Samuel M. 1981. "Some Perspectives on the New York City Economy in a Time of Change." In B. J. Klebaner, ed., *New York City's Changing Economic Base*. New York: Pica Press.

Foner, Nancy. 1983. "Jamaican Migrants: A Comparative Analysis of the

New York and London Experience." *Occasional Paper No. 36.* Center for Latin American and Caribbean Studies, New York University.

Hendricks, G. 1974. *The Dominican Diaspora.* New York: Teachers College Press, Columbia University.

Hughes, James W. and G. Sternlieb. 1978. *Jobs and People, New York City 1985.* New Brunswick, N.J.: Center for Urban Policy Research.

Immigration and Naturalization Service. 1965–1979. *Annual Reports.* Washington, D.C.: U.S. Government Printing Office.

Jaffe, A. J., R. M. Cullen, and T. D. Boswell. 1980. *The Changing Demography of Spanish Americans.* New York: Academic Press.

Klebaner, Benjamen J., ed. 1981. *New York City's Changing Economic Base.* New York: Pica Press.

Marshall, Adriana. 1983. "Immigration in a Surplus-Worker Labor Market: The Case of New York." *Occasional Paper No. 39.* Center for Latin American and Caribbean Studies, New York University.

—— 1984. "Immigration, Labor Demand, and the Working Class." *Politics and Society* 13:425–453.

McClelland, Peter D. and A. L. Magdovitz. 1981. *Crisis in the Making—the Political Economy of New York State Since 1945.* New York: Cambridge University Press.

New York State Department of Labor. 1978. "Occupational Employment Statistics, Manufacturing, New York State, April-June 1977." Fall.

—— 1982. "Employment by Occupation, Manufacturing, New York State, April-June 1980." March.

Perez, Glauco A. 1981. "The Legal and Illegal Dominican in New York City." Paper presented at Conference on Hispanic Migrants to New York City, New York University.

Portes, A. 1979. "La Inmigración y el Sistema Internacional: Algunas Características de los Mexicanos Recientemente Emigrados a los Estados Unidos." *Revista Mexicana de Sociología* 41:1257–1277.

Steinberg, Stephen. 1981. *The Ethnic Myth.* New York: Atheneum.

Urrea Giraldo, Fernando. 1982. "Life Strategies and the Labor Market: Colombians in New York in the 1970s." *Occasional Paper No. 34.* Center for Latin American and Caribbean Studies, New York University.

U.S. Bureau of the Census. 1981. *1980 Census of Population.* Vol. 1. Washington, D.C.: U.S. Government Printing Office.

Waldinger, R. 1980. "Immigration and Industrial Decline." MIT-Harvard University. Mimeo.

4. The Dominicans: Women in the Household and the Garment Industry

Patricia R. Pessar

Dominicans are the largest group of immigrants to New York City in recent years and, as among many other new immigrant groups, women predominate. In New York, nearly all Dominican women, at some point, enter the work force, very often taking jobs in the garment industry. Dominican women's participation as garment workers has implications for the city's garment industry as well as for the lives of the women themselves. This essay thus focuses on two related issues: (1) how the presence of Dominican female garment workers has helped to bolster the New York apparel industry and (2) how Dominican women's status as wage workers has improved their position in the household and modified their orientation to an eventual return to the Dominican Republic.

In describing the experiences of Dominicans in New York City, I adopt what anthropologists often call an "etic" approach. In contrast to an "emic," or "native," view, an etic approach is a derivative analytical construction that builds and elaborates upon interviews with informants as well as participant observation. Therefore, while my conclusions are based on several years of ethnographic research in the Dominican Republic and New York (1980–83) and while I have shared many of my claims with key Dominican informants to check and refine their veracity, the conclusions I reach were never expressed, as such, by my informants.

There is a danger in generalizing about a population of many thousands from ethnographic research in which only several hundred were interviewed. Therefore, throughout this essay, I alert the reader to the nature of the population and data sources upon which my assertions are drawn. The generalizations reached about immigrants' experiences in the United States are based on structured interviews with informants, as well as casual conversations and participant observation in households, workplaces and social gatherings over a two-year period. Two principal groups form the basis for much of the data and analysis presented below: the senior female member of fifty-five immigrant households who provided information over a year's period on topics such as social networks, decision making, income, control over budgeting, and beliefs about sex roles; and sixteen female garment workers who were interviewed about the above topics as well as the nature of their workplace and beliefs about their role as workers.

In selecting these informants, some diversity was sought to explore how the immigrant experience was affected by such variables as class background, time of arrival, age, marital status, household composition, and work history. Informants were obtained through various means, including previous contacts with them or their relatives in the Dominican Republic and introductions by other informants and community leaders.[1]

THE DOMINICAN IMMIGRANT STREAM

According to the 1980 census, 169,100 persons of Dominican birth were residing in the United States with 127,700 of them (76 percent) in the New York metropolitan area (Kraly, this volume).[2] Other counts, assuming a very large undocumented population missed by the census, are much higher, and some estimate that as many as 400,000 Dominicans live in the New York metropolitan area. Dominicans in Manhattan are concentrated in Washington Heights and the Lower East Side. In the other boroughs the largest numbers of Dominicans are found in the South Bronx, the Greenpoint section of Brooklyn, and in the Jackson Heights section of Queens.

Economic motivation predominates in Dominican emigration (see Pessar 1982a, 1986; Grasmuck 1982, Bray 1984): many aim to bolster a precarious middle-class standing in the Dominican Republic by accumulating savings to be invested back home. Nonetheless, the experience or fear of political repression have also been expulsive factors, and there were major increases in the numbers of Dominicans emigrating after the overthrow of President Juan Bosch in 1963 and the election years of 1974 and 1978 (Bray 1984; Georges 1984). At least Dominicans have been able to leave in recent years. During the Trujillo era (1930–60) restrictive emigration policies made it extremely difficult for Dominicans to move to the United States. It was only after the dictator's death in 1961 that the migration to the United States became significant (Georges 1984). The 1980 census shows that more than three-quarters of the Dominicans in the United States arrived after 1970 (see Kraly, this volume).

Contrary to conventional wisdom as well as early ethnographic accounts of Dominican emigration (Hendricks 1974; González 1970, 1976), the immigrant population is neither predominantly rural nor from the ranks of the chronically unemployed or underemployed. According to the *Diagnos* national survey conducted in 1974 in the Dominican Republic (see Ugalde et al. 1979) and the Hispanic Settlement in New York City Survey conducted in 1981 among Dominicans in Queens and northern Manhattan (see Gurak and Kritz 1982), the migration stream is predominantly urban and middle-class. The *Diagnos* survey found that about a quarter of the migrants were from rural areas, and nearly three-quarters of the urban migrants were middle-class. While this survey did not provide information on class differences among the rural population, research conducted in the Dominican Republic and the United States documents that migrants from rural areas mainly come from fairly prosperous households. These are middle-sized and large land-owning households that engaged in petty commodity production using household labor and/or paid agricultural workers (see also Grasmuck 1982; Bray 1984; Pessar 1982a, 1982b).

The 1981 probability survey, based on interviews with 560 Dominicans in New York, gives data on other characteristics of the immigrants. It is worth describing the findings in some detail for they provide a useful picture of the New York Dominican population. Women migrants outnumbered men, with females comprising 60.4 percent of the immigrant population surveyed. The average age at arrival for women was 22.2 years and the median level of education was 8.0 years. The majority of the women (53 percent) were married; 12 percent had never married, and 35 percent were divorced or separated. While only 31 percent of the women had been employed prior to emigration, 91.5 percent had worked for pay at some time since moving to the United States. In fact at the time of the survey, half were in the labor force (employed or seeking employment). The mean income in 1981 for female migrants was $6,884 as compared to $9,430 for males.

As for men, the 1981 survey showed that their average age at arrival was 22, and the median level of education was 9.4 years; 65 percent were married, 23 percent were never married, and 12 percent were divorced or separated. The majority of the men (64 percent) had been employed prior to migration; 91.3 percent had worked for wages at some time during their residence in the United States, and 87.6 percent were in the labor force when interviewed.

The median income for Dominican immigrant households surveyed in 1981 was $11,800. The nuclear household was the most common type (48 percent), but female-headed units accounted for 37 percent of the households. During 1980–81, 55.7 percent of the Dominican women were receiving or had received some form of public assistance (Gurak and Kritz 1982).

Table 4.1. Occupation of Dominicans in New York

Occupation	Males (%)		Females (%)	
No occupation	33	(14.8)	162	(48.1)
Professional workers	11	(4.9)	11	(3.3)
Managers, proprietors, officials	11	(6.3)	3	(0.9)
Clerical workers	11	(4.9)	15	(4.5)
Sales workers	10	(4.5)	4	(1.2)
Domestic services	0		15	(4.5)
Other service workers	39	(17.5)	12	(3.6)
Farmers, farm laborers, miners, etc.	0		1	(0.3)
Skilled, blue-collar, or craft workers	14	(6.3)	4	(1.2)
Semiskilled operatives	68	(30.5)	81	(24.0)
Unskilled nonfarm laborers	23	(10.3)	27	(8.0)
Unknown	0		2	(0.6)
(n)	223		337	

Source: The 1981 Hispanic Settlement in New York City Survey (Douglas Gurak, personal communication).

In terms of occupation in New York, table 4.1 indicates that most Dominican men and women in the work force were semiskilled operatives, service workers, and unskilled nonfarm laborers.

Most relevant to this essay is the concentration of women workers in the garment industry. In 1981, 61 percent of all Dominican women active in the New York labor force were engaged in manufacturing; and 42 percent of these workers were employed in the garment industry, making it the largest employer of Dominican women (Gurak and Kritz 1982:5).

THE SUPPLY OF LABOR FOR THE NEW YORK APPAREL INDUSTRY

Almost from its inception, the New York garment industry has depended on immigrant labor. Irish, Swedes, and Germans comprised the first flow, and later, by the turn of the century, Jews and Italians made up the majority of the industry's labor force (Fenton 1975; Fitzpatrick 1971). Immigrants were an exceptionally productive source of labor, whose capacity for hard work and long hours compensated in part for the deficiencies of New York's production facilities (Helfgott 1959:85).

Black women from the South and Puerto Rican women began to enter the apparel industry in the 1930s. They responded to a growing shortage of European immigrant labor, a consequence of restrictive immigration legislation in the previous decade. And, as was the case for earlier immigrants, these black and Puerto Rican women concentrated in the lowest-level, least remunerative jobs (Helfgott 1959:85; Hill 1968). In fact with the economic boom of the 1950s, job recruiters from New York went to Puerto Rico in search of garment workers for sweatshops (Smith 1980:55). In 1969, 33 percent of the workers in the New York City apparel industry were Puerto Rican and 17 percent were blacks and other nonwhites (Smith 1980:55).

While from the 1960s onward wages were falling in apparel relative to other manufacturing industries in New York, other opportunities were evolving for the key labor force groups, mainly earlier European immigrants, Puerto Ricans, and blacks, upon which the garment industry had depended. With improvements in the general labor market situation in the 1960s, many of these workers were able to move out of manufacturing. Furthermore, political developments, such as militance among low-income groups, reduced discrimination in hiring, and improvements in real wages in other sectors of the economy, provided important incentives for blacks and Puerto Ricans to leave low-wage, unstable manufacturing jobs[3] (Abeles et al. 1983:28).

Over this period important changes were taking place in the New York apparel industry. Stable, standardized production moved first from the Northeast to the Southern United States in the 1960s, and more recently it has relocated abroad (NACLA 1977). New York has become transformed into a "spot market," specializing in the unstable components of demand. The components include: (1) fashion-sensitive product lines, where demand fluctuates seasonally as well as in accordance with vagaries in consumer demand; and (2) reorders of standardized lines which cannot be managed by larger, more routinized manufacturers (see Waldinger 1984).

In the face of New York's transformation from a production center to a "spot market" and the need of employers to remain competitive within the entire global organization of apparel production, the exodus of key labor force groups posed a serious threat. Whereas the productivity of New York's immigrant labor force had previously compensated for production inefficiencies, New York firms now found themselves relying upon aging and increasingly uncommitted workers whose ability to work rapidly and under highly pressured conditions was declining steadily.[4] In the early 1970s employers complained about shortages of workers.

New immigrants were drawn into this labor vacuum. They included Chinese, Dominicans, Colombians, Haitians, Central Americans, and Ecuadorians. The garment industry has been invigorated by an abundant supply of immigrant workers (Chishti 1983). Not only has this new flow infused the industry with younger, productive workers but it has weakened the upward pressure on wages. New York's wage differential, which inched up in the early 1970s, moved downward in the latter half of the decade. In sum, the new immigration has not simply stemmed the decline of the garment industry but has actually provided the resources needed to secure a more viable, if still highly competitive, market niche for New York (see Waldinger 1985:333–336).

Industries that employ large numbers of immigrants, such as apparel, impose direct control over workers to maintain a disciplined, productive work force. Firms in the competitive sector of the economy require labor-supply flexibility (e.g., shift work and ease of hiring and firing) and flexibility in other inputs (e.g., the use of obsolete and hazardous equipment in substandard workspaces). Immigrants' status as foreigners (often as temporary labor), their lack of familiarity with union politics, and their frequent segregation from native workers both in the workplace and the community, all combine to make them unusually compliant, dependent on their employers, and difficult to recruit by labor organizers (Sassen-Koob 1981; Edwards 1979; Piore 1979).

The argument so far, like most current discussions of labor market segmentation, has been largely framed from the perspective of labor demand (Portes 1981; Sassen-Koob 1980), looking at how segments of the market require workers with certain characteristics, such as compliance. This emphasis on labor demand in the new discourse on migration—and the tendency to ignore those who supply labor— is no doubt a reaction to the traditional approach, which stressed workers' individual and cultural characteristics and neglected structural labor market factors (cf. Sowell 1981; Light 1972). But critical as it is to stress labor demand, it is also important not to overlook the beliefs and behavior of immigrant workers. There is a need to balance and complement arguments that emphasize labor demand with an examination of forces not directly determined by the labor market that make immigrants "good" workers and available to the competitive sector. In the case of Dominican workers, this means exploring ideological constructs and social relations among them, the subject of the section that follows.

THE SOCIAL CONSTRUCTION OF LABOR: A SUPPLY-SIDE VIEW

Immigrant Ideology

Political economists commonly attribute immigrant workers' compliance to negative sanctions. Docility is purported to be the outcome of potential coercion by the State and of manipulation by owners in paternalistically organized workplaces (Sassen-Koob 1980; Portes 1981). Such a big-stick explanation, however, is inadequate as well as deceptive. Positive orientations to work also underlie immigrant workers' compliance and make them a highly desirable workforce, especially, in this case, given the organization and constraints under which most garment firms operate in New York's "spot market." Despite the characterization of garment work as low-skilled and transient, employers in the highly volatile New York market require workers with sufficient experience and skills to conform to rapid and pressing demands for style change, who strive for productivity, and who are loyal and committed workers when the pace of work escalates. Under these conditions attachment to the workplace and general job satisfaction are far preferable dispositions by which to secure a reliable and productive work force than fear and vulnerability.

In-depth interviews with sixteen Dominican female garment workers reveal that immigrants' orientation to employment helps explain why despite unfavorable conditions in many garment factories morale is maintained and militancy avoided. Admittedly, the number of informants is very small, and the women interviewed are not representative in a statistical sense. However, in keeping with an ethnographic approach they were chosen as persons who embody and perform characteristic domestic and productive roles found in the Dominican immigrant community and the garment industry. An open-ended questionnaire containing over 200 questions was administered to each woman during several home visits. It included questions on the division of labor in the workplace and household, beliefs about the role of women in work and in the family, and levels of satisfaction with the roles of worker, wife, and mother. Contacts were maintained with many of the informants once formal interviewing had ended through visits and phone calls over the year. These latter discussions often fleshed out and helped in the interpretation of statements the women had made when responding to the earlier questionnaire.

The sixteen informants ranged in age from 17 to 62, and they had lived in the United States from one to twenty years with nine years being the average. Their marital status was as follows: Six were married, one was widowed, two were separated, four were divorced, and three were single. Most claimed to come from the ranks of the middle class in the Dominican Republic. Four had been sewing machine operators in the Dominican Republic, two nurse's aides, one a nurse, one a saleswoman, one a maid, three students, and four had done housework in their own or parental home. In New York, nearly all were sewing machine operators with the exception of two floor-workers and one samplemaker.

Of the sixteen women interviewed, all but two said they were satisfied with their jobs. The most plausible explanation for this high degree of job satisfaction is that employment in the apparel industry is experienced as a means to attain the main goal of emigration: material and social advancement.

Objectively, garment workers in this country are classified as lower working class and they are viewed as occupants of dead-end, poorly remunerated jobs. Given this characterization, it is surprising that the majority of the Dominican garment workers interviewed indicated satisfaction with their employment, believed they were progressing, and identified themselves as middle class. How is this apparent paradox to be explained? A critical factor is the meanings and symbolic markers of social mobility for these and other newly arrived immigrants.

One of the characteristics of an increasingly interdependent world economic system is that social status is measured and marked by access to prestigious consumer goods available on the international market. As a way of extending markets for commodities and labor, core capitalist countries export new consumer goods and create a demand for them (Alba 1978). Consequently, a transnational symbolic system of stratification has emerged. However, there is not only an unequal distribution of these consumer goods among social classes in each country but, more significantly, among the *same* social classes in different countries. Many consumer goods enjoyed by lower-class Americans, for example, are completely beyond the reach of members of the lower class in less developed countries. It is this disparity between the United States and less developed countries, like the Dominican Republic, over access to prestigious consumer goods that makes emigration a viable strategy for social mobility (see Grant and Herbstein 1983). As Kessler-Harris (1981:145) observes, consumerism in the United States has for many decades "raised the level of 'necessary' goods to the point where telephones, refrigerators, and automobiles were rarely optional." But while these commodities are deemed necessities in most American households, even members of the middle class in the Dominican Republic are not assured them. Uneven development in the Dominican Republic has meant that the expectations of the middle strata of landowners, merchants, professionals, technocrats, and wage earners for easy access to middle-class consumption goods often have not been met. Structural transformations that would have ensured a comfortable income to sustain a stable Dominican middle class are missing (Bray 1984).

The precarious hold many Dominicans had on a middle-class standard of living, as measured in household income and commodities, has been strengthened in the United States. Thus, when Dominican garment workers moved to the United States and acquired "prestigious" consumer goods like modern kitchen appliances, color televisions, and automobiles, many felt they had solidified, if not improved, their status, and they accordingly perceived themselves as middle class.

It is important to emphasize that *pooled* household, rather than individual, income enables many of the Dominican garment workers to maintain what they perceive is a middle-class standard of living. In other words, the structure of many Dominican immigrant households and their organization of income accumulation and allocation facilitate consumerism (see Pessar 1984). The value of multiple wage earners who pool low wages is apparent when we compare the women who defined themselves as middle class with those who said they were poor.

The four women who considered themselves "poor" reside in households with an average of 1.5 wage earners and a dependency ratio of 3:1. In contrast, among the nine who claimed to be middle class, there are 2.5 wage earners and the dependency ratio is 1:1. The differences in the consumer power between these two groups was apparent in their diet, housing, furnishing, and use of leisure time. To take two extreme examples, Esperanza, a divorced woman who defined herself as poor, lived with six children and one grandchild in a one-bedroom apartment with only three beds; Ivalise, who said she was middle class, lived with her husband and a twenty-four-year-old daughter in a spacious garden apartment, complete with guest room, living room, and den.

Clearly, then, the Third World reference for standard of living and social mobility gives many Dominican workers the sense that they have improved their position in the United States, and this satisfaction affects their behavior in the workplace. In contrast, Helen Safa's (n.d.) recent study of women production workers in a relatively large New Jersey plant suggests that native-born workers, oriented to the U.S. status system, have much higher aspirations than immigrants and are much less likely to feel they have made significant gains. Even though most of the white ethnic, black, and second-generation Hispanic women in Safa's study had children in white-collar occupations, nearly 70 percent of the women said that social mobility is *not* easily attained in the United States. Significantly, an affirmative reply was strongly correlated with a relatively high household income that few immigrant households could match.

Important as improved living standards are, it is also possible that the lower-middle-class origins of most of the sixteen Dominican workers plays a role in their middle-class identification (see Gurak and Kritz 1982; Foner 1983). Many may see themselves, and be thought of by Dominican friends and relatives in New York, in terms of their former class position in the Dominican Republic rather than in terms of their present low occupational status. The key point is that the workers' middle-class identification has significant consequences for the garment industry. In my opinion, this identification and satisfaction with improvements in life-style dampen the collective sentiments and solidarity that are potentially nurtured and ignited in the workplace.

The structured interviews, as well as more casual conversations with the sixteen Dominican garment workers, showed that the women brought an individualistic rather than collective orientation to issues such as social advancement and employment. When asked to choose the most effective means for social advancement—the legislative process, collective action of the Hispanic community, unions, or education—all but one woman selected education. The women's beliefs accurately reflect their behavior. *All* of the women with children in their late teens and twenties had at least one child attending college part-time or full-time; none of the women participated in political associations; and only one belonged to a social club and its orientation was recreational. The women's clear rejection of the legislative process as an effective means for Hispanic advancement reflects both the belief that as Dominicans they could expect no political assistance from the U.S. government and a more general lack of confidence in the political process. One woman commented, "It isn't a good thing getting involved in politics" ("No está bien meterse en política"). Another said, "an individual comes to no good involving him or herself in politics" ("La persona se va abajo con la política"). While most of the informants favored unions in the abstract, their individualistic orientation to work emerged in their discussion of their own experiences with unions. As one woman put it, "Unions can be good. But in my shop it has caused trouble. The shippers always complain, disrupt work, and try to draw in others. I just want to be left alone to work hard. If there is too much noise and agitation, I can't make more than the piece rate. And there's no gain there for me."

The view that social mobility is an individual responsibility rather than a collective achievement of ethnic or class-based coalitions was further evident in the informants' explanations for poverty in the United States and in the Dominican Republic. According to one woman, "in the United States people are poor, because they are lazy or want the government to take care of them. No one needs to be poor in the United States if they work hard. I tell people when I go home (to the Dominican Republic) that we are a poor people, because we don't know how to work hard." Another stated, "a poor person in Latin America may struggle from dawn to dusk and always be poor because the land is infertile or the boss is a great exploiter. Perhaps there, political associations and unions that struggle for the poor are necessary. But here, thank God, there are so many chances for the person who works hard that each person should be left alone to progress as he chooses."

In the structured interview, if the informant said that since arriving in the United States, it has become increasingly difficult for Dominicans to find work in the garment industry, she was asked who is the most and least responsible for this problem (1) the owners, because they close their factories here and move to other sites in the U.S. or abroad; (2) the U.S. government for not having placed quotas upon imported products; (3) the unions, because they inflate the salaries forcing factories to close or move their operations to another site where the salaries are lower; or (4) the large number of legal and undocumented immigrants who compete for a diminishing number of jobs.

The majority of the informants perceived the problem of unemployment and underemployment in neoclassical terms of supply and demand: there were too many immigrants competing for a limited number of jobs. Moreover, nine women said that factory owners were *least* responsible for the increased difficulty in finding jobs. Three women stated that the United States government's failure to impose quotas on imports was most responsible for the diminishing job supply. This is a position fostered by labor unions (see Chaikin 1976). At its root, it pits more exploited foreign workers against less exploited domestic workers. Only one informant perceived the problem as one between the conflicting interests of owners and workers. Not surprisingly, she is the only woman who consistently identified herself in the Dominican Republic and the United States as working class, using such terms as "we" and "they" when speaking of fellow workers and employers.

In this section I have indicated that one factor contributing to the individual orientation of most of my informants is their lower-middle-class origin and their current self-identification as middle class. This analysis suggests that appeals for collective action in the workplace based upon working-class values and interests will come up against the fact that most Dominicans do not have a working-class self-image.[5] Thus, while the type of organization of garment shops—section work, close supervision, etc.—may heighten the collective sentiments of workers, there are countervailing tendencies embodied in the type of labor the industry has recruited that modulate the potential for conflict and struggle.

Social Networks and Household Organization

Dominican workers' compliance is an important asset not just to American-born owners but to owners who are immigrants themselves. And it turns out that immigrant owners are especially likely to benefit from their immigrant workers' social networks and household organization.

Within the apparel industry a large number of immigrant owners and workers face highly uncertain and often unfavorable conditions. Most immigrant entrepreneurs and workers are found in contracting shops,[6] a highly volatile, risky, and competitive segment of the industry. On the one hand, owners of contracting shops must maintain access to a pool of productive workers, especially during peak intervals. On the other hand, since employers have to minimize costs they must also be able to lay off their employees without creating undue ill will. This elasticity is evident in figures that show that between 1977 and 1980, employment in women's sportswear during peak periods exceeded the base level by 16 percent (Waldinger 1984:155). Had the smallest productive units, sweatshops and domestic out-work, been included the differential would have been even greater.

In addition, many subcontractors may attempt to remain competitive by engaging in illegal practices such as paying subminimum wages and violating labor codes. To pursue this strategy successfully, owners must rely on a compliant controllable work force. In this section, I will go beyond the discussion of immigrant ideology to examine how additional factors, social networks and household organization, enable many immigrants to fulfill these labor requirements.

A recent study of the New York apparel industry shows that immigrant owners are clustered in the most competitive tier as subcontractors (Waldinger 1984). Immigrant employers are often able to maintain a pool of surplus labor predisposed to work irregularly as well as a core of steady employees who are willing to respond loyally to production speed-ups and rapid changes in orders. Patron-client ideology and relations underlie the attachment between the employer and both categories of immigrant workers.

The owner often assumes the role of patron, dispensing work and various favors, as well as offering protection, in return for the loyalty of his "worker-clients." The core of the work force is often attached to the owner through kinship and friendship ties. Waldinger found, for example, that relatives and friends made up the entire work force in an eighteen-person factory owned by three Dominican brothers. In another Dominican family-owned firm, the parents and their two adult children worked alongside employees who originated from their home town and neighboring hamlets (1984:170). Waldinger concludes that a familylike ambiance and social networks associated with patron-client relationships have important benefits for immigrant owners.

In fact, because non-Hispanic owners are unlikely to have family or friendship ties with, or assume the role of patron to, their workers, they experience higher turnover rates and absenteeism than Hispanic owners (Waldinger 1984:164–165).

The benefits of the patron role for immigrant owners are especially apparent when it comes to the group of irregular or "semiattached" workers. In immigrant-owned firms, this group tends to consist of immigrant women with young children, students, and the elderly— that is, individuals whose social characteristics and responsibilities place them outside the formal labor market and make them undesirable to most American employers. At first glance, immigrant employers may appear to be magnanimous by temporarily employing workers who other employers do not want. However, these workers fulfill the immigrant owners' critical need for flexibility. Because the "owner-patrons" grant many temporary workers extra-workplace favors, like loans, these workers feel obligated to meet the owners' erratic and pressing demands and to work long, grueling hours when called upon. In fact, women with young children frequently have to rely on free child care by relatives and friends so they can put in this time at work.

If social networks between immigrant owners and workers help to maintain the loyalty and flexibility needed in this highly volatile segment of the apparel industry, so do social networks among immigrant workers themselves and among workers and their household members. The impression often created by social scientists who discuss the role of social networks for immigrant settlement is that social networks somehow come with the status of immigrant and need no further explanation. What has gone unacknowledged is that underlying and sustaining these social ties are transfers of labor and goods which require large expenditures of time and limited resources. Furthermore, while such help among immigrants is external to capitalist relations, it often serves extremely useful functions for employers, as an analysis of the garment industry makes clear.

First, the fact that workers often recommend their relatives and friends to employers significantly reduces the costs of recruiting and screening apparel workers. Second, immigrants' ability to call on the assistance of people in their social networks helps to reduce the likelihood that employers who fail to pay unemployment insurance taxes will be detected. Many informants I interviewed who were laid off never had to apply for unemployment benefits because they quickly obtained employment through people in their social networks. Others chose not to apply for benefits because they found the bureaucratic process confusing and they enjoyed the temporary financial support of household and family members. Third, the likelihood that workers will report their employers' labor code violations is reduced through network hiring. Immigrants frequently recommend that their employers hire relatives or friends who are undocumented aliens or welfare recipients. Individuals who are legally not supposed to be working are reluctant to complain to the authorities for fear that their illegal immigrant status will be discovered or their welfare payments suspended.

One reason immigrants, especially women, often accept jobs that pay subminimum wages, provide few or no benefits, and offer no job stability, is that their households and extended kin networks subsidize their low or unstable wages through pooling income and providing various services. The following case histories are illustrative.

Case 1

Marina, a thirty-eight-year-old divorcee, has resided in New York for thirteen years. She currently lives with her nine-year-old daughter, her sister, brother-in-law, and their three children. All of the adults work and the children attend parochial school. Marina's transnational household consists of the above members as well as a Dominican-based contingent comprised of her two teenage daughters and her mother.

After ten years of employment in a stable sportswear firm, Marina found herself unemployed when the plant closed. Subsequent employment was arranged by the union, but she remained in this job only a few months because the commute was too long.

Through a niece's efforts, Marina found a job closer to home in a nonunion shop. The problem this job poses is that wages fluctuate widely and there are periods when she is temporarily laid off. Although Marina is eligible for unemployment benefits during these periods, her reported wages are so low that she receives very little income.

When her weekly paycheck falls below $100, the only way Marina can meet her own basic expenses and send a monthly stipend of $100 to her two teenage daughters is by reducing her weekly contribution to the New York household's budget. This occurred eleven times during 1982–1983. Although no records were kept by the coresidents, when Marina was able to work overtime on weekdays and on Saturdays, she increased her budgetary contributions. She commented, "I do not think I have ever caught up since taking this job over a year ago. But in the past, I helped out the others so now it is my turn."

Case 2

Ana, twenty-eight, resides with her husband and two children aged three and one. She is an illegal alien, having overstayed her tourist visa two years ago. While Ana would like to work full time, her husband insists that she assume the primary role in child care. With this constraint, Ana cannot apply for better-paying, more secure jobs for which workers must be willing to labor thirty-five to forty hours a week. Instead she has had to find jobs in neighborhood sweatshops which have flexible work schedules and allow her occasionally to bring her eldest child to the shop.

When the workload is heavy, Ana works three nights a week for three to four hours and all day on Saturdays. A teenaged niece, who lives in the same apartment building, babysits at night and is compensated with occasional gifts of clothing and pocket money. Ana's mother, who works full time, cares for the children on Saturdays. Given Ana's low wages, approximately $50.00 a week, there would be little financial gain to working were she not able to rely on the child care services of her relatives.

Furthermore, the low, irregular wages and lack of benefits Ana receives are counterbalanced by her husband's employment situation. He works full time as an elevator operator, earning over $1,000 a month, and his health benefits cover the entire family.

These and many other cases highlight the relationship between the structure of multi-wage-earning households, in which pooling and cooperation are the norm, and immigrants' behavior at work. Immigrants' willingness to work irregular shifts and be loyal and undemanding, despite low wages and insecurity, are, I conclude, not necessarily due to individual traits—a frequent claim of employers when they compare immigrant workers to native-born employees. The social relations and resource base of immigrants' domestic groups provide a competitive advantage which native-born workers may not have.

Having explored the way in which the New York garment industry has benefited from the ideology and social networks of its Dominican female workers, let us now turn to the reciprocal side of the immigrant experience: how life in New York has affected the Dominicans.

THE IMPACT OF NEW YORK ON
DOMINICAN IMMIGRANTS: WOMEN'S
IMPROVED STATUS IN THE HOUSEHOLD

Observers of the family in the Dominican Republic have distinguished two basic forms of domestic organization, the single-mate and multiple-mate patterns, each associated with specific forms of authority (see Brown 1972; Ferrán 1974; Instituto Dominicano de Estudios Aplicados 1978; González 1970, 1976; Tancer 1973; Pessar 1982c). In the single-mate household, authority resides largely with the senior male; in the multiple-mate unit, women tend to command authority (see Brown 1972; Ferrán 1974). With Dominican settlement in New York, a third pattern of domestic authority has emerged in many immigrant households. There has been a movement away from the hegemony of one sex over decision making and control of domestic resources to a more egalitarian division of labor and distribution of authority.

Since the single-mate pattern predominates among the middle strata in the Dominican Republic, and since most Dominican immigrants come from this strata, changes in domestic authority generally involve a movement away from patriarchal relations and values toward greater egalitarianism. These changes have been most evident in three areas: beliefs about household authority, the allocation of household members to housework tasks, and budgetary control.

For most Dominicans the status of household head is equated with the concept of "defending the family" (quien defiende la familia). This "defense" is conceived of largely in material terms. Now that women contribute a larger share of the household income in New

York, they begin to expect to be partners in "heading" the household. Thus, when I asked the sample of fifty-five immigrant women to state who headed their household now and who headed it before they emigrated, the majority (70 percent) echoed the words of the following woman:

"We both are the heads. If both husband and wife are earning salaries then they should equally rule in the household. In the Dominican Republic it is always the husband who gives the orders in the household (manda en la casa). But here when the two are working, the woman feels herself equal to the man in ruling the home (se siente capacitada de mandar igual al hombre)."

Immigrant women reported that in New York men are more willing to help out in the house and this reduces, at least to some extent, their double burden. Women complain that it is unjust if they alone are forced to toil in the home after work and on weekends when they, like their husbands, are generating an income by working outside the home—something that is much more common in New York than in the Dominican Republic. The "compromise" reached in the households of most women I interviewed involves the husband's minor participation in housework. The degree of his participation usually depends on the domestic cycle and gender composition of the household. The man's contribution is greatest when his children are young and decreases once daughters are old enough to help their mothers. The most commonly shared domestic tasks are cooking and weekly shopping.

The other domain in which renegotiation and change has occurred is in household budgeting. Interviews with the fifty-five immigrant women showed that in the Dominican Republic, before emigration, men controlled the household budget in 69 percent of their households, even though women, either as wives or daughters, contributed income in many of these households on a regular or semiregular basis. Of the thirty-eight households where men controlled the budget, 26 percent were characterized by the traditional, patriarchal form in which members gave all or part of their wages or profits to the senior male who, in turn, oversaw the payment of household expenses; 74 percent operated with the household allowance pattern, that is, the wife was given a housekeeping allowance to cover such basic expenditures as food and clothing. When women in households with the household allowance pattern generated income, it was most commonly used for household rather than personal items of consumption. And these household purchases tended to be "luxuries," rather than staples. Both objectively and symbolically, the direction of these women's savings to nonessential prestige items reinforced the image of the man as the breadwinner and the woman, at best, as the bestower of modern status goods and, at worst, as the purchaser of "tonterias" (frivolities). Finally, 31 percent of these fifty-five premigration households were characterized by what I term a "pooled household income pattern." All but two of these seventeen households were headed by a woman, with no senior male present, so that pooling of income occurred among a woman head and her dependents.

In the United States, there has been a profound change in budgetary allocation for Dominican households. Far fewer households have a patriarchal form of budget control, and many more pool their income. Not only is pooling more common in the United States but it is increasingly found in households with a senior male present. Thus, only two of the fifty-five migrant households in New York follow the traditional patriarchal pattern of budgetary control. And in most of the households where women received a household allowance, the wife was either not employed or was engaged in industrial homework. The dominant pattern, found in 69 percent of the fifty-five households in New York, was to pool income, and of these thirty-eight domestic units, 58 percent were nuclear and 42 percent were female-headed. When nuclear families pool income, the husband, wife, and working children pool a specific amount of their wages or profits for shared household expenses such as food, rent, and electricity. Sometimes, they also pool the rest of their salaries; in other cases, household members keep the rest of their incomes for personal expenses and savings.

Income pooling within nuclear households brings women advantages that were unknown in the Dominican Republic. Responsibility for meeting the household's basic subsistence costs are distributed among members regardless of gender, thus mitigating the invidious comparison between "essential" male contributions and "supplementary" female inputs. Moreover, according to informants, men's greater participation in domestic tasks generally assigned to women in the Dominican Republic, such as developing strategies for stretching the food budget, has led them to appreciate more fully the experience and skills women bring to these activities.

Women recognize that strides have been made in the United States in that they now have much greater control over the fruits of their labor. In some cases, women have had to struggle with husbands and fathers to acquire this right. Indeed, when husbands are recalcitrant, immigrant women sometimes leave them. Of the fifty-five women in my sample, eighteen were divorced or separated from a partner while in the United States, and in most instances the man's reluctance to temper his patriarchal attitudes and behavior was a crucial factor leading to the breakup. Nonetheless, in most cases the senior male adapted relatively easily to a more egalitarian form of domestic organization. Several factors are important contributors to this change. First, the orientation to emigration as a cooperative effort to improve the status of the household appears to lessen social distance and power inequities. Second, both Dominican women and men have expressed a desire to emulate what they believe is a more modern and less conflict-ridden American pattern of sharing household decision making between men and women. And finally, there is an important material element operating: immigrant women's contribution to the household budget. Indeed, when a woman significantly reduced these financial contributions, either in the United States or in the Dominican Republic on return, the man commonly asserted his dominance by allocating a household allowance to his wife and reducing her authority over budgetary and other domestic decisions.

Because wage work has brought immigrant women many personal gains, including greater household authority and self-esteem, they are much more active agents than men in prolonging the household's stay in the United States (see Pessar 1984, 1987). When they left the Dominican Republic, most women looked forward to going back to live. This orientation has changed in New York. Women realize that if they returned to the Dominican Republic they might well end up cloistered in the home since the sexual division of labor in the Dominican economy militates against productive employment for women of their training and class background.

FROM NEW IMMIGRANTS TO A
DOMINICAN ETHNIC COMMUNITY

We have seen how many Dominican immigrants have improved their living standards in New York by pooling resources in their households, and I have argued that this success has promoted satisfied workers. I have also noted that members of many immigrant households come to prolong their stays, often at the instigation of working women. When the second generation comes of age, will they be as satisfied and satisfactory workers as their immigrant parents? This is unlikely for several reasons.

While members of the first generation tend to measure their well-being and progress by material standards, they seek *both* material and occupational advancement for their children. In a 1981 survey of 301 Dominican immigrants I conducted with Sherri Grasmuck, we found that the vast majority wanted their children to enter the professions—and definitely did *not* want their children to go into their own type of work.

There is, however, an emerging contradiction between immigrants' aspirations for their children and the future structure of employment in the Dominican Republic and the United States. Many immigrant parents hope that their educated children will return to the Dominican Republic where they can apply their U.S. training. Unfortunately, there is little reason to believe that the Dominican economy will develop sufficiently to absorb the U.S.-educated cohort. Already Dominican technical schools and universities, which have expanded tremendously in the last decade,[7] are turning out increasingly large numbers of well-educated students who often cannot get jobs commensurate with their training or expectations. In fact, quite a few university-educated Dominicans have moved to the United States due to lack of job opportunities in the Dominican Republic. As for prospects for the immigrants' children in the United States, these, too, are bleak. Many social scientists point to an increasingly profound bifurcation in the U.S. labor market between high-skilled white-collar jobs and low-skilled secondary-sector jobs (O'Connor 1974; Sassen-Koob 1984; Tienda et al. 1984). As competition increases for positions at the top of the employment hierarchy, it is likely that Hispanics will cluster at the bottom levels, due to blatant discrimination as well as more subtle limitations such as lack of access to prestigious social networks.

In short, the latest wave of immigrants may find that the occupational mobility enjoyed by earlier groups of second-generation ethnics will be much more circumscribed for them in the United States. Unless structural changes occur in the Dominican Republic or unless the most recent predictions about the U.S. labor market prove erroneous, the social mobility Dominicans anticipate for their children may indeed prove illusory. An Hispanic lower working class may become a more or less permanent feature of the United States' political economy.

Needless to say, members of the second generation are also likely to be frustrated and disappointed if they end up in low-level jobs since they, too, have higher occupational aspirations for themselves. Moreover, unlike their parents, who were gratified by jobs that led to improved living standards in the United States, the second generation, who evaluate their consumer power and lifestyle by American, rather than Dominican, standards are bound to be dissatisfied with the low-status jobs many will be forced to accept.

CONCLUSION

Although the New York garment industry has suffered setbacks in part due to fierce international competition, it has nonetheless benefited from the influx of labor from many of the very countries where garment firms have been relocating (see Sassen-Koob 1981; Fernández-Kelly 1983; Teitelbaum 1985). Immigrant laborers, like the Dominican women described here, bring a set of beliefs, values, and social relations from the home and community to the workplace that make many satisfied and committed workers. In addition, the changes that new work opportunities and exposure to American sex roles have brought to Dominican women have reinforced their positive disposition toward employment in the United States. There is, however, reason to suspect that second-generation Dominican garment workers will not be so content. Because they are oriented to American standards of living and will not likely experience such dramatic changes in gender roles within their own households, second-generation Dominican garment workers will undoubtedly be far less satisfied and compliant workers than their mothers.

NOTES

1. The ethnographic research was funded by the National Institutes of Health, the National Science Foundation, and New York University's New York Research Program in Inter-American Affairs. I want to thank my research assistant, Catherine Benamou, for her help in designing and administering the questionnaire used in the garment worker study.
2. It should be noted that New York City and other plaintiffs filed suit in August 1980 against the Bureau of the Census and other defendants, claiming that the Bureau had undercounted the population of the state and city in the 1980 decennial census. Thus there are many, including this author, who believe that the total number of Dominicans residing in the United States far surpasses the current census figures.
3. The 1970 census revealed that black sewing machine operators had significantly more years of schooling than their white counterparts, suggesting that racial discrimination had limited black workers' job opportunities and had impeded their mobility out of the garment industry (Abeles et al. 1983:28).
4. According to the 1970 census, the average sewing machine operator was 47 years of age or older. A key contributing factor was the declining labor force participation of Puerto Rican women in New York City (down from 36 percent in 1960 to 29 percent in 1970). This decline in labor force activity was steepest among younger Puerto Rican women aged 25–44, the mainstay of the apparel industry's workforce (Abeles et al. 1983:27–28).
5. Another contributing element is the immigrant ideology of self-made individuals and families which the Dominicans carried with them to the United States and have found reinforced in the Spanish and English language media, in schools, and in churches.
6. Contractors are independent firms that perform operations according to the specifications set by manufacturers. They generally sew and complete garments.
7. In 1965 there were only two Dominican universities. By 1976 the number had increased to seven and matriculation had expanded from 6,963 to 58,907, that is, by approximately 850 percent (Ureña and Ferreiras 1980:153).

REFERENCES

Abeles, Schwartz, Haeckel, and Silverblatt, Inc. 1983. *The Chinatown Garment Industry Study*. New York: ILGWU.
Alba, Francisco. 1978. "Mexico's International Migration as a Manifestation of Its Development Pattern." *International Migration Review* 12:502–513.

Benamou, Catherine. 1984. "La Aguja: Labor Union Participation Among Hispanic Immigrant Women in The New York Garment Industry." *Occasional Paper No. 44*. Center for Latin American and Caribbean Studies, New York University.

Bray, David. 1984. "Economic Development: The Middle Class and International Migration in the Dominican Republic." *International Migration Review* 18:217–236.

Brown, Susan. 1972. "Coping with Poverty in the Dominican Republic: Women and Their Mates." Ph.D. dissertation, University of Michigan.

Chaikin, Sol. 1976. "The Needed Repeal of Item 807.00 of the Tariff Schedules of the United States." Report presented to the Subcommittee on Ways and Means, U.S. House of Representatives.

Chishti, Muzaffar. 1983. "Blaming the Victim." *ILR Report* 20:22–24.

Edwards, Richard. 1979. *Contested Terrain*. New York: Basic Books.

Fenton, Edward. 1975. *Immigrants and the Union, A Case Study: Italians and American Labor 1870–1920*. New York: Arno Press.

Fernández-Kelly, María Patricia. 1983. *For We Are Sold, I and My People: Women and Industrialization in Mexico's Frontier*. Albany, N.Y.: State University of New York Press.

Ferrán, Fernando. 1984. "La Familia Nuclear de la Subcultura de la Pobreza Dominicana." *Estudios Sociales* 27:137–185.

Fitzpatrick, Joseph. 1971. *Puerto Rican Americans*. Englewood Cliffs, N.J.: Prentice-Hall.

Foner, Nancy. 1983. "Jamaican Migrants: A Comparative Analysis of the New York and London Experience." *Occasional Paper No. 36*. Center for Latin American and Caribbean Studies, New York University.

Georges, Eugenia. 1984. "New Immigrants in the Political Process: Dominicans in New York." *Occasional Paper No. 45*. Center for Latin American and Caribbean Studies, New York University.

González, Nancie. 1970. "Peasants' Progress: Dominicans in New York." *Caribbean Studies* 10:154–171.

—— 1976. "Multiple Migratory Experiences of Dominican Women." *Anthropological Quarterly* 49:36–43.

Grant, Geraldine and Judith Herbstein. 1983. "Immigrant Mobility: Upward, Downward or Outward?" Paper presented at the Annual Meeting of the Society for Applied Anthropology, San Diego, Ca.

Grasmuck, Sherri. 1982. "The Impact of Emigration on National Development: Three Sending Communities in the Dominican Republic." *Occasional Paper No. 33*. Center for Latin American and Caribbean Studies, New York University.

Gray, Louis. 1975. "A Socio-Economic Profile of Puerto Rican New Yorkers." Regional Report No. 46. New York: U.S. Department of Labor, Bureau of Labor Statistics.

Gurak, Douglas and Mary Kritz. 1982. "Settlement and Immigration Processes of Dominicans and Colombians in New York City." Paper presented at the Annual Meeting of the American Sociological Association, San Francisco.

Helfgott, Roy. 1959. "Women's and Children's Apparel." In Max Hall, ed., *Made in New York: Case Studies in Metropolitan Manufacturing.* Cambridge: Harvard University Press.

Hendricks, Glenn. 1974. *The Dominican Diaspora: From the Dominican Republic to New York City—Villagers in Transition.* New York: Teachers College Press, Columbia University.

Hill, Herbert. 1968. "The Racial Practices of Organized Labor: The Contemporary Record." In Julius Jacobson, ed., *The Negro and the American Labor Movement.* Garden City, N.Y.: Doubleday.

Immigration and Naturalization Service. 1961–1980. *Annual Reports.* Washington, D.C.: U.S. Government Printing Office.

Instituto Dominicano de Estudios Aplicados. 1978. "La Condición de la Campesina Dominicana y su Participación en la Economia." Secretaria de Estado de Agricultura, Santo Domingo, Dominican Republic.

Kessler-Harris, Alice. 1981. *Women Have Always Worked.* Old Westbury, N.Y.: Feminist Press.

Light, Ivan. 1972. *Ethnic Enterprise in America.* Berkeley: University of California Press.

Marshall, Adriana. 1983. "Immigration in a Surplus-Worker Labor Market: The Case of New York." *Occasional Paper No. 39.* Center for Latin American and Caribbean Studies, New York University.

NACLA (North American Congress on Latin America). 1977. "Capital's Flight: Apparel Industry Moves South." *NACLA Report on the Americas* 11:1–25.

O'Connor, James. 1974. *The Fiscal Crisis of the State.* New York: St. Martin's Press.

Pessar, Patricia. 1982a. "The Role of Households in International Migration." *International Migration Review* 16:342–364.

—— 1982b. "Kinship Relations of Production in the Migration Process: The Case of Dominican Migration to the United States." *Occasional Paper No. 32.* Center for Latin American and Caribbean Studies, New York University.

—— 1982c. "Social Relations Within the Family in the Dominican Republic and United States: Continuity and Change." In Office of Pastoral Research, ed., *Hispanics in New York: Religious, Cultural and Social Experiences.* New York: Archdiocese of New York.

—— 1984. "The Linkage Between the Household and Workplace in the Experience of Dominican Immigrant Women in the United States." *International Migration Review* 18:1188–1211.

—— 1987. "The Constraints Upon and Release of Female Labor Power: The Case of Dominican Migration to the United States." In Daisy Dwyer and Judith Bruce, eds., *Women, Income and Poverty.* Stanford: Stanford University Press.

Piore, Michael. 1979. *Birds of Passage: Migrant Labor and Industrial Societies.* Cambridge: Cambridge University Press.

Portes, Alejandro. 1981. "Modes of Structural Incorporation and Present Theories of Labor Immigration." In M. Kritz, C. Keely, and S. Tomasi, eds., *Global Trends in Migration: Theory and Research on International Population Movements.* New York: Center for Migration Studies.

Safa, Helen. n.d. "Work and Women's Liberation: A Case Study of Garment Workers." Manuscript.

Sassen-Koob, Saskia. 1980. "Immigrant and Minority Workers in the Organization of the Labor Process." *The Journal of Ethnic Studies* 8:1–34.

—— 1981. "Exporting Capital and Importing Labor: The Role of Caribbean Migration to New York City." *Occasional Paper No. 28.* Center for Latin American and Caribbean Studies, New York University.

—— 1984. "The New Labor Demand in Global Cities." In D. Smith, ed., *Cities in Transformation.* Beverly Hills, Ca.: Sage.

Smith, Carol. 1980. "Immigrant Women, Work and Use of Government Benefits: A Case Study of Hispanic Women Workers in New York's Garment Industry." Ph.D. dissertation, School of Social Work, Adelphi University.

Sowell, Thomas. 1981. *Ethnic America.* New York: Basic Books.

Tancer, Shosona. 1973. "La Quesqueyana: The Dominican Women, 1940–1970." In Ann Pescatello, ed., *Female and Male in Latin America.* Pittsburgh: University of Pittsburgh Press.

Teitelbaum, Michael. 1985. *Latin Migration North.* New York: Council on Foreign Relations.

Tienda, Marta, Lief Jensen, and Robert Bach. 1984. "Immigration, Gender and the Process of Occupational Change in the United States, 1970–1980." *International Migration Review* 18:1021–1044.

Ugalde, Antonio, Frank Bean, and Gil Cardenas. 1979. "International Migration from the Dominican Republic: Findings from a National Survey." *International Migration Review* 13:235–254.

Ureña, Ernesto and Araceles Ferreiras. 1980. "Modelo de Dominación y Sectores Medios en la Republica Dominicana: 1966–1978." B.A. thesis in sociology, Universidad Autonoma de Santo Domingo.

Waldinger, Roger. 1984. "Ethnic Enterprise and Industrial Change: A Case Study of the New York City Garment Industry." Unpublished doctoral dissertation, Department of Sociology, Harvard University.

—— 1985. "Immigration and Industrial Change in the New York Apparel Industry." In Marta Tienda and George Borjas, eds., *Hispanics in the U.S. Economy.* New York: Academic Press.

5. The Haitians: The Cultural Meaning of Race and Ethnicity

Susan Buchanan Stafford

Although Afro-Caribbean immigrants form an increasingly large proportion of the immigrants currently settling in New York City, the effects of this migration on the city, as well as on the immigrants, have only recently become the subject of scholarly attention. The impact of Afro-Caribbean immigrants on the multiethnic, multiracial setting of New York City is evident in revitalized neighborhoods, new music and art forms, festivals to celebrate Caribbean and island heritages, bilingual programs in schools, and emerging community centers which meet the immigrants' special needs. Equally important, the lives and the perceptions of the immigrants themselves have been transformed in their new sociocultural, economic, and political environment.

This essay examines shifts in the symbolic meaning of race and ethnicity among Haitian immigrants in New York City.[1] In attempting to understand these changes and their effects on Haitians' lives, the structure of race and ethnic relations in New York is obviously crucial. As a population of foreign immigrants who are phenotypically black, Haitians occupy an ambiguous position in New York. They are a minority within a minority, often viewed simply as black by the white majority, but, at the same time, distinguished within the black population from other black immigrants and from black Americans by cultural and linguistic characteristics. Important as the structure of race and ethnic relations is, we must also consider the cultural conceptions and historical heritage Haitians bring with them for these factors also influence Haitians' racial and ethnic identity in New York.

Beyond analyzing the meanings and perceptions of race and ethnicity among Haitians in New York, this essay also shows that these meanings and perceptions have practical consequences for behavior and social relationships—not only between Haitians and other populations in New York, but also within the Haitian community itself. As the analysis indicates, Haitians are not merely passive players, simply molded or shaped by social conditions in their new home; they are also active agents in the process of change and adaptation (cf. Barnes 1977).

Before exploring these issues, I briefly outline the history of Haitian emigration to the United States and provide a demographic overview of the Haitian population. I also describe some features of the Haitian community of New York City and discuss some effects Haitian immigrants have had on certain neighborhoods in the city.

HAITIAN EMIGRATION TO THE UNITED STATES

Although Haitian emigration to the United States is generally perceived to be a very recent phenomenon, it actually dates back to the eighteenth century.

French colonists and freed mulattoes, accompanied by their slaves, fled the revolutionary turmoil of Saint Domingue (Haiti's colonial name) in the late 1790s and established colonies along the American Eastern seaboard in cities such as New Orleans, New York, Philadelphia, and Charleston. Notable Saint Dominguan émigrés in this period include Jean Baptiste Pointe du Sable, a trader who is credited with being the first permanent settler on the site of Chicago (Graham 1953:174; Spear 1967:5); John James Audubon, the naturalist, who arrived in 1803; and Marie Laveau, the "Voodoo Queen of New Orleans," born of Haitian émigré parents. Ottley and Weatherby (1967:47) note the presence of émigrés in New York City during this time: "Creoles from Haiti flounce through the streets clad richly in West Indian materials; 'coal black negresses,' in flowing white dresses and colorful turbans made of mouchoir de madras strolled with white or mixed creoles. . . ."

During the early part of the twentieth century, Haitian emigration to the United States increased as Haiti suffered continuous political unrest. Reid (1939:97) in his history of West Indian emigration to the United States, records the presence of approximately 500 Haitians in New York City during the early twentieth century. Most of these Haitians were engaged in industry, trade, or white-collar professions and many of them became politically active in the Marcus Garvey "Back to Africa" movement and in other aspects of the Harlem Renaissance.

Following the end of the American occupation of Haiti (1915–1934), American marines who had Haitian mistresses, wives, and children made special efforts to bring them to the United States. Teachers College of Columbia University also recruited Haitian students through an educational and cultural exchange program. After World War II, Haitian women were attracted to New York, Washington, Chicago, and Los Angeles by opportunities to work as sleep-in domestics in American homes (Woldenmikael 1980).

The greatest outmigration from Haiti began in the late 1950s when François Duvalier assumed power and instituted a reign of terror which stripped citizens of their rights and forced political opponents, intellectuals, and professionals to seek a safe haven abroad. The first wave of political refugees emigrated to Francophone Africa, Canada, France, Latin America, and to nearby Caribbean countries as well as to the United States. During the 1960s, as many of these countries closed their doors, the United States became the major haven for expatriates, mainly from the Haitian middle class.

By the mid 1960s, Haitians from the less privileged sectors of society joined the urban middle class and elite as the Haitian economy continued to fail and political terrorism worsened. Well over half of the legal immigrants from Haiti to the United States entered after 1968. There has also been a large influx of undocumented Haitian immigrants into the United States. After the 1965 Immigration and Nationality Act went into effect, requiring labor certification for all but immediate relatives of U.S. citizens and permanent resident aliens, "illegal" entry became more feasible and faster than legal entry, which often took, and still takes, up to two years or longer to effect.

As a result, during the 1970s, Haitians from all strata of society cla-
moured for tourist visas and many simply "overstayed" their visit,
thus joining the ranks of the undocumented. Many came without
visas at all. Between 1978 and 1981, over 40,000 risked their lives to
make the 800-mile voyage between Haiti and the United States, or
fled the Bahamas which had threatened to deport Haitian workers.

Motivation for Emigration

Migration in Haiti is a positively sanctioned strategy to achieve employment and upward mobility for both men and women. Within
Haiti, it is normal—and frequent—for individuals to migrate from a
rural area to a larger town for purposes of education or employment.
Port-au-Prince, the nation's capital, has doubled in size over the past
ten years and it serves as a major "commercial" center for travel
agents whose business is emigration. Migration—both internal and
international—is thus part of the Haitian sociocultural and economic
environment; it is an alternative employment strategy for individuals
in an impoverished country with a chronically high unemployment
rate, a subsistence economy, and little opportunity for its educated
middle class to advance. As in the case of immigrants from other
countries, the United States has held out the promise of unbounded
opportunity for those willing to work. It has also served as a safe
haven for political opponents of the Duvalier regimes (François Duvalier, "Papa Doc," and his son, Jean-Claude Duvalier, "Baby Doc")
and for those whose livelihood and security were threatened by the
arbitrary enforcement of the law by the Tonton Macoutes.

The reasons Haitians themselves gave for migrating reflect the grim
economic and political situation in Haiti. For both men and women
I interviewed, the major motivating factors were lack of employment
and lack of opportunity for upward social and economic mobility in
Haiti. These reasons for migrating were given by individuals from
the middle as well as the lower class. Indeed, nearly all Haitians,
except those with political connections or who belong to the elite by
virtue of wealth or family background, view Haiti as a closed society.
As Haitians express it, "Ou pa kapab fè mouvman an Ayiti" ("You
cannot move up in Haiti") or, "Ou pa kapab fè lavi an Ayiti" ("You
cannot make a living in Haiti"). Especially before the fall of "Baby
Doc," these statements carried strong political undertones. In the

view of most Haitians, Haiti has offered so little social and economic opportunity because for so long the government has paid little attention to the well-being of its population.

In the early years of the outmigration to the United States, upper and middle-class Haitians fleeing the Duvalier regime could afford—or had—to emigrate as family units. Now, however, few families have sufficient funds to leave Haiti together. The average payment to a travel agent to arrange for the necessary, usually false, papers is $1,500–$2,000. Even Haitians who have entered the United States by boat have often paid similar prices, the exact fee depending upon their mode of entry, that is, small sailing boat, commercial trawler, etc. Typically, a Haitian family will select one family member to lead the way, choosing someone most likely to obtain the necessary documents from Haitian and American immigration authorities. Women are often chosen partly because they can qualify for labor certification more easily than men. Women, too, can more easily obtain tourist visas since immigration officials seem to feel that women are less likely than men to overstay visas since they will want to return to their children in Haiti. And once in the United States, women are able to find work as domestics, an avenue of employment generally not open to men, and one that offers the possibility of achieving permanent resident status through an American sponsor.

Haitian migration to the United States is thus primarily a chain migration (MacDonald and MacDonald 1964) in which one or two individuals establish a household in the host society and begin to recruit a series of relatives and friends to join them. This means that few Haitians now enter the United States without an established network of kin and friends who can offer initial assistance with housing, daily expenses, and employment. Clérismé (1975) found a particularly dramatic case when studying a cluster of Haitian emigrants in Brooklyn who came from Bassin Bleu, a town in northwestern Haiti. This cluster of thirty-six owed its origins to one woman who immigrated in 1966 and was later joined by real or fictive kin from her home community.

Demographic Overview of the Haitian Population

We do not know exactly how many Haitian immigrants live in the United States, mainly because of the large number of undocumented

Haitian aliens who, obviously, do not appear in Immigration and Naturalization Service (INS) figures on legal admissions and who also were undercounted in the 1980 census.

Between 1953 and 1979, 50,002 Haitian women and 44,157 Haitian men were legally admitted to the United States as immigrants (U.S. Department of Justice 1953–1979). These immigrants tended to be young, with most arrivals in the age range of ten to thirty-nine years. Among the so-called Haitian "boat people" who arrived en masse between 1978 and 1981, Haitian men comprise about 70 percent of the arrivals and Haitian women, 30 percent. They too are a young population with the majority of arrivals falling within the twenty- to twenty-nine-year-old age range (U.S. Department of Health and Human Services 1981).

Haitians have settled in various parts of the United States, with the largest communities in New York, Miami, Chicago, Boston, Washington, and Philadelphia. Estimates of the total Haitian population in the United States vary widely. Laguerre's estimate (1984:24–25), based upon INS data and talks with community leaders, is as high as 600,000 for the early 1980s, and he guesses that roughly 325,000 were undocumented arrivals who had not yet regularized their status. The 1980 census figures record that 92,400 persons of Haitian birth reside in the United States, of whom 52,600—or 57 percent—live in the New York-New Jersey metropolitan area (see Kraly, this volume). Nearly 90 percent of these New York-New Jersey residents arrived after 1965, and 60 percent have come since 1970 (see Kraly, this volume).

The majority of Haitians, especially new arrivals, work at unskilled or semiskilled jobs in factories, service industries, and domestic service. A small but growing percentage of earlier immigrants hold professional, technical, or managerial positions, or own small businesses, often in Haitian communities. Lack of documentation places many Haitians in a vulnerable legal position that affects their employment opportunities—and also precludes return visits home. The undocumented flow continues from Haiti, but, at the same time, many undocumented Haitians are in the process of trying to regularize their status and a minority of permanent residents have become U.S. citizens.

THE HAITIAN COMMUNITY
OF NEW YORK

Settlement Patterns

New York is, by far, the city with the largest concentration of Haitians in the country. Within New York City, Haitians tend to cluster in particular areas. Haitian enclaves have developed in Brooklyn, Manhattan, and Queens as new arrivals swell the ranks of earlier settlers and as successful earlier immigrants establish residence in new, more desirable areas. This geographical concentration of Haitians in specific New York City neighborhoods reflects not only their desire to live among kin, friends, and fellow Haitians, but also their socioeconomic and racial status. Given their economic position, it is not surprising that most Haitians live in low-income areas. Moreover, as Laguerre (1984:49) notes, "they must join a black or racially mixed neighborhood." Even Haitians who have moved to more affluent areas of Queens, for example, find themselves in changing neighborhoods whose white population is being replaced by black Americans and Afro-Caribbean and Hispanic immigrants.

The residential patterns of new Haitian immigrants clearly influence their lives in many ways. These patterns also have a decided impact on New York City itself. As Haitians cluster together in particular neighborhoods, they have given these areas a distinct Haitian character and have affected various institutions in them.

Brooklyn is home to the largest number of Haitians in New York City. The run-down sections of Crown Heights, Bedford Stuyvesant, Bushwick, and East New York house many poor Haitians in apartment buildings whose elegant names, such as "The Paradise" and "The Martinique," and grand exteriors belie their dilapidated, rat- and roach-infested interiors. Some Haitians in these areas own their homes, usually small brownstone-type buildings in various stages of disrepair, but most are apartment dwellers. Haitians consider their residence in these areas temporary until they can afford to move to more secure, less crime-ridden neighborhoods in Brooklyn or Queens.

The lower-middle-class sections of Crown Heights on the southern side of Eastern Parkway, Park Slope, Prospect Heights, East Flatbush, and Flatbush are natural areas of expansion for Haitians as these neighborhoods offer better housing and a safer environment, plus good access to public transportation and shopping areas. Many Haitians have purchased homes here, mainly attached houses, preferring to do this than to move to the less easily accessible neighborhoods of Queens. Rutland Road and Utica Avenue form the core of the Haitian business district in Brooklyn.

The Haitian presence in Brooklyn has affected many existing institutions—and has even created some new ones. In the Haitian sections of residence, a growing number of Catholic and Protestant churches hold French or Haitian Creole services. Many Haitian businesses have emerged—beauty parlors, restaurants, record stores, auto body shops, grocery markets, and so on. Several Haitian community centers have opened in parts of the borough and, with other centers in Manhattan and Queens, operate under the organizational umbrella of the Haitian Centers Council. Many primary and secondary schools offer bilingual programs for Haitian children and several private schools have been opened for Haitian students. Other institutions, such as banks and health care facilities, have responded to the Haitian presence by printing their clinic cards and instructions in Haitian Creole and French.

A second major location for Haitians in New York City is lower-middle-class and working-class sections of Queens. Haitians who initially settled in Brooklyn and Manhattan later often move into the Queens neighborhoods of Cambria Heights, Hollis, Queens Village, Springfield Gardens, Elmhurst, Flushing, and Corona. In many of these areas there are clean, tree-lined streets and a quiet atmosphere which attract Haitians who find the ambiance slightly reminiscent of Haiti. Many Haitians in Queens own single-family houses—usually small brick or clapboard homes on small lots—in neighborhoods whose population has recently shifted, or is still shifting, from middle-income white to lower-middle-income black Hispanic or Afro-Caribbean. Rosedale, Bellerose, and Elmont on the Nassau County border are considered particularly desirable areas. Again, where Haitians have clustered in Queens, so too, Haitian businesses flourish, churches celebrate French/Haitian Creole masses, and Haitian children are a marked presence in the school systems.

In Manhattan, the largest concentration of Haitians is on the Upper West Side in the eighties and nineties, an area which has become increasingly gentrified and populated by affluent whites. In the 1960s and 1970s, transient and resident hotels in the area provided new Haitian arrivals with temporary housing until they located apartments in the area or in the other boroughs. Many of these hotels, as well as numerous tenements and brownstone buildings which have served as homes to Haitians, have been transformed into condominiums and cooperatives, thus reducing the Haitian population there, as well as that of other low-income minority groups. The Haitian presence, however, is still felt at the institutional level: two community centers exist to meet the social service needs of the populace, Haitian children attend bilingual programs, and local churches serve not only the spiritual needs of the Haitian parishioners, but also as meeting places for the general New York Haitian population.

There are no large concentrations of Haitians in the Bronx or Staten Island, but a number of communities in Westchester and Long Island, particularly in the southshore area, have attracted both relatively well-off professionals and blue-collar workers. Spring Valley and Nyack in Rockland County are close to industrial areas of New Jersey where many Haitians have found work in factories. Several organizations—both Haitian and non-Haitian—have developed social service and language programs to meet the special needs of this Rockland County population.

Social Organization

Family and kinship ties are the most important bases of social organization within the Haitian community. As I indicated already, kinship ties have been crucial in the migration process itself. Earlier immigrants helped their relatives move to New York and clusters of kin often settled in the same area. Once in New York, extended family members and a wider network of kin (every Haitian has a myriad of "cousins," both related and fictive) are bound together in reciprocal social and exchange networks. They assist each other in a variety of ways, ranging from giving support in times of crisis to providing each other with loans of money. Kin who live nearby see each other regularly, and informal visits—as well as such formal occasions as weddings, funerals, birthdays, confirmations, and holidays—bring together relatives from all over the city.

In addition to family and kinship ties, Haitians often socialize with, and live among, people from the same village or general region of Haiti. Indeed, one finds many pockets of residents from the same Haitian town, such as Hinche or Jacmel, in the same neighborhood. These immigrants also belong to village associations which provide the basis for social occasions and for sending aid back to fellow villagers who remain in Haiti. Within apartment buildings, networks of economic exchange often arise, particularly if people can trace some kinship tie, lived in the same *quartier* (section) of a town or village in Haiti, or attended the same school on the island. Even if people from the same community or family do not live near each other, the *télédjòl*, or gossip network, quickly disseminates information, rumors, and scandals among them.

In addition to gossip networks, a number of journals, reviews, and newspapers spread news among Haitian immigrants in New York City. *Haiti-Observateur*, an anti-Duvalier newspaper with a conservative political stand, is the longest-running weekly publication and circulates nationally and internationally. Because many Haitians are illiterate, radio programs in Creole attract a larger audience than the printed media.

Voluntary associations also link Haitians together within New York—and they abound. There are Haitian social clubs, student organizations, cultural and artistic groups, religious groups, youth and fraternal organizations, political cliques, rotating credit associations, and associations for professionals. Theatrical groups, choral groups, dance troupes, and other cultural groups provide much of the entertainment at the myriad dances, fêtes, cultural programs, and recitals that occur regularly in the "community."

One particularly important social institution that has developed recently is the Haitian Centers Council which unites six Haitian community centers in the New York area: Haitian Americans United for Progress (Queens); the Haitian Neighborhood Service Center (Manhattan); the Charlemagne Peralte Center, the Brooklyn Haitian Ralph and Good Shepherd Center, and the Evangelical Crusade Center (Brooklyn); and the Haitian American Cultural and Social Organization (Spring Valley). Although each center maintains its separate identity and organizational structure—and provides social, legal, and employment services to the Haitian community—the Haitian Centers

Council coordinates the centers' program development and funding efforts and serves as a clearinghouse for information.

And finally, there is religion which forms the focal point in many Haitians' lives. Most Haitians are Catholic, but the evangelical Protestant churches, such as the Seventh Day Adventists and Baptists, which have made inroads in Haiti, have their congregations here also. The Catholic church has responded to the influx of Haitian parishioners by offering services in French and Creole in several churches where Haitian priests are assigned. Many Haitians in New York also continue to practice the less formally institutionalized Voodoo religion through propitiation of the family *loa* (deities) and participation in rituals led by *houngans* (priests) and *mambos* (priestesses), particularly on special occasions, such as the celebration for Guédé on All Souls Day.

Haitians in New York have thus developed both formal and informal means for maintaining ties throughout the boroughs and beyond. Over the past ten years, the Haitian impact on institutions in the city has grown considerably so that the Haitian population is a more noticeable presence in the New York urban social landscape.

THE STRUCTURE OF INCORPORATION— RACE AND ETHNICITY

As a nation of immigrants, the United States has an extraordinarily diverse population, and in large urban centers ethnic diversity is a recognized fact of life. Although ethnic differences have long received informal political recognition (Sutton and Makiesky 1975:127), they have only recently been given formal legitimation by governmental bodies. Such recognition has come through a number of federally sponsored programs aimed at minority populations, especially in the field of bilingual education, that are designed to maintain and preserve cultural heritages and ethnic identities at the same time as they assist integration into the mainstream. Responding to institutional interest in ethnicity, as well as to their own desire to preserve their heritages, even older immigrant populations have been caught up in the resurgence of ethnicity. Ethnicity, as Glazer and Moynihan (1970) observe, forms the constitutive basis for many interest groups (see also Glick 1977; Schiller et al. 1985).

Differences based on race have, of course, also been highly significant in American social history, going back to the days of slavery. Racial differences "have been formally recognized" throughout American history and "non-white groups . . . have been 'differentially incorporated' into the polity" (Sutton and Makiesky 1975:127). In fact, the position of subordinate racial groups in American society, unlike that of white ethnic groups, is, as some scholars argue, like that of colonized peoples (see Blauner 1972; Katznelson 1973). Distinguishing race and ethnicity is not always easy, and Blu (1980:209) notes that "ethnicity and race are currently intertwined in popular as well as social scientific conceptions" with "the racial aspects of ethnic groups . . . being emphasized in a way that they formerly were not, and cultural aspects of race [being] added or stressed." Analytically, however, we can separate race and ethnicity: the symbols representing racial distinctions are drawn from physical appearance and the symbols representing ethnic distinctions are taken from such domains as national origin, language, religion, and food (Blu 1980:215–216). Although more emphasis has recently been placed on ethnicity in the social science literature, racial divisions still pervade American society and are an important source of social differentiation and inequality.

Race *and* ethnicity are significant among Haitian immigrants to the United States. As a population with African, European, and Amerindian heritages, the Haitian population is phenotypically and genetically diverse. Most Haitians are dark-skinned with African features; a small percentage is light-skinned with various European features. According to the racial classification system in the United States, which is primarily based on skin color, most Haitians, including those who are light-skinned with European features, are perceived as "black" or, according to more recent and more ambiguous terminology, "nonwhite." From the perspective of white Americans, Haitians are thus categorized with the native black American population and other blacks.

Because Haitian immigrants have distinctive linguistic, cultural, and historical characteristics, they can also be perceived as an ethnic population. In fact, differences of culture, language, and colonial heritage set Haitian immigrants apart from native black Americans and other Caribbean immigrant populations.

Thus, Haitians as a group and as individuals occupy an ambiguous position in American society; they can be perceived and categorized as either a racial or an ethnic population (Sutton 1973:145; see also Foner 1985 for a similar discussion of race and color among Jamaican migrants in New York City). This ambiguity creates some contradictions for them. Their perceived "blackness" can render them invisible, as both immigrants and black immigrants, from the perspective of white Americans (Bryce-Laporte 1972). They are relegated to the same low status as native black Americans and their special needs as immigrants may be left unattended. They are, however, also very visible to black Americans as foreigners with a distinctive cultural background—and they have recently become more visible to white Americans as well since the arrival of the "boat people."[2] According to Bryce-Laporte:

Black immigrants operate—as blacks and immigrants—in the United States under more levels of cross-pressures, multiple affiliations, and inequalities than either native blacks or European immigrants. These levels include . . . their being treated as blacks and recognized as foreigners. (1972:48)

Such multiple affiliations and cross-ties do give Haitians some flexibility, providing them with a number of social identities which they can choose—and manipulate—according to circumstances at hand. They can, for example, emphasize their "Haitianness" in some situations or their "blackness" in others, as I show in a later section.

Given the structure of race and ethnic relations that Haitians encounter in the United States, several questions thus arise: What impact does this new racial and ethnic context have on Haitians' perceptions of themselves and the cultural categories they bring with them when they migrate? How do Haitians deal with—and perceive—their various new statuses in American society?

THE CHANGED MEANING OF COLOR

Haitians come from a society where they have experienced considerable conflict and ambivalence about their racial identity (see Labelle 1978 for an interesting discussion of the ideology of race and social class in Haiti; see also Buchanan 1979). Haitians of all social classes tend to accept the ranking of whiteness as superior to blackness, and privileged Haitians have traditionally been fair-skinned with European features while the underprivileged have generally been dark-skinned with African features. Color in Haiti, as in other Caribbean countries, refers "to a position on a continuum of racial mixture between European and African, and not merely to one's color of skin. Determination of position on such a continuum depends upon the evaluation of hair form and facial features, as well as of color of skin" (Dominguez 1975:31–32).

But if there is a white bias in Haiti and if a certain color or racial prejudice exists there, it is also true that color is not automatically equated with social superiority or inferiority. Being black does not necessarily relegate a person to a low social status in Haitian society. Factors other than color are also important. Most Haitians believe that people are excluded from social participation not because they are black, but because they are lower class. Many well-off and politically important Haitians are in fact very dark-skinned. One can change social color in Haiti, that is, be thought of as culturally lighter if one acquires the manners, education, wealth, and other accoutrements of high social class standing.

Haitians are well aware that the American racial classification scheme differs from their own and they know that color cannot be "changed" by cultural factors as was possible in Haiti. Race, they also know, plays a critical role in determining social position and social identity in the United States where black skin carries a stigma of inherent inferiority. One consequence, then, of Haitians' move to the United States is a shift in the symbolic significance of color.[3] Although shade distinctions and the association of light skin with high social status are still important in Haitian immigrants' relationships with each other, these factors lose their significance in relations with whites. As Sutton and Makiesky note, shade distinctions

have little relevance to the larger white society which if it acknowledges them at all, sees them as internal divisions in a group whose primary categorical identity is as black people—with all that implies in the history of United States black-white relations. (1975:129)

Haitians' realization that color has a different meaning for Americans than it did in Haiti is apparent in the feeling by many Haitians that, no matter what distinctions they themselves make, in the eyes of white Americans, "Nou tout noua isi" ("We're all black here"). This realization is most painful to both light- and dark-skinned Haitians who had high social status in Haiti, but who find that whites in the United States put them in the same category as dark-skinned, lower-class Haitians.

Although the vast majority of Haitians are defined as "black" by whites in New York, a very small number have benefited from the U.S. racial system. Very light-skinned persons with European features from the lower social classes in Haiti—and who were not accorded high status in Haiti—may experience some upward mobility in New York if they can "pass" as white and be accepted as indistinguishable from the native white population. Light-skinned Haitians with European features who had high status in Haiti may also be able to "pass" in this way. One Haitian psychiatric social worker told me that some mulattoes can pass for Canadians or Europeans and, as whites, they gain advantages in American society. "Dark-skinned Haitians," he said, "resent this pretension at being white and the denial of Haitian origin. There is some resentment and jealousy here too. Mulattoes aren't immediately perceived or classified as black Americans by whites whereas darker-skinned people are and they don't like that at all."

Whiteness, as well as blackness, has a different symbolic significance for Haitians in New York. Despite the white bias in Haiti, dating back to prerevolutionary days of white rule, the fact is that, unlike other Caribbean islands, Haiti gained its independence early, in 1804, and did not have a dominant white minority after this time. Since the revolution, the ruling elite has mainly been drawn from the mulatto sector, and mulattoes (and some blacks) have enjoyed social and economic as well as political advantages. In the United States, by contrast, the dominant majority is white, and Haitians have become acutely aware that "nou pa gin pouvoua nan péyi-a" ("Blacks have no power in this country") and that social and economic privileges accrue to whites. Whiteness thus becomes firmly associated with social and economic power—and blackness with minority group status and powerlessness.

RACE AND ETHNICITY IN
HAITIANS' DAILY LIVES

The fact that Haitians are labeled as blacks in New York has a profound effect on their daily lives and their reactions to American society. They have migrated from a society where blacks are a majority
and where, as one informant put it, "You can feel comfortable being
black," to a society where blacks constitute a minority and racism is
institutionalized. Most Haitians had some previous knowledge of the
racial situation in the United States, based either on tales returning
migrants told about racism in America or on stories about the prejudice exhibited by U.S. marines during the American Occupation of
Haiti in 1915–1934.[4] Nonetheless, few arriving Haitians fully appre-
ciated or understood how their perceived color would affect their
personal lives in New York. One man depicted the attitude of newly
arrived Haitians:

"A lot of Haitians coming here don't even know they're black. Some
of them think of themselves as 'colored Frenchmen.' They certainly
don't think of themselves as the equivalent of black Americans or
imagine that they will be treated the same way."

The consequences of their perceived color become only too apparent in New York where they are the target of racial slurs and prejudice and subject to discrimination in employment, housing, and
education. For poor Haitians and new arrivals, their blackness means
sharing the ghetto experience with poor nonwhites—that is, crime-
ridden neighborhoods where drugs are a problem, poorly maintained
apartment buildings, and, if they cannot afford private schools, an
education for their children that is "so poor that it can, in no con-
ceivable way, serve as the path of assimilation and upward mobility"
(Dominguez 1975:54–55). Even Haitians who experience upward economic mobility find that lower-middle-class or middle-income areas
available to them are generally those in transition or inhabited mainly
by black Americans, Hispanics, Haitians, and other Caribbean immigrants. Friends who have settled in predominantly white neighborhoods usually meet with difficulties. In one case, a Haitian family
encountered resistance from the block association when buying their
home and, once settled, they were harassed by neighborhood chil-

dren. A young Haitian woman living in Queens described her experience:

"This neighborhood is mostly white. Our neighbors won't even say Hello, and they will not allow their children to play with ours. Even though my husband can pass for white, I am dark-skinned and so is one of my sons. The neighbors treat us this way because they see us as black. We don't expect to be bosom friends with them, but they could at least be courteous. Nobody welcomed us when we moved in and no one would even tell us the neighborhood routine, such as when to put out our garbage."

Haitians respond to such offenses to their dignity in various ways. They often claim that they do not understand derogatory terms such as "nigger" or they rationalize that the abusive person is simply ignorant and unworthy of further consideration. Haitians tend to regard the United States system of racial classification as illegitimate, as applied to them, and they assert a sense of moral superiority, arguing that "the same thing would never happen in Haiti." Haitians also have a highly developed sense of self-worth, drawn from their history as the first independent black nation in the Western hemisphere and, for many, from the social class position they occupied in Haiti. This sense of self-worth tends to minimize the impact of barbs of racism.

Haitian ethnicity also reduces some of the stigma of being black in New York. Despite class and other divisions among Haitian immigrants (see Buchanan 1980, 1983), the distinctiveness of being Haitian marks them off in their own eyes—and they hope in the eyes of white Americans—as superior to black Americans. Whereas the content of ethnic identity expressed in the United States has been a matter of considerable debate among Haitians who can draw on both their African and French heritage for cultural symbolism (see Buchanan 1979, 1980), they do often find it advantageous to set themselves apart as Haitians.

Haitians often insist that they are not prejudiced against other blacks, but are merely different from them by historical accident. Despite these assertions, however, Haitians tend to hold negative stereotypes about black Americans. Some of these perceptions about black Americans developed in Haiti where the media has spread a negative image of black Americans and where members of the elite were, and are, often assured by white Americans that their manners, culture, and educational level far surpass those of black Americans. One young Haitian in New York told me that "people from the Caribbean are susceptible to being brainwashed. They have the idea that every time a black American enters some place, he spits on the floor. They pick up this nonsense from the [Haitian] media." Whatever the attitudes they bring with them, once in New York, Haitians' desire to differentiate themselves from native blacks and their exposure to racist beliefs affirm and intensify already established prejudices. Perhaps, too, as one well-educated informant suggested, Haitians' stereotypes about black Americans are reinforced by the fact that most Haitians mainly interact with lower-class black Americans and have little, if any, contact with members of the black American middle class.

The particular stereotypes most Haitians have about black Americans closely resemble those held by many white Americans. Although Haitians are often conscious that "the white majority has brutally mistreated its black population . . . there is a tendency to rest part of the blame on black Americans themselves for not showing more 'initiative' in the face of opportunities" (Sutton and Makiesky 1975:125). An excerpt from my field notes gives an example of Haitians stereotypic thinking about black Americans:

At a church discussion group, the question of black Americans arose. One young man in his late twenties (from the Haitian middle class) expressed the opinion that Haitians do not want to be identified with black Americans because they are savages. He then proceeded to imitate a black American man's loose, swinging walk with slouched posture, gestures, and tone of voice—all 'bad form' for a respectable person. He also said that he does not associate with American blacks because they are rude and ill-mannered and because they reject any effort by foreigners to be friendly. He told of an incident in his apartment building in which he saw a black child playing outside his door in the hallway. When the child's father came outside, he asked the man if the child were his, attempting to strike up a conversation. Much to his bewilderment, the man told him to go away and started shouting at him. The Haitian young man reiterated his feeling that black Americans are savages, although a Haitian priest urged him not to be so harsh in his judgment.

Given such views, and the views of most white Americans, it is not surprising that Haitians are eager to emphasize their differences from black Americans. Like other foreign blacks, Haitians have learned that the presentation of "proper credentials"—that is, cultural, behavioral, and linguistic features perceived as superior to those of black Americans—often brings tangible and intangible benefits from white Americans (see Green 1975; Reid 1939). Many Haitians I met recounted experiences where, once their identity as Haitians had been made known, they received preferential treatment from whites at work or in other social situations.

Playing upon white Americans' fascination with and stereotypes about the French language and culture, many Haitians present themselves as culturally and linguistically French. Lest white Americans mistake them for American blacks, Haitians often let whites know they come from a country that has been independent for nearly two hundred years and that the slave revolution in 1791 began Haiti on its road to independence from the French. They also emphasize various symbols of "French" culture, especially manners, *fomasion* (social and moral training), education, and language.

Haitians' presentation of themselves as French-speaking individuals or as belonging to a French-speaking people is not restricted to those who actually speak French. In fact, only the educated elite and middle class in Haiti, a small minority, are fluent in French. Most Haitians in Haiti speak only Creole, which derives much of its vocabulary from French, but is a distinct language. Monolingual Creole speakers in New York, nonetheless, also stress their "French" language in relations with whites.[5] Even when Haitians speak English, their accents distinguish them from black Americans, as most Haitians speak with a distinct cadence and lilt to their voices.

Many incidents during my field work showed how Haitians evoke symbols of French culture and Haitian history to distinguish themselves from black Americans and elicit favorable responses from whites. At one baptismal party, for example, I was introduced separately to four different Haitian men. Each one immediately asked me if I understood that Haitians are not at all like black Americans. Without further questioning from me, they each explained that Haitians differ from black Americans because they fought a revolution to free themselves from white oppressors. They went on to say that black Americans failed to follow the Haitian lead and remained slaves. Each of the four men also stressed that Haitians are different because of their French culture and upbringing. Haitians, they said, know how to behave genteelly and properly; they are well-informed and well-educated; and they know how to speak correct French. I was made to understand that I should expect, and would receive, much better treatment from Haitians than I could ever expect from black Americans.

The same features that draw positive responses from white Americans may also lead to resentment and hostility from black Americans and reinforce negative stereotypes of Haitians as snobbish, clannish, and arrogant. The case of William, a former artist in Haiti and a factory worker in New York, illustrates this point. William's employer, a Frenchman from Alsace-Lorraine, brought his daughter to work one day and introduced William to her as an educated man who spoke their native tongue, French. They conversed for some time. When William returned to his job, his coworkers, mostly black Americans, denounced him for currying favor with the boss and for trying to assert his superiority over the rest of them. William told me that no one would eat lunch with him after this incident and, on the assembly line, his coworkers allowed material to accumulate so that he could not keep up with the pace. The hostility continued and, eventually, he lost his job.

In some situations, "hiding" one's ethnicity from black Americans is a more useful strategy than displaying it—though, of course, this is not always possible. In fact, many of my Haitian friends have experienced discrimination not only from whites, but also from black Americans. One thirty-year-old man with a white-collar job at a bank told me that he always eats lunch alone. The black American workers there, he said, do not like him because he is Haitian and the white Americans do not care for him because he is black. Another man explained his similar feeling of isolation from black as well as white Americans:

"We Haitians are *isolé* [isolated][6] from white Americans and from black Americans. I moved to this particular part of Brooklyn because I knew there were Haitians here and I have friends. I have some white friends from work who have invited me to some big events, like marriages, but I never really feel I am friends with them. I am not at ease in an all-white milieu. Sometimes, you have a white friend, but he won't invite you to his home because you might embarrass him. He's too concerned about what other people think to risk being friends with you. On the other hand, I find it very hard to make friends with black Americans. I've tried a lot of times without success to develop solid friendships, you know, the kind where you feel comfortable visiting that person's family at his home. I find that they have a stereotype about people from the Caribbean—that black Americans think foreign blacks look down on them. So they immediately think you are prejudiced and won't accept you."

Haitian youths often find that their national origin and language arouse animosity among black American and Caribbean youths who interpret their speaking Haitian Creole or French among themselves as a sign of clannishness and snobbishness. Frequently, they are taunted with the labels of "Frenchie" and "French-fried" and, according to teachers with whom I have spoken, they are sometimes beaten up after school. One teacher in a Manhattan bilingual program told me that she often kept her Haitian students an extra fifteen minutes after class in the hope that non-Haitian students would go home rather than wait to pounce upon the Haitians. At several primary schools, teachers in bilingual programs said that the Haitian students often get into fights with black American and Dominican students. The teachers also pointed out that Haitian students sometimes exacerbate tensions by acting very aloof. To avoid conflict, some Haitian young people group together and isolate themselves from non-Haitian students. Others deny or try to hide their Haitian identity by speaking only English.

Although the negative stereotypes Haitians and black Americans have about each other contribute to resentments between them, there are times when their common racial identity becomes more salient than ethnic differences. In some instances, Haitians have moved to establish closer ties, particularly political ones, with black Americans. A striking example is the support Haitians garnered from black American politicians, particularly those in the Congressional Black Caucus, for the Haitian refugee issue. The unwillingness of the U.S. government to admit Haitians to the United States as refugees or to grant most applicants status as political asylees was interpreted by the Haitian community not only as a foreign policy issue, but also as a racial issue. Whereas the U.S. government contended that Haitians did not fulfill the definition of refugee because they were allegedly seeking employment opportunities only, Haitians and their supporters maintained that Haitians were denied their rightful status because the United States supported the Duvalier regime in Haiti *and* because Haitians were black. Black American support was gained not only on humanitarian grounds but also because the refugee issue was seen as an example of racial discrimination and bias. Thus, on a collective level, issues affecting Haitians have also become a focal point for black American politicians. As more Haitians become citizens and exercise their right to vote, perhaps these political ties to black Americans will become closer.

Also looking ahead to the future, a common racial identity will probably bring Haitian immigrants' children, who were born in the United States, together with black Americans. In school, on the streets, in daily interaction with non-Haitian peers, and through the media, members of the second generation develop a racial consciousness from early childhood. Unless their Haitian heritage is strongly reinforced by their parents, their primary identity will be as blacks within a white society, with their ethnic identity as Haitians playing a much less important role than it did for the immigrant generation.

RELATIONS WITH OTHER
CARIBBEAN POPULATIONS

To understand Haitians' racial and ethnic identity in New York, we also have to consider their relations with other Caribbean peoples. Haitians arrive in New York with a sense of distinctiveness from other Caribbean peoples based on Haiti's early independence, historical insularity, and their language and culture. Haitians in New York say that these factors, especially the linguistic difference, isolate them from other Caribbean immigrants, and there is some truth in this perception. One reason why Haitians have so little to do with English-speaking West Indians, even though they often live in the same neighborhoods, is the language barrier between them. Island rivalries and national stereotypes also divide *moun ki sot non Antilles* (Antilles peoples) in New York City, as Haitians themselves say.

Haitians take pride in their French cultural and linguistic heritage which, in the words of one Haitian, makes them "krouè yo gro pi pasé tout nèg" ("believe they're better than all other blacks"). English-speaking West Indians resent this implied superiority and point out the underdeveloped and preindustrial condition of Haitian society in comparison to their own more developed nations. English-speaking West Indians claim that Haitians are clannish and snobbish and do not wish to mingle or socialize with them. Haitians make similar accusations about English-speaking West Indians and thus they blame each other for their lack of interaction.

Haitians generally classify Puerto Ricans, Dominicans, and Cubans under the category *pagnol* (Spanish). In racial terms, Haitians characterize themselves as "black people" in relation to Hispanic immigrants who, as Haitians note, tend to be physically lighter and closer to whites in appearance than most Haitians. In terms of their culture, however, Haitians often emphasize their superiority. While Haitians express grudging admiration for Cubans because Cuba is an advanced island nation, they tend to stereotype Dominicans and Puerto Ricans as lackadaisical, unambitious, and content to live on welfare. In general, Haitians often stress their "French heritage" which they feel white Americans rank higher than Hispanic ancestry.

It is not only that objective cultural differences distinguish Haitians from other Caribbean immigrants and that Haitians seek to maintain a separate ethnic identity. The American political system has also encouraged ethnic divisions among Caribbean immigrants by providing special services and programs to members of particular ethnic groups and by indirectly fostering competition among these groups for government resources (Glick 1975, 1977; Susser 1973; Susser and Glick 1971). Individually and collectively, Haitians have benefited from special neighborhood centers that were established to help them deal with employment, educational, language, housing, and legal problems and from bilingual programs for Haitian children in public schools. Religious institutions, particularly the Catholic church, have also paid special attention to the Haitians and their unique language and problems. Participation in, or assistance from, these programs and institutions requires presenting oneself as Haitian, thus making this ethnic identity particularly useful.

Although there are clearly sharp divisions between Haitians and other Caribbean immigrants in New York—and although most Haitians marry and tend to socialize with other Haitians—many of my informants mentioned individual friends from different Caribbean islands.[7] Since many Haitians speak Spanish, they have a basis for rapport with Spanish speakers, particularly with Dominicans, their island neighbors. Haitians also participate in Caribbean-wide activities in New York City such as festivals, Carnival, dances, and theatrical events, and in West Indian and Hispanic organizations. Politically active Haitians who are concerned with the fate of other Caribbean peoples periodically join in political activities with them. Indeed, Sutton and Makiesky (1975:130–131) argue that similarities between Haitians and English-speaking West Indians in life-style and position with respect to the dominant society "create shared understandings which are beginning to be articulated in the growing interest in the Caribbean as a region and in community forms of political action and socializing."

To most Haitians in New York, however, their ethnic identity as Haitians is primary—and a broader Caribbean or West Indian identity is secondary, if present at all. The label "West Indian" is still more often assigned by white Americans rather than used by Haitians to describe themselves. As one young woman explained:

"Haitians don't have any trouble with the idea of accepting a West Indian identity, but that is more of a label put on Haitians coming here by Americans who consider Haitians to be part of the West Indian migration. The first time I heard the term "West Indies," I did not really know what was meant. I thought it strange that mail sent to Haiti from the United States must be marked West Indies [in order not to confuse Haiti with Tahiti]. I did not know that Haiti is in the West Indies. Part of Haiti's lack of West Indian identity also comes from its long history of isolation from other islands, especially under Papa Doc who did not want to participate in any of the economic or political federations. Part of the isolation is cultural and linguistic."

CONCLUSION

This analysis has shown that the perceptions of race and ethnicity that Haitians bring with them to New York are infused with new content and meaning in the new social setting.

Haitians' racial and ethnic identities in New York are shaped by a complex set of factors: the racial and ethnic context of New York as well as the cultural heritage Haitians carry with them when they immigrate. Moreover, Haitians' ethnic and racial identities are not fixed or static. They vary—and sometimes are manipulated—depending upon the social situation. Indeed, this discussion has indicated that Haitians are not simply acted upon by external forces that shape their identity. Haitians themselves are actively involved in making choices as they develop strategies to cope successfully in New York.

Such strategies entail emphasizing certain aspects of their ethnic and racial identities in some situations, downplaying them in others. Thus, I indicated how in New York, where Haitians find themselves forced to come to grips with their status as members of a racial minority, some very light-skinned immigrants try to pass for white. Most others, for whom this option is not available, emphasize their ethnic distinctiveness—and presumed superiority to black Americans—as a way to gain advantages in relations with whites. Haitians also stress their ethnic identity in relations with black Americans and Caribbean immigrants, a fact that frequently causes tensions and conflict. However, they may at times also emphasize their common racial bond with other blacks not only as a way to get along, but also for political reasons. Collectively, Haitians have begun to carve out a place for themselves as a particular black immigrant population and have used ethnicity as a means of gaining access to resources.

The presence of a large Haitian population in New York City has added a new dimension and dynamic to the ethnic composition of the sociocultural landscape. The Haitian impact on New York neighborhoods is marked by the introduction of Haitian community centers, French and Creole religious services in Catholic and Protestant churches, Haitian-owned stores, bilingual programs for Haitian students, cultural and political events celebrating Haitian tradition and history, and simply by the sounds of Haitian Creole and French on the streets. The Haitian impact on the wider city will be increasingly felt as Haitians become more involved in community and city politics, as more Haitians become legal residents and American citizens, and as the Haitian immigrant population grows in number.

NOTES

1. Material for this paper is drawn from my doctoral dissertation, "Scattered Seeds: The Meaning of the Migration for Haitians in New York City." The Charles Kriser Foundation and the Department of Anthropology of New York University generously provided funding for the research, which took place mainly among the Haitian populations of Brooklyn and Queens between 1974 and 1977. The main methods of data collection were informal and structured interviews with over one hundred Haitians as well as participant observation. For several reasons—a highly charged political atmosphere within the Haitian community at the time, fueled by rumors of Haitian expatriates' return to the island under new leadership; Immigration and Naturalization Service raids upon residential neighborhoods and workplaces; and a general Haitian tendency to be suspicious of outsiders—I collected data by developing an extensive social network within the community rather than administering questionnaires or using other survey techniques. Most of my contact was with members of the Haitian *petit bourgeoisie* or *classe moyenne* (middle class), although I spent considerable time with individuals from all social backgrounds. All quotations in this paper are in Haitian Creole and all personal names are pseudonyms.

2. Since my field work was conducted before the massive influx of the Haitian boat people, this essay does not—apart from a few comments on political ties between black Americans and Haitians on the refugee question—investigate the impact that this influx has had on Haitian identity in New York City. For a beginning attempt in this direction, in relation to Haitian organizations in the city, see Schiller, Brutus, and DeWind (1985).

   In the past few years, the drama of the Haitian boat people has focused the American public's attention on the Haitian population, unfortunately often in a negative way. More positively, the availability of government funding for resettlement and social services to this segment of the Haitian population, i.e., those with the status of "Cuban/Haitian Entrant (status pending)," has provided Haitian community agencies with a focal point for gaining access to resources. Thus, Haitians have collectively gained more visibility as a special subset of the black population in the United States, namely, as a particular population of black immigrants.

3. See Foner (1978:24–53, 238) for an analysis of the changed symbolic meaning of race and color among Jamaicans in London.

4. The racial prejudice exhibited by U.S. military personnel during the American Occupation of Haiti (1915–1934) left Haitians very bitter. The American failure to recognize Haitian color distinctions and their contemptuous and often brutal treatment of the populace antagonized all sectors of Haitian society.

5. For a more complete discussion of the use and meaning of language

among Haitians, including debates within the Haitian community about emphasizing Creole or French as a symbol of group identity, see Buchanan (1979, 1980).
6. Educated Haitians from the middle class and the elite tend to have more non-Haitian acquaintances and friends in their social networks than do Haitians of other social class backgrounds. However, the feeling of isolation as a population extends throughout all social classes.
7. A tabulation of marriages from the records of a Brooklyn Catholic church shows 18 marriages with non-Haitians (mostly with individuals from other Caribbean islands) out of a total of 344 marriages performed between 1956 and 1975.

REFERENCES

Barnes, Barry. 1977. *Interests and the Growth of Knowledge.* London: Routledge and Kegan Paul.
Blauner, Robert. 1972. *Racial Oppression in America.* New York: Harper and Row.
Blu, Karen I. 1980. *The Lumbee Problem: The Making of an American Indian People.* New York: Cambridge University Press.
Bryce-Laporte, Roy S. 1972. "Black Immigrants: The Experience of Invisibility and Inequality." *Journal of Black Studies* 1:29–56.
Buchanan, Susan Huelsebusch. 1979. "Language and Identity Among Haitians in New York City." *International Migration Review* 13:298–313.
—— 1980. "Scattered Seeds: The Meaning of the Migration for Haitians in New York City." Unpublished doctoral dissertation, New York University.
—— 1983. "The Cultural Meaning of Social Class for Haitians in New York City." *Ethnic Groups* 5:7–30.
Clérismé, Renald. 1975. "Dependency and Migration, A Case Study: Bassin-Bleuans in Brooklyn." Unpublished Master's thesis, New York University.
Dominguez, Virginia R. 1973. "The Spanish-Speaking Caribbeans in New York City: The Middle Race." *Revista Interamericana/Interamerican Review* 3:135–142.
—— 1975. *From Neighbor to Stranger: The Dilemma of Caribbean Peoples in the United States.* New Haven: Antilles Research Program, Yale University.
Foner, Nancy. 1978. *Jamaica Farewell: Jamaican Migrants in London.* Berkeley: University of California Press.
—— 1985. "Race and Color: Jamaican Migrants in London and New York City." *International Migration Review* 19:708–727.
Glazer, Nathan and Daniel Moynihan. 1970. *Beyond the Melting Pot.* Cambridge: MIT Press.
Glick (Schiller), Nina. 1975. "The Formation of a Haitian Ethnic Group." Unpublished doctoral dissertation, Columbia University.
—— 1977. "Ethnic Groups Are Made, Not Born." In George L. Hicks and

Philip E. Leis, eds., *Identity and Ethnicity*. North Scituate, Mass.: Duxbury Press.

Graham, Shirley. 1953. *Jean Baptiste Pointe du Sable, Founder of Chicago*. New York: Julian Messner.

Green, Vera. 1975. "Racial Versus Ethnic Factors in Afro-American and Afro-Caribbean Migration." In Helen I. Safa and Brian M. Du Toit, eds., *Migration and Development: Implications for Ethnic Identity and Political Conflict*. The Hague: Mouton.

Katznelson, Ira. 1973. *Black Men, White Cities: Race, Politics, and Migration in the United States, 1900–1930 and Britain, 1948–1968*. London: Oxford University Press.

Labelle, Micheline. 1978. *Ideologie de couleur et classes sociales in Haiti*. Montreal: Les Presses de l'Université de Montreal.

Laguerre, Michel S. 1984. *American Odyssey: Haitians in New York City*. Ithaca: Cornell University Press.

MacDonald, John S. and Leatrice D. MacDonald. 1964. "Chain Migration, Ethnic Neighborhoods, and Social Networks." *Milbank Memorial Fund Quarterly* 42:82–97.

Ottley, Roi and William Weatherby. 1967. *The Negro in New York: An Informal Social History*. Dobbs Ferry, N.Y.: Oceana Publications.

Reid, Ira de A. 1939. *The Negro Immigrant: His Background, Characteristics, and Social Adjustment, 1899–1937*. New York: Columbia University Press.

Schiller, Nina Glick, Marie Lucie Brutus, and Josh DeWind. 1985. "'Right Here on Flatbush Avenue': The Development of Multiple Organizational Identities among Haitian Immigrants." Paper presented to the American Anthropological Association, Washington, D.C., December.

Spear, Albert. 1967. *Black Chicago: The Making of a Negro Ghetto, 1890–1920*. Chicago: University of Chicago Press.

Susser, Ida. 1973. "A Comparative Approach to Ethnicity." Unpublished Master's thesis, University of Chicago.

Susser, Ida and Nina Glick. 1971. "Ethnicity in a New York City School." *Student Anthropologist* 3:133–142.

Sutton, Constance R. 1973. "Caribbean Migrants and Group Identity: Suggestions for Comparative Studies." *Migration: Report on the Research Conference on Migration, Ethnic Minority Status, and Social Adaptation*. Publication No. 5. Rome: United Nations Social Defense Research Institute.

Sutton, Constance and Susan Makiesky. 1975. "Migration and West Indian Racial and Ethnic Consciousness." In Helen I. Safa and Brian M. Du Toit, eds., *Migration and Development: Implications for Ethnic Identity and Political Conflict*. The Hague: Mouton.

U.S. Department of Health and Human Services. 1981. *Monthly Reports*. Cuban Haitian Task Force. Office of Refugee Resettlement.

U.S. Department of Justice. 1953–1979. *Annual Reports*. Immigration and Naturalization Service. Washington, D.C.: U.S. Government Printing Office.

Woldenmikael, Teklemarian. 1980. "Maintenance and Change of Status in a Migrant Community: Haitians in Evanston, Illinois." Unpublished doctoral dissertation, Northwestern University.

6. The Vincentians and Grenadians: The Role of Voluntary Associations in Immigrant Adaptation to New York City

Linda Basch

The demographic landscape of New York City has changed dramatically in the past twenty years. In large part a result of 1965 changes in U.S. immigration legislation, there has been a heavy influx of immigrants from the English-speaking Caribbean to New York.[1] Peoples from the English-speaking Caribbean figure prominently among the fifteen largest ethnic groups entering New York City between 1975 and 1980,[2] and according to the 1980 census, of the approximately 750,000 immigrants arriving in the New York area since 1970, about one-fifth were from the English and French-speaking Caribbean (U.S. Department of Commerce 1983:4).[3]

This rapid ethnic restructuring has had a profound cultural impact on the city. As one observer points out: "In Crown Heights and East Flatbush, American candy stores have given way to Jamaican restaurants, Puerto Rican bodegas and Trinidadian roti shops. In Cambria Heights and Laurelton, the manicured lawns and newly painted homes proclaim the presence of the Caribbean bourgeoisie. On Boston and Gunhill Roads, the record stores belt out the pulsating lyrics of the soca [the picong of calypso],[4] and the lilting rhythms of reggae"

(Moore 1984:13). West Indian[5] people have also made their political mark on New York. The politicians Hulan Jack, Shirley Chisholm, George Fleary, Percy Sutton, Herman ("Denny") Farrell, and Ronald Blackwood, the newly elected mayor of White Plains, as well as the judge Constance Baker Motley, all of West Indian origin, are but a few of the names that stand out in a growing list of West Indian-American legislative and judicial officials.

Just as West Indian immigrants have made a cultural imprint on the city, so the urban environment has affected them. Many of the activities of these immigrants are shaped by the established institutions and structures of New York City. This assertion is supported through analyzing the role of voluntary organizations among West Indian immigrants from two small agricultural islands in the eastern Caribbean, St. Vincent and Grenada, each with a population of approximately 100,000.

The research on which this essay is based was undertaken among Vincentians and Grenadians in New York City between 1982 and 1984. The study utilized two basic methods: (1) participant observation among immigrants in their homes, voluntary organizations, and at political meetings and other kinds of social and cultural gatherings; and (2) systematic in-depth interviews with 105 Grenadians and Vincentians in seventy-eight households on such matters as their work experiences, kin and gender relations, associational ties, linkages with relatives and friends in their home societies, and their assessments and perceptions of the migration experience.[6] Life history information was also gathered on selected community leaders.

The literature on voluntary or ethnic associations demonstrates that these organizations provide an important mode of adaptation for immigrants in new urban environments. Such associations historically have been a prominent feature of the sociocultural landscape of New York, and in the early decades of this century, ethnic organizations of Italian, Irish, and Jewish immigrants served as the primary mechanism for the articulation of these groups with political and economic institutions in the city. The voluntary associations of Vincentian and Grenadian immigrants in New York City are particularly interesting on two counts: (1) organizational participation was not a significant aspect of these immigrants' lives in their home societies,[7] and

(2) ethnic voluntary associations are not found among comparable groups of Vincentian and Grenadian immigrants in Trinidad.

According to the U.S. census, there were some 5,000 Grenadians and 2,700 Vincentians in New York City in 1980 (City Planning Commission 1985), although if undocumented immigrants were included, the total figure would probably jump to 15,000 or even higher.[8] While the absolute numbers of these two immigrant groups are small relative to the larger West Indian population—for example, according to Immigration and Naturalization Service (INS) figures some 181,000 Jamaicans entered the United States between 1967 and 1979—these groups nonetheless are a representative and continuing component of the West Indian presence in New York City. In addition, their impact on the city is marked by several noteworthy features. They have contributed two ambassadors to the United Nations, one each from St. Vincent and Grenada; spawned a support group to reelect Mayor Koch; and given rise to an "ecumenical cultural celebration" now held annually at St. Patrick's Cathedral in Manhattan replete with steel band and a chief celebrant flown in from the Caribbean. They have also given the city calypsonians, steel drum players, and cricketeers; a major bakery in Brooklyn; at least three small shipping companies; the president of the influential New York district branch of the Hotel and Hospital Workers Union; a columnist for the largest Afro-American weekly, the *Amsterdam News*; and a novelist, the late Orde Coombs, who enjoyed international repute.

IMMIGRANT VOLUNTARY ASSOCIATIONS IN ANTHROPOLOGICAL PERSPECTIVE

Voluntary associations have been widely explored in the anthropological literature on migration and urbanization. This work has generally looked at voluntary organizations as mediating forces between immigrants and their new environment, and the emphasis has been threefold. One focus has been on voluntary associations as mechanisms enabling immigrants to adapt to new urban contexts, where they often experience rapid change and cultural disorientation. This instrumental view has been prominent in studies of rural Latin American (Doughty 1970; Mangin 1959; Roberts 1979) and tribal African

(Grillo 1974; Little 1967; Mitchell 1959; Parkin 1966; Schildkrout 1975; Smock 1969) peasants who moved as low wage laborers into developing urban centers. In these cases, voluntary associations were seen as instrumental in the early adaptation process, assisting immigrants with housing, employment, and problems arising from sickness and a range of personal and family crises.

Another emphasis in the literature has been on the cultural dimensions of urban voluntary associations, with a stress on their role in reproducing the home society's cultural institutions in the new environment. While some observers have viewed the lingering focus on cultural processes from the home society as retarding the immigrants' adaptation to the new environment (Hendricks 1974), most researchers have interpreted the reproduction of home-based cultural patterns in urban associations more positively. They have seen these associations as providing an arena in which the group can reaffirm its traditional heritage and ethnicity in an alien context (Doughty 1970; Little 1967; Meillassoux 1968). Moreover, some analysts have argued that traditional institutional forms, regardless of how they might appear, are, in fact, reworked and modified in voluntary associations in response to conditions of the new urban context (Sassen-Koob 1979; Sutton 1975) in ways that ease new immigrants' adjustment.

A third focus of the literature has been on the role voluntary associations play in fostering immigrants' links to the home community and society—through encouraging or reinforcing a continued home orientation as well as involvement in the community and political life of the sending area. This phenomenon has been noted among migrants in Africa (Mitchell 1959; Parkin 1966; Smock 1971), some of whom circulate between city and home and, more recently, among Dominican immigrants in New York (Georges 1984).

Vincentian and Grenadian voluntary associations in New York are an interesting case in that they reveal all three dimensions noted in the literature. They emphasize the immigrants' common ethnicity through reminding them of, and reaffirming, the group's traditional beliefs and cultural practices. In this way they galvanize the community into a cohesive force and provide an important means of reproducing the group's ethnic identity in the diaspora situation. These associations also are continuously involved with the economic development and political life of the home societies where, in fact, they make an impact. Finally, they increasingly, if hesitantly, address the instrumental needs of immigrants in the host society. In this respect they give support to Little's (1973) observation of West African associations, that the emphasis on ethnicity—by increasing the associations' hold over their members' actions—enables these organizations to teach members new standards and ways.

Vincentian and Grenadian voluntary associations in New York also serve an additional function generally overlooked in the literature. They link the immigrants to both the home and host societies simultaneously and in so doing join the two societies in a single field of action. This means that contrary to findings among other immigrant groups in New York (see Georges 1984), the activities of Vincentian and Grenadian associations in the home society need not detract from their involvement in New York—and vice versa.

In addition to examining the ways Vincentian and Grenadian associations link the host and home societies, this chapter shows that the function and orientation of these associations are products of the interaction between structural and cultural factors in both the home society and New York (compare Georges 1984; Sassen-Koob 1979). I will argue that the very existence of these associations and the strong role they play in Vincentian and Grenadian immigrant life are at base a response to the dominant structures of the New York urban environment, namely those of race and ethnicity, and the way these structures affect and are perceived by the immigrants. Part of the proof for this argument derives from the absence of these immigrant associations among the socially and culturally similar Grenadian and Vincentian immigrants in Trinidad.

VINCENTIANS AND GRENADIANS IN NEW YORK

Vincentians and Grenadians, like other West Indians, have been emigrating to New York since the early part of the twentieth century, although the larger influx began in 1968 following the loosening of immigration restrictions for non-Europeans. Even before these flows, however, migration had become a way of life for nationals of these resource-impoverished islands who, in search of employment, began moving to the growth poles within the Caribbean region—Panama, Costa Rica, Guyana, Barbados, Trinidad—in the latter third of the nineteenth century. With the labor needs arising in the colonial metropoles after World War II, many Vincentian and Grenadian emigrants shifted their direction to England, and in more recent years, they have headed for Canada as well. For the majority of these emigrants at the present moment, however, the more buoyant economies of New York and Trinidad serve as the primary destination points.[9]

These patterns of migration have created an entrenched migration tradition within the English-speaking Caribbean, an orientation reflected in the life histories of many migrants interviewed in the study. Although for the majority of Vincentians and Grenadians interviewed the move to New York was their first migration experience, some 72 percent reported that family members had migrated before them. And of these, 55 percent listed four or more emigrants in their families, while 13 percent could provide names of at least nine relatives who had migrated (Basch 1985).

At base, international migration is an effect of world processes of unequal economic development in which the more vigorous economies of relatively developed countries attract the labor surpluses of less developed nations. For individuals in particular countries, however, the decision to migrate is a response to perceived opportunities in the host society measured against conditions at home. For both Vincentians and Grenadians, it is clear that neither the resource bases nor the levels of economic development in their home countries are adequate to meet their needs and aspirations. Agriculturally based, both economies are dependent on a few crops produced mainly for export in the world market. Bananas, arrowroot, and various ground provisions are the mainstay of St. Vincent, while nutmeg, cocoa, and bananas provide the basis of Grenada's economy. These crops are highly vulnerable to local climatic conditions—to hurricanes and, in the case of St. Vincent, to volcano eruptions as well—and to fluctuations in world market prices. Considering these conditions, it is no surprise that the revenues of these two countries have been insufficient to maintain stable, viable economies: both societies have among the lowest per capita incomes in the Caribbean (Toney 1985), and unemployment, a chronic problem at all socioeconomic levels, is reported to be well over 20 percent in each island.

As a consequence, there has been little opportunity for the development of local managerial, entrepreneurial, and technical skills in either country, and those who have such skills tend to emigrate. The absence of these skills, combined with the lack of financial resources, has constrained the development of viable manufacturing sectors in both places. Despite their continuing economic underdevelopment, St. Vincent and Grenada have highly literate populations—literacy rates are well over 85 percent (Wiltshire-Brodber and Wiltshire 1985). In these economic circumstances, however, such educational levels only provide another inducement to emigration.

The relatively fragile political arrangements in both St. Vincent and Grenada have also increased emigration flows during certain periods. In St. Vincent in the late 1970s, when wide-scale strikes in both education and health care were harshly suppressed, large numbers of teachers and nurses left for New York. Whereas 1,564 Vincentian immigrants entered the United States between 1970 and 1974, the number almost doubled to 2,705 between 1975 and 1979 (Bouvier 1984b:6). Although the strikes abated, no visible changes were made in the country's economic or political policies. The relatively high emigration rates to the United States continued, with 3,750 Vincentians entering between 1980 and 1984.

Political turbulence and instability have played an even stronger role in emigration from Grenada. In the mid and late 1970s, the atmosphere of manipulation and repression created by then prime minister Eric Gairy spawned relatively high levels of outmigration: over 1,000 Grenadian immigrants were admitted to the United States each year between 1977 and 1979. The subsequent rise and then fall of Maurice Bishop's People's Revolutionary Government between 1979 and 1983, followed by the American invasion of Grenada, again produced high levels of outmigration; at least 1,000 Grenadians were legally admitted to the United States annually during this period as well (see Bouvier 1984a:7).

The push factors generated by the St. Vincent and Grenada political economies dovetailed with changes taking place in the structure of New York's economy in the 1970s that created a particular pull for

Caribbean labor supplies. An important component of this economic restructuring for West Indians has been the increase in employment opportunities in several white-collar service industries: namely, finance, insurance, real estate, educational services, communications and the media, business services, entertainment, and social services (Sassen-Koob 1985:303). Many of these are the very employment areas to which West Indians have gravitated. Several Vincentians and Grenadians interviewed are employed in banking as tellers, loan officers, and clerical workers; in health care; and in real estate, data processing, import-export firms, communications, and the media, where they fill low- to middle-level technical, managerial, and administrative positions.

Several in the sample also constitute part of what has been described as an "enclave employment sector." That is, they occupy jobs generated and controlled by the immigrant community (see Sassen-Koob 1985:321). These jobs encompass a range of professional and technical positions as well as a widening array of entrepreneurial activities which service the expanding and increasingly income-stratified West Indian immigrant community. Vincentians and Grenadians in New York own small shipping companies, beauty shops, record and music stores, and restaurants and catering establishments that employ other West Indians. There are a number of entertainers as well as arrangers, directors, and producers of musical, dance, and theatrical productions. And a few write for and own newspapers that cater to West Indians or serve as physicians, dentists, accountants, and lawyers to this community (Basch 1985).

Despite the severe economic conditions in St. Vincent and Grenada, research among the immigrants in New York indicates that they do not come from the lowest socioeconomic sectors in their societies, a pattern found among other Caribbean immigrants in New York as well (see Foner 1983; Georges 1984; Pessar 1982; Sassen-Koob 1979). Many Vincentian and Grenadian immigrants in the sample possessed the educational backgrounds and skill levels which eventually enabled them to move into white-collar positions: 82 percent of those interviewed had some secondary school education prior to emigration and almost one-third had skill training, primarily in the teaching and health care fields.[10] This education and training, however, did not prepare them to move into technically skilled, administrative, or entrepreneurial positions immediately. Similar to other newly arrived immigrants from low-wage developing countries, most immigrants in the study experienced downward or lateral mobility in their first jobs. They worked as tradesmen, security guards, domestic workers, building superintendants, and low-level clerical workers. They were poised and motivated, however, to take advantage of the many educational and training opportunities in New York to augment their basic educational and skill levels. Sixty percent of the sample went beyond a high school diploma and 27 percent gained a university or postgraduate degree in New York. Armed with this training, several were able to move into supervisory and managerial positions by their second jobs.

For the majority in the study, both their migration to New York and their early adjustment were facilitated by the previous chain migration from their islands and the family reunification provisions contained in the 1965 immigration law. As a result, a receiving network of kin and friends from home was already in place for most Vincentian and Grenadian immigrants. Over 90 percent in the New York sample had such networks and almost two-thirds were able to move into the households of kin or friends when they first arrived. Many of these friends and relatives helped the new arrivals with immigration papers or sponsorship, with locating employment, and with financial assistance and moral support.

Most of the Vincentians and Grenadians interviewed were able to "make good" materially as have other Caribbean immigrants in New York (see Foner 1983; Georges 1984; Marshall 1981). Roughly 33 percent of the 130 employed individuals in the households studied[11] earned annual incomes between $11,000 and $20,000 and another 20 percent brought home between $21,000 and $30,000. Fifteen percent earned between $30,000 and $50,000 while less than 30 percent drew incomes smaller than $10,000 in a given year (Basch 1985). Regardless of how these salary levels may seem by U.S. standards, they are high relative to incomes in St. Vincent and Grenada. More to the point, they allow the immigrants to accumulate property in both New York and their home societies—for example, fully 50 percent of the immigrants in the study owned their homes—as well as valued material possessions such as stereos, pianos, cars, video recorders, and home computers.

The ability to buy homes and many consumer goods often depends on the participation of at least two household members in the labor force at a given time. Three-quarters of the seventy-eight households studied had more than one employed member and at least one-third reported between three and four workers. In many families young adult children continue to live at home and to contribute to household incomes, rather than moving into their own apartments as do many of their American peers.

That Vincentians and Grenadians live in an immigrant enclave also contributes to their material gains. Many goods and services produced and provided by the West Indian community in Brooklyn such as child care, cooked foods, hair styling, tailoring, repair services, and professional services cost less than they do in the wider society.[12] In fact, when these immigrant-produced goods and services circulate outside the Caribbean community into the fashionable apartments and offices of Manhattan, their prices generally escalate considerably (Sassen-Koob 1985).

Many of the people interviewed, then, are satisfied in that they and their children have advanced educationally and economically in New York. Also important to many is their exposure to new ideas and knowledge in New York, which they feel expands their perspective. As a Vincentian said:

"You get more information from the media and other sources not available at home. You can buy books in Harlem, Brooklyn, and on 23d Street. You meet a tremendous number of people with different experiences. That, you could never find in St. Vincent."

Yet despite their material and experiential gains, Vincentians and Grenadians perceive the urban environment as hostile and ominous. The images they invoke to characterize New York City—lonely, crime-ridden, racially biased, cold, dirty—convey their sense of alienation. To lessen this loneliness and isolation, Grenadian and Vincentian immigrants cluster in West Indian enclaves in the Crown Heights and East Flatbush sections of Brooklyn, their immediate neighbors usually from their home islands. Some more affluent Vincentians and Grenadians have also begun to move to Queens—namely, the Laurelton section—where many of their neighbors are also West Indians. Social life in New York focuses around extended kin and close friends from home. These were the people migrants usually mentioned when asked about their social networks and who they felt they could count on most. Almost all social activities outside the home are anchored in the shops, restaurants, pubs, churches, and avenues of Brooklyn, which project a distinctly West Indian tone.

Voluntary associations provide an important texturing to this cultural milieu through the many activities they sponsor. These associations, along with the cultural tempo of Brooklyn life and the support provided by kin and friends, create the aura of a reconstituted West Indian community in Brooklyn and play an important role in the adjustment of Vincentian and Grenadian immigrants to New York.

VOLUNTARY ASSOCIATIONS AND
THE IMMIGRANT COMMUNITY

There are eighteen voluntary associations within the Vincentian community in New York and twenty among the Grenadians. Of these, about half have emerged since the 1970s in response to the rapid expansion of these two immigrant populations. Vincentian and Grenadian organizations, which are fairly similar, can, for the sake of analysis, be divided into nine broad categories. It should be recognized, however, that, in reality, associations listed under the different categories often are involved in similar activities and that some individuals belong to more than one organization. A breakdown of these organizations follows.

1. Benevolent societies, some dating back to 1910, were organized to facilitate the individual's adjustment to American society through financial benefits (i.e., primarily sickness and death) and moral support to members. Benevolent societies were prominent at a time when the size of these immigrant communities was very small and few family members were in New York to provide assistance. Their members constituted a relatively undifferentiated group since, whatever their social position at home, in New York they filled a range of menial occupational positions such as domestics, factory workers, porters, bellhops, elevator operators, and janitors.

2. Sports and social clubs, which focus on recreational and social activities and have also been in existence since the early days of West Indian immigration, organize competitive events with other clubs. In

so doing, they provide a means of forging linkages with the wider West Indian immigrant community.

3. Welfare associations are primarily concerned with the economic well-being of communities at home and they regularly send money and equipment for particular institutions—schools, hospitals, and scholarship funds, for example. They also address the social well-being of their memberships in New York and, like most of the voluntary associations, sponsor social functions which attract immigrants from home well beyond the numbers in their associations.

4. Occupational associations are usually based on occupations in the home society—for example, nursing, teaching, and the police. They address the economic conditions of members in New York, most of whom left these professions following migration because their credentials were not transferable. They also keep abreast of the economic as well as the political situations of fellow professionals in the home society.

5. Educational and cultural clubs focus on the culture of the home society through such activities as cultural festivals, discussions of folklore and local literature, and artistic performances. These activities enable immigrants to maintain and rework their cultural traditions in New York. The workshops and group discussions they sponsor also make immigrants aware of relevant social, cultural, and economic issues in both the United States and the home society.

6. Political clubs function as support groups for political parties in the home society. There is only one such organization in the Vincentian community, although several organizations show interest in political parties at home, and individual members of a number of organizations have given public support to specific candidates. The Grenadian community has been more highly politicized than the Vincentian in response to the engulfing political realities and marked ideological differences prominent in Grenada. Several organizations, some of which have stated political goals and others which do not, have given strong support to political groups at home, and active support committees for particular candidates have been formed before elections. In fact, political issues from home have so pervaded the Grenadian community in New York that some immigrant associations have had difficulty functioning during periods of unrest in Grenada, such as at the height of Gairy's regime and during the rise

and demise of the Bishop government. Indeed, the cleavages from home have to some extent been reproduced in New York's Grenadian community.

The above organizational types are found in both the Grenadian and Vincentian communities in New York. In addition, the Grenadian community alone has:

7. A performing cultural club which both preserves and furthers the Africanized cultural traditions of the island of Carriacou (a dependency of Grenada), largely through performance groups focused on dance, drumming, and recitation.

8. A woman's group which, responding to the emphasis on women's rights during the Bishop government, addressed the social and political welfare and economic participation of women in Grenada. Since the fall of the Bishop government this organization has been inoperative in New York.

Finally, the St. Vincent community has:

9. An umbrella group, the St. Vincent Anniversary Committee, which first mobilized around the island's political independence in 1979. It was strengthened by efforts to organize relief for the Soufrire volcano eruption, which occurred later that same year and inflicted heavy damage in St. Vincent. After a few dormant years, the committee was resuscitated in 1984 under its present name to organize a weekend of activities celebrating the anniversary of St. Vincent's independence and it has continued, if haltingly, into the present. Comprised of two representatives from each voluntary association in the Vincentian community, the umbrella association has been mandated by Vincentian member organizations to continue on a year-round basis, with the caveat that it confine its activities to the anniversary celebrations. This organization has the potential to mobilize the immigrant community around joint interests and already has defined specific activities for member organizations and collected funds from these organizations to use in planning events.

Most organizations today have between twenty-five and fifty members who are of similar background and who are often recruited on the basis of friendship networks. Members of an association typically come from the same age group and the same educational and occupational background back home and they enjoy similar social and economic status in New York. As it turns out, members also frequently share a common political orientation concerning the home society.

The rise and decline of voluntary associations reflect the ways the Vincentian and Grenadian communities have been changing—and expanding—in recent years. Not only are the two communities growing in numbers but they are becoming increasingly differentiated economically and socially due to the growth of educational programs at home and an increasing array of economic opportunities in New York.

Consider the changing importance of benevolent associations. At their peak, in the 1940s, 1950s, and early 1960s, when the immigrant communities were less differentiated, some benevolent associations had as many as 500 participants. Today, benevolent associations have been eclipsed in importance by other types of associations. In part, this is because Vincentian and Grenadian immigrants have become more affluent and have less need of such groups. As compared to earlier immigrants who generally worked in menial jobs in New York, recent immigrants have had greater educational opportunities both at home and in New York as well as a wider choice of occupational positions in New York. They also look to family members, which most now have in New York—and even to insurance salesmen, many from their home islands—for the assistance and support benevolent associations traditionally provided.

The recent proliferation of Vincentian and Grenadian associations in New York reflects the increasing occupational and class differentiation within the two immigrant communities as well as the immigrants' more comfortable economic position (see Georges 1984 and Sassen-Koob 1979 on the New York Dominican community). Some now middle-aged immigrants who have attained relatively well-paid positions in New York as nurses, bank tellers, entrepreneurs, and mid-level administrators have formed clubs comprised of similarly successful individuals. Many of these associations focus on charitable causes at home such as orphanages, schools, and hospitals. Similarly placed younger immigrants—many having arrived since the mid 1970s—have organized educational and cultural clubs as well as occupational associations based on their jobs at home.

If the growing number of voluntary associations expresses the internal stratification within the Vincentian and Grenadian communities there is, at the same time, a countervailing tendency. Immigrant associations are marked by an egalitarian ethos which emphasizes the similarity and basic equality of all immigrants as well as the jointness of their interests. In large part this ethos is related to certain leveling factors in New York: the subordinate status of immigrants, and especially black immigrants, and the desire of Vincentians and Grenadians, like many West Indians today, to distinguish themselves from Afro-Americans. The egalitarian ethos,[13] which is reflected in the fact that many association activities such as dances, cocktail "sips," fashion shows, athletic events, and cultural programs are open to all immigrants, welds the community together. Whether or not one is a member of the sponsoring organization is irrelevant. Everyone can, and many usually do, attend these functions. As one Vincentian said of New York associational life:

"Look at everyone mixing. They appear to be the same even though they're not. At home you would never see some of these people attending the same function together."

The opposition between the ideology of equality and actual social differentiation developing among immigrants creates certain tensions. The planning of the 1984 anniversary celebrations by the St. Vincent Anniversary Committee is a case in point. The committee had heated discussions, which consumed the agenda of two meetings, over whether to hold the anniversary dance at locations in Queens or Brooklyn. The Queens site was an exclusive Italian-owned catering hall that would cost $40 a person, including dinner and drinks. Given the cost and small size of the Queens building, attendance would be limited. The alternative was to have the function of a larger hall in Brooklyn—a public school gymnasium—charge $10 per person, and sell drinks, an option that would open the dance to many more segments of the community. In keeping with the egalitarian ideology which currently underpins the community, the Brooklyn hall was chosen. Allegedly, the dance netted significantly more money than it would have at the catering hall in Queens.

The emphasis on equality can also restrict the scope of an association's and its leaders' activities. In setting up the St. Vincent Anniversary Committee, organization representatives quickly put restrictions on its activities in order to prevent the chairman and other

officers from becoming too powerful. As one organization leader observed: "In every organization you have leaders and followers. With
West Indians, everyone wants to be the leader. No one trusts the
other." This concern about leaders' allegiances is partly shaped by
West Indian colonial history: leaders, because they were more ac-
countable to colonial power holders who appointed them than to
their followers, were perceived by the bulk of the population as un-
trustworthy (see Basch 1978; Carmody 1978; Makiesky-Barrow 1976;
Sutton 1969). The racial and ethnic dynamics in New York reinforce
these traditional attitudes.[14]

Despite the intrusion of various tensions into organizational activities, voluntary associations perform important unifying functions
within their respective communities. They reinforce and strengthen
a sense of common ethnicity among immigrants through their newsletters as well as their many activities—dances, sporting events,
church services, beauty contests, seminars, cultural festivals and performances. (These activities occur with such frequency that a club
often has trouble scheduling a weekend dance when it will not compete with a function sponsored by another organization from the
same home island.) This common ethnic identification, in turn, provides the basis for a horizontal linking among immigrants that can
potentially be mobilized for wider group efforts, as was the case with
the Anniversary Committee's activities. Voluntary organizations also
unite the immigrant community around a common ideology and set
of cultural symbols which acknowledge the group's heritage and traditions and emphasize the immigrants' worth and basic integrity.
This is critical in the New York context where West Indians, by virtue
of their racial characteristics and immigrant status, are ascribed to a
subordinate social position.

ORGANIZATIONS AND THE
SENDING SOCIETY

With independence in St. Vincent in 1979 and the changes in political
regime in Grenada in 1979 and again in 1983, Vincentian and Grenadian immigrants in New York have felt an increased commitment
to their home societies. Beyond the level of the individual family,
one means of keeping their connections to home alive and viable,

particularly at the community and national levels, has been through voluntary associations. Voluntary organizations in New York perform a number of mediating functions between Vincentian and Grenadian immigrants and their sending societies and assist migrants in maintaining an involvement with home emotionally, politically, and economically.

Their meetings and newsletters constantly bring issues of the home society into the consciousness of immigrants. A recent newsletter (St. Vincent and the Grenadines Ex-Teachers Association 1985), which has a mailing list of 600 names, was dedicated to the upcoming Carnival in St. Vincent. It described the joys and meaning of Carnival and printed the actual Carnival schedule. While the same issue addressed a number of topics specific to immigrants in New York, it also contained a lengthy cultural article on a community at home (Union Island), a page with the words to St. Vincent's national anthem, and a report on a meeting in New York between the organization's officers and the treasurer of the St. Vincent teachers' union. An earlier newsletter of an educational and cultural club, with a similarly large mailing list, included articles assessing the dominant political ideologies in the Caribbean and analyzing the implications of "the Grenada invasion by American troops" for the Caribbean region.

Voluntary organizations further solidify connections with home by sponsoring excursion flights at Carnival and Christmas. These organizations also maintain strong linkages with the sending country through the contributions they send for disaster relief, the support of schools, churches, and hospitals, and the provision of scholarships. More than 60 percent of the New York sample reported making contributions, through voluntary organizations, to institutions in the sending country.

The fact that some voluntary organizations have operating budgets as high as $10,000 means that these associations can make an impact on development in the home society. Government officials have long recognized this potential and attempt to tap immigrant resources. Various government officials from both St. Vincent and Grenada visit New York at least three times a year to discuss development plans and solicit investments from immigrant associations. On these occasions, the government consulates in New York organize large community meetings in coordination with the voluntary organizations. The following announcement of a meeting held in Brooklyn with the foreign minister from St. Vincent illustrates the close linkage between home governments and these organizations:

To All Vincentian Nationals and Friends

The Vincentian Organizations of New York with the Consulate of Saint Vincent and the Grenadines Cordially Invite You to a Community Meeting at which The Honorable Hudson K. Tannis, Minister of Foreign Affairs, Tourism, and Internal Security of Saint Vincent and the Grenadines Will Deliver an Address and Answer Questions.

Keep in Touch with Your Country.
Tell and Bring Your Friends.
Don't Miss This Opportunity to Get the Facts About Conditions at
   Home.

The St. Vincent and the Grenadines Consulate has worked hard in other ways to harness resources from the immigrant community. The consulate invites representatives of the voluntary organizations to social functions during the year, thus serving to consolidate ties among these associations in the community. Representatives of the consulate also attend meetings of the voluntary organizations. The consulate, moreover, actively supported the institutionalization of the umbrella St. Vincent Anniversary Committee.

From the point of view of the home country government, this umbrella organization is very useful. Beyond creating cohesion within the immigrant community, it can channel contributions from various organizations in New York to single development projects in St. Vincent. One complaint made by the government has been that the diffuse nature of immigrant associations' financial contributions to the island—distributed in relatively small amounts to many different projects and institutions—has minimized the overall development impact of these inputs. Significantly, the various voluntary organizations in New York, working together through their representatives on the Anniversary Committee, recently agreed to sponsor the development of a cultural center for the performing arts in St. Vincent. This center may well boost "migrant tourism" since it will house the Carnival shows so popular with visiting migrants.

Vincentians and Grenadians in New York also maintain linkages with political affairs at home. In the New York sample, one-third actively supported a political party at home and half reported having frequent discussions about home politics with other Vincentians or Grenadians. These connections are furthered by voluntary organizations, many of which maintain active involvement with political processes at home. The president of one organization said that his club can actually "have more impact on politics at home than [they] are prepared for," and this is despite the fact that his organization is formally nonpolitical. This organization sees itself as a potential "pressure group," however. The club has a strong image at home through its various activities—its New York newsletter, which is read at home, the excursions it sponsors at Carnival, and its popular cultural festivals in New York.

Politicians and government officials nurture this involvement with home. The president of the organization mentioned above is interviewed on radio and television when he visits home and he has been invited, along with other club members, to "speak with" the prime minister on these occasions. And this past year at Carnival in St. Vincent, the president and secretary of the umbrella Anniversary Committee were called to the stage during the main Carnival performance to formally present the organization's $500 contribution for the cultural center to the government.

Before elections at home, active support committees in New York for political candidates are formed, drawing on voluntary organization memberships. This has been most evident in the Grenadian community. For example, in the past election many candidates visited New York and sums of up to $1,000 were collected to further their campaigns. Some members of the New York-based support committees also return to the Caribbean to campaign for candidates during elections. They are perceived as effective campaigners because they have influence with family and local community members by virtue of their success abroad and the monetary remittances they send. As one organization leader said of his intention to return home to campaign in the recent Grenada election: "If people at home see prominent people coming back behind X, it will make a difference."

There is a reciprocal aspect to political involvement with the home community. Some organizational leaders, through their involvement with political life in the home country, find themselves dubbed for important governmental positions. Two ambassadors to the United Nations and one minister-counselor were activists in the New York immigrant community. Moreover, some organizational leaders, who see political activity as a possible avenue for return migration, talk of going home in the near future to run for office. Clearly, immigrants who want to assert themselves politically would find it easier to do so in their smaller home societies, among their own people, than in New York.

Others speak of making political connections that could help in establishing themselves in business at home. In this regard, it is significant that more than half of the New York sample expressed an intention to return home on retirement. Undoubtedly, for those who are active in voluntary associations, the continued involvement of these organizations with the home society encourages immigrants to contemplate actual return. This orientation to home is reinforced by the many visits to New York by politicians from home as well as by relatives and friends. In general, concrete involvement with the home country through voluntary associations benefits the immigrants as well as the home society. Not only does it provide possible future opportunities—and options—for those who may return, but it provides moral support to immigrants who feel demeaned both as immigrants and blacks in New York.

MEDIATION WITH THE HOST SOCIETY

Voluntary associations also link Vincentian and Grenadian immigrants with organizations and institutions in New York and help them adapt to the society in which they now live. Voluntary associations assist immigrants in reworking their traditional cultural forms in New York, thereby helping them to reduce the discrepancies between the host and home environments. For example, a recent newsletter of a cultural club published a "reinterpretation" of a portion of the novel *Madame Bovary*, utilizing a distinctly West Indian slant. By focusing on home cultural models and forms of interaction, these organizations provide an important refuge for Vincentians and Grenadians in New York and serve as a buffer against the alienating atmosphere and structures of the city.

Voluntary organizations also play an instrumental role in New

York in that they increasingly address ways that immigrants can tap into the city's resources. In the past three decades, an increasing number of urban services have been available to immigrants and these organizations publicize and try to make members aware of programs and issues in such areas as housing, community improvement, citizenship, and health care. One way they do this is through their newsletters. For example, a recent organization newsletter published a review of proposed changes in the Simpson-Mazzoli immigration bill, an article giving information on training and education programs in New York, and an article on the "creative financing" of real estate. This same newsletter also assessed the implications of Jesse Jackson's bid for the presidency for West Indians.

In addition, newsletters provide role models for immigrants through descriptions of "successful" immigrant personalities in New York, ranging from union organizers to small entrepreneurs who cater to the West Indian community. Voluntary organizations also make members aware of opportunities and political and legal issues by holding seminars on such topics as the pros and cons of U.S. citizenship, the New York City educational system, investments, and real estate. Although these meetings are poorly attended relative to the more distinctly West Indian cultural events, the important point is that they are being organized with increasing regularity by immigrant organizations.

Vincentian and Grenadian organizational leaders also emphasize the role of ethnic associations in obtaining services for immigrants in the pluralist context of New York. They frequently invoke the imputed successes of Jewish and Italian organizations as models of how immigrant groups can "make it" in New York. Leaders stress two principles for action: direct demands on the city for resources, information, and services; and the mobilization of large numbers to make these demands.

Vincentian and Grenadian leaders are beginning to make direct political forays into the wider urban arena as well. One association leader organized a Caribbean trade fair in Brooklyn in partnership with a U.S. government agency. He is also trying to obtain city funds to develop a Caribbean-American Chamber of Commerce to foster West Indian entrepreneurial activities. A Vincentian has become president of the board of a city-funded day care center; approximately six Vincentians and Grenadians sit on neighborhood community and school boards; a coalition of activists, largely from the Grenadian community, initiated a support group for Mayor Koch's reelection; and some Vincentian leaders were active in Carol Bellamy's campaign. These initiatives, in large part, have been built on membership and participation in voluntary organizations.

It has been more difficult to organize political activities that mobilize a large number of immigrants from the home society. While activists in voluntary organizations emphasize the common ethnicity and common interests of all Vincentians and all Grenadians, each immigrant community is bedeviled by a colonial legacy which emphasized narrow social and class divisions that continue to place a brake on collective action, even in New York. Nonetheless, the umbrella St. Vincent Anniversary Committee is a potential structural base for the political mobilization of Vincentians in New York across class lines. The web of voluntary organizations in both the Vincentian and Grenadian communities also has the same potential. Acting together, voluntary associations have organized large meetings—some attracting more than 500 immigrants—to hear politicians from home. Although these efforts remain largely inchoate and incipient at the moment, they do attest to "the demographic and potential political strength" of these immigrant communities (Georges 1984).

Mobilizing pan-West Indian action is even more problematic. Despite the historical and cultural similarities of all West Indians, there is a strong island identity and parochialism. In addition to geographic distances between islands, the Caribbean variant of colonialism stressed metropolitan connections to the exclusion of intra-Caribbean relationships and made "mixing" between residents of different islands, other than at university or in migration situations, nearly impossible. These factors constrain joint West Indian action in New York, although there are indications, especially in the cultural realm, that boundaries dividing West Indians from the different islands are softening.

Cooperation with black Americans through voluntary associations and political mobilization has, interestingly, become less paramount in recent years. Before the large-scale West Indian migration in the late 1960s, Vincentians and Grenadians, like most other West Indians, saw their interests tied to those of Afro-Americans. There were a number of occasions when Vincentians and Grenadians—through their organization leaders or through other West Indian leaders— joined forces with Afro-Americans in black political clubs and through their vote. Today, Vincentians and Grenadians, including those who belong to and lead associations, see their interests as more distinctly Vincentian or Grenadian, and in the wider urban arena as West Indian. This is due not only to the increased size of the two immigrant populations and their longer experience in New York, but also to the loosening of rigid racial structures resulting from the civil rights movement, which makes alliances with Afro-Americans seem less imperative at the moment (see Basch 1987 for a fuller analysis of these processes).

Thus, like other Caribbean immigrant associations in New York, Vincentian and Grenadian organizations have become more involved in initiating "active exchanges with the wider society" for political goods (Sassen-Koob 1979:329) as the immigrant population has grown, as immigrants have lived in New York longer, and as association leaders are more likely to fill middle-class occupational positions in New York (cf. Georges 1984; Rogler 1972; Sassen-Koob 1979). But whereas other studies of Caribbean immigrant associations observe that this increased articulation with U.S. political processes is accompanied by a movement away from a focus on politics in the home society (Georges 1984), my own study shows that this is not so for Vincentians and Grenadians.

On the contrary, many community activists as well as ordinary members of associations have maintained an interest in political processes in St. Vincent or Grenada as well as in New York. In fact, some of the organizational leaders most active in maintaining links with St. Vincent and Grenada are the very ones who lead New York organizations concerned with greater West Indian involvement in urban matters and with mobilization of joint West Indian action. The chairman of the pan-Caribbean support committee to reelect Mayor Koch was also chairman of the support committee to elect the current prime minister of Grenada. Similarly, a St. Vincent delegate to the UN was previously a member of the community board in his Brooklyn neighborhood and at the same time the chair of the umbrella St. Vincent volcano relief committee.

It is this meshing of home and host community into a single field of action through migrants' activities that enabled a Grenadian dentist, who has had a Brooklyn practice and been a U.S. citizen for over twenty years, to be named Grenada's most recent ambassador to the UN. To many in the diplomatic community this man's participation in the two arenas seemed discrepant, and a *New York Times* report indicated that outsiders in general saw the appointment as aberrant (Sciolino 1985). Viewed from the perspective of a single unitary field of immigrant action, however, the appointment was logical, particularly considering Grenada's scant resources.

VOLUNTARY ORGANIZATIONS AND STRUCTURAL CONSTRAINTS OF THE HOST SOCIETY

In objective terms, the Vincentians and Grenadians described here have enjoyed considerable economic success. Many have reached lower-middle- or even middle-class status in New York in terms of occupational and material criteria. The particular structuring of race and ethnicity in American society, however, complicates the issue of social mobility. Within the American racial context, West Indian immigrants, regardless of occupational position, find themselves excluded from certain residential areas, jobs, and educational institutions. Several in the sample related experiences of being refused housing because landlords "were not renting to black people." Others had similar tales regarding their job searches.

The racial organization of the New York urban environment means that West Indians are segregated from whites in most spheres of daily interaction. They have little, if any, contact with whites in informal contexts—in their communities or on the job—where they can get to know them personally on an equal basis. Rather, their contacts with whites are usually confined to asymmetrical, and socially and culturally distancing, situations in which whites are employers, supervisors, doctors, bankers, agency administrators, teachers, or school principals. In these situations, subtle, and sometimes blatant, instances of racial discrimination occur. The majority of Vincentians and Grenadians interviewed said that they felt negatively perceived by whites and vulnerable to racism. At least half reported personal experiences involving racial discrimination.

For Vincentians and Grenadians in New York, as for most West Indians, social reproduction largely takes place in a separate, somewhat insulated, social system localized in Brooklyn. The shops, catering establishments, and other businesses in this "immigrant enclave" are increasingly West-Indian owned, and many professional and other services are provided by West Indians. The children attend schools heavily populated by West Indians, and some are even sent to West Indian-controlled private schools where they can learn appropriate West Indian "self-discipline, self-control, and self-direction" (Foner 1983:41). Similarly, the rich cultural life that has evolved is decidedly Anglo-Caribbean. Perhaps most importantly, the norms and values that govern interactions in this subculture are West Indian in origin.

Dovetailing and reinforcing the racial exclusion that permeates U.S. society is the ethnic structuring of New York City which focuses attention on ethnicity and encourages groups to organize around, and thus reproduce, their ethnicity. For example, the Mayor's Ethnic Advisory Council sponsors fifteen annual awards to "representatives of the city's diverse ethnic groups" in recognition of their "contributions to their community and the quality of life in the city" (*Carib News* 1985:10). Grants for community services, which are awarded through community boards that are residentially—and hence ethnically—based, serve as another force emphasizing ethnicity. Moreover, ethnic groups in New York have long mobilized their constituencies to elect ethnic candidates who represent their interests (see Katznelson 1981).

Within this complex structuring of ethnic and race relations, West Indians are subject to a multiplicity of "dominant" and "lesser" messages leading to a fragmented and even "situational sense of self" (see Blanc-Szanton 1985:10). At various moments, depending on the context, they perceive themselves as Vincentians or Grenadians, West Indians, blacks, and even Americans. It is in this context of racial exclusion and ethnic organization and of shifting identity constructs that voluntary organizations take on particular salience. By stressing pride in their community and a sense of distinctiveness, they enable Vincentians and Grenadians "to turn inwards and to embrace other nationals rather than outwards to an acceptance of an inferior status" and "the stigma attached to blackness" (Toney 1986:145).

Voluntary associations, moreover, provide a means by which Vincentians and Grenadians can distinguish themselves from Afro-Americans. To be sure, these immigrants, like all West Indians, interact and cooperate with Afro-Americans, especially politically. Afro-Americans remain an important reference group and mediating force for West Indians in their dealings with the wider society, particularly when it comes to applying pressure on host institutions for goods and positions. However, Vincentians and Grenadians want to establish some social distance from Afro-Americans with whom they are lumped by dominant groups in New York, but from whom they feel culturally different and in some ways superior. Voluntary organizations also increasingly provide immigrants with institutional mechanisms, including leadership and networks (Schiller 1977), that allow them to play a continuing role in their home societies and at the same time to compete in the pluralistic social and political structures of New York, organized as they are around competing ethnic and immigrant categories.

The particular configuration of race and ethnic relations in the host society thus plays a decisive role in the generation of immigrant organizations. This becomes clearer when we compare the situation confronting immigrants in New York with that in Trinidad, a resource-endowed Caribbean country that has been the destination for many thousands of Grenadian and Vincentian migrants over the last century. In contrast to the hierarchical ordering of racial and ethnic groups in New York, relations in Trinidad between the two numerically equal and dominant racial/ethnic groups—Afro-Trinidadians and Indo-Trinidadians[15]—are relatively symmetrical. Far from confronting racial barriers and severe racial discrimination, as they do in New York, Vincentians and Grenadians find that Afro-Trinidadians are open to the immigrants' participation in host institutions and organizations. Because Afro-Trinidadians compete with and want to maximize their numbers vis-à-vis Indo-Trinidadians, they minimize the more subtle cultural differences between themselves and Vincentian and Grenadian immigrants. A sense of commonality deriving from their shared African origins and similar colonial experiences predominates. As a Vincentian immigrant said: "In Trinidad, Vincentians and Grenadians become Trinidadized so quickly that they cannot form organizations."[16]

The more open social environment of Trinidad, where legal Vincentian and Grenadian immigrants have the same access to dominant structures as Trinidadians, is not therefore a fertile environment for immigrant voluntary associations. Indeed, a recent attempt by some Vincentian immigrants to form an ethnic association failed, in part because many would-be members were already active in Trinidad voluntary organizations.

CONCLUSION

Vincentians and Grenadians, as part of the larger West Indian population in New York, have had a profound demographic and cultural impact on New York City. By moving into sections of the city in clusters, improving the housing, and creating a sense of community through a rich cultural and social life, they have contributed to urban neighborhoods and increased the ethnic diversity of city life. An important component of their adaptation has been their voluntary associations. This essay has documented the multiple roles these organizations play within the Vincentian and Grenadian communities and the way they reflect the concerns and needs of immigrants in their new home.

Voluntary organizations provide a means of knitting the immigrant communities together, albeit into a loosely textured fabric. Although the large number, and continuing proliferation, of associations reflect generational, social class, and political differences among the immigrants, the openness of their activities emphasizes the basic similarity of all Vincentians and all Grenadians. Moreover, despite various divisions and a general mistrust of leaders, the embryonic St. Vincent Anniversary Committee attests to the potential for unified action around joint interests in the New York context.

While the voluntary associations have a definite West Indian flavor and orientation, their development in New York, I have argued, is a response to the inequalities and constraints imposed by racial and ethnic divisions in the city. Regardless of their material and occupational success, West Indian immigrants confront discrimination in housing, employment, and innumerable daily encounters. Their reaction, similar to that of other racial and ethnic groups, has been to live in immigrant enclaves where they are shielded from the assaults of the wider society. Here they can develop their own patterns of interaction, based largely on norms and values brought from home and reinforced by constant interactions with their home societies. And here, among Vincentians and Grenadians, voluntary associations that strengthen and foster a pride in their ethnic identity flourish.

The contrast between the host situations of New York and Trinidad is especially illuminating. In Trinidad, where race and ethnic relations are symmetrically rather than hierarchically organized and where shared cultural traditions and historical experiences link the immigrants to Afro-Trinidadians, Vincentians and Grenadians have not formed separate ethnic associations. There, a need for organizations that will further immigrant interests or provide a base for political action does not exist—rather, immigrants are absorbed into existing Trinidad organizations.

In the New York context, Vincentian and Grenadian voluntary associations perform the functions frequently associated with immigrant organizations: they facilitate adaptation to the host society by addressing instrumental needs such as employment, housing, and community services; they reaffirm and even rework the group's traditional beliefs and weld the immigrants into a cohesive unit by creating a set of common symbols; and they perpetuate the immigrants' relationship with their home societies.

I have argued, however, that these associations serve a function that has received insufficient attention in the literature: they link immigrants to the host society and home society simultaneously. The case of Vincentian and Grenadian immigrants thus challenges the view that ties to the home society distract immigrants from forging instrumental links in New York that would enhance their social and economic position. Indeed, a number of immigrants who have been economically and politically successful in New York have also retained strong involvements with St. Vincent or Grenada.

Ties to home, I have suggested, provide immigrants in the racially demeaning New York context with an alternate arena—the home society—of prestige and action. That they receive respect from those at home for their achievements in New York bolsters immigrants' self-esteem and imbues the migration experience with positive meaning. In addition, migrants' continuing involvement with their home societies through their organizations lays the groundwork for possible return some day. Finally, within this unitary field of action consisting of home and host societies, political capital—that is, prestige and position—that organizational leaders and activists gain in the home society can be transferred to the New York immigrant community, and vice versa.

In conclusion, then, this analysis of Vincentians and Grenadians in New York shows that the two arenas of action—host and home— are not, as is implicit in much migration research, opposing poles. Indeed, from the perspective of Vincentian and Grenadian immigrants, they have become merged into a single transnational field of activities. And voluntary associations, through linking the home island and New York ideationally as well as concretely, have contributed to the development of a "transnational" world view—creating a more integrated image of the two societies for the immigrants.[17]

NOTES

1. The data on which this essay is based derive from a larger comparative study of the adaptive strategies of Vincentian and Grenadian immigrants in New York and Trinidad. The research was funded in various parts by the International Development Research Centre of Ottawa, Canada and the United States Agency for International Development. Seed money was provided by the United Nations Fund for Population Activities, and material support was given by the United Nations Institute for Training and Research and the Institute of International Relations at the University of the West Indies in Trinidad and Tobago. The study was a collaborative project undertaken with Dr. Rosina Wiltshire-Brodber of the Institute of International Relations, University of the West Indies, St. Augustine, Trinidad; with Joyce Toney of St. Vincent; and with Winston Wiltshire of Trinidad. I would like to thank these three collaborators for the many suggestions and ideas they provided in discussions, which helped in writing this essay. I also express my appreciation to Colin Robinson, Isa Soto, and Margaret Souza, research assistants in New York, for their many insights into West Indian life in New York, and to Milton Benjamin, who assisted with the interviewing. Finally, I thank the many Vincentian and Grenadian immigrants interviewed in New York, who shall

remain unnamed to preserve their confidentiality, but who generously provided the information on which this analysis is based.

2. The fifteen largest ethnic groups entering New York City between 1975 and 1980, listed in order of relative size of the group, are from the following countries: Dominican Republic, USSR (Jews), China (including Hong Kong, Taiwan, and the Mainland) and Vietnam, Jamaica, Guyana, Haiti, Korea, Colombia, Trinidad and Tobago, India, Ecuador, Philippines, Greece, Italy, and Barbados (City Planning Commission 1985).

3. This figure should probably be even larger, considering the large number of undocumented Caribbean immigrants in New York City who are undercounted in the census.

4. "Calypso," a musical form indigenous to Trinidad and Tobago, is in its truest expression a satirical commentary on political and social issues. "Picong" refers to the sharpness of the satire, and is the basis of good calypso.

5. The term West Indian in this paper refers to the former British Caribbean territories. The term Caribbean refers to all islands lying in the Caribbean Sea between North and South America as well as to particular countries along the northern rim of South America, namely, Surinam and French Guyana.

6. The study focused on individuals over eighteen years of age who had been in New York a minimum of two years, but who had arrived in the United States after 1965, when changes that liberalized the immigration law were enacted. The sample was gathered through a snowball method: through migrants' networks and through contacts with church leaders, community activists, and the Missions to the U.N. from St. Vincent and Grenada. Relatively equal numbers of women and men were interviewed. A concerted effort was made for the sample to be representative of the sociocultural spread in the Vincentian and Grenadian communities. But since there are no censal or survey data available to provide information on these groups' characteristics, the findings in this study represent a beginning attempt to develop such profiles.

7. There are, of course, organizations like sports clubs and rotating credit associations in St. Vincent and Grenada but formal associations appear to be less prominent aspects of social life than among immigrants in New York.

8. Statistics on immigrant populations are imprecise, and counts vary. According to estimates of the Population Reference Bureau (PRB) in Washington, D.C., between 1960 and 1980, 10,391 Grenadians entered the United States legally (Bouvier 1984b:7), and 6,041 Vincentians were admitted between 1960 and 1979 (Bouvier 1984a:6). Because New York is the destination for the majority of Vincentians and Grenadians, it is probable that more are settled in New York than the U.S. census indicates.

9. There is some indication that as many Vincentians now move to the geographically proximate island of Barbados, chiefly as cane cutters and domestic workers, as to Trinidad. Many immigrants work in Trinidad as skilled artisans and domestics, and a number fill positions at the upper end of the occupational scale, as engineers, lawyers, doctors, managers, and university professors.

10. The success of these Vincentian and Grenadian migrants may reflect the network method through which the sample was selected. Because of the paucity of information—census data, INS figures, or other studies—it is not clear how representative the immigrants in this study are of the wider Vincentian and Grenadian populations in New York. It should be noted, too, that the data in the larger comparative study on migrant streams to Trinidad indicate that lower status Vincentians and Grenadians are more likely to migrate there than to New York.

11. Employment information was gathered on all employed members of the seventy-eight households in the sample. The figure of 130, however, refers only to heads of households and their spouses.

12. This lowered cost of immigrant subsistence has an important effect in New York in that the immigrants are therefore more willing—and able— to work outside the immigrant community for low wages (see Sassen-Koob 1985).

13. This egalitarian orientation has also been noted in the Caribbean by observers of West Indian working-class and peasant behavior (see Austin 1983; Jayawardena 1963; Makiesky-Barrow 1976; Manning 1973; Rubenstein 1976; Wilson 1973). It is viewed as a response to the colonial experience. By emphasizing the sameness of all island folk and the positive value of traditional ways, this ethos countered the socioeconomic differentiation emerging among the population, which threatened the unity of their opposition to the dominant and alien structures of colonial control.

14. Members' suspicions of the current leader of the St. Vincent Anniversary Committee were aroused when he became involved in Brooklyn political activities. Members worried that the Anniversary Committee, rather than being the leader's primary interest, was viewed by him as a stepping stone to realizing his interests in the wider urban arena.

15. These groups are descendants of the African slaves and Indian indentured laborers imported by the white colonial plantocracy to develop Trinidad agriculturally. Since political independence in 1962, the white group, which today constitutes a minute fraction of the population, has receded into the background. Today, Trinidad is run by the African and Indian descendants of the early inhabitants, and the two groups are relatively equal in number.

16. Despite the overriding sense of commonality, there are subtle tensions between the immigrants and Afro-Trinidadians. After all, Vincentians

and Grenadians are small islanders, and almost by definition, therefore—within the context of the Caribbean—have had a narrower range of experiences and more limited educational and occupational opportunities. In Trinidad they are viewed as clients, a status tinged with an aura of inferiority. Emphasizing this point is the restrictive immigration legislation enacted by the Trinidad and Tobago government in recent years, aimed at curbing the number of Vincentians, Grenadians, and other West Indian immigrants entering the country, in light of the country's own limited resource base.

17. The concept of "transnational field of action" linking the home and host societies, particularly through political activities—including voluntary associations—and kin and friendship networks, evolved out of joint discussions between Rosina Wiltshire-Brodber, Winston Wiltshire, and myself. This linking of host and home has been noted in other research. Sutton and Makiesky-Barrow (1987) discussed the bidirectional flow of political ideology in which black power ideas were circulated between New York and the West Indies. This linking has also been noted in child fostering (Soto 1987) and Carnival celebrations (Kasinitz and Friedenberg-Herbstein 1987).

REFERENCES

Austin, D. J. 1983. "Culture and Ideology in the English-Speaking Caribbean: A View from Jamaica." *American Ethnologist* 10:223–240.

Basch, L. 1978. *Workin' for the Yankee Dollar: The Impact of a Transnational Petroleum Company on Caribbean Class and Ethnic Relations.* Ann Arbor: University Microfilms International.

—— 1985. "Caribbean International Migration: Implications for Development." Final Report. New York: United Nations Institute for Training and Research.

—— 1987. "The Politics of Caribbeanization: Vincentians and Grenadians in New York." In C. Sutton and E. Chaney, eds., *Caribbean Life in New York City: Sociocultural Dimensions.* New York: Center for Migration Studies.

Blanc-Szanton, C. 1985. "Ethnic Identities and Aspects of Class in Contemporary Thailand." Southern Asian Institute, Columbia University. Mimeo.

Bouvier, L. F. 1984a. *St. Vincent and the Grenadines: Yesterday, Today and Tomorrow.* Washington, D.C.: Population Reference Bureau. Occasional Series, *The Caribbean.* March.

—— 1984b. *Grenada: Yesterday, Today and Tomorrow.* Washington, D.C.: Population Reference Bureau. Occasional Series, *The Caribbean.* April.

Carib News. 1985. "New York City Ethnic Award." November 19, p. 10.

Carmody, C. 1978. *First Among Equals: Antiguan Patterns of Local-Level Leadership.* Ann Arbor: University Microfilms International.

City Planning Commission. 1985. Private communication.

Club St. Vincent. 1984. *Newsletter 5*. February.

Doughty, P. L. 1970. "Behind the Back of the City: 'Provincial' Life in Lima, Peru." In W. Mangin, ed., *Peasants in Cities*. Boston: Houghton Mifflin.

Foner, N. 1983. "Jamaican Migrants: A Comparative Analysis of the New York and London Experience." *Occasional Paper No. 36*. Center for Latin American and Caribbean Studies, New York University.

Georges, E. 1984. "New Immigrants and the Political Process: Dominicans in New York." *Occasional Paper No. 45*. Center for Latin American and Caribbean Studies, New York University.

Grillo, R. D. 1974. "Ethnic Identity and Social Stratification on a Kampala Housing Estate." In A. Cohen, ed., *Urban Ethnicity*. London: Tavistock.

Hendricks, G. L. 1974. *The Dominican Diaspora: From the Dominican Republic to New York City—Villagers in Transition*. New York: Teachers College Press, Columbia University.

Jayawardena, C. 1963. *Conflict and Solidarity on a Guianese Plantation*. London: Athlone Press.

Kasinitz, P. and J. Friedenberg-Herbstein. 1987. "Public Celebrations in New York City: The Puerto Rican Parade and West Indian Carnival." In C. Sutton and E. Chaney, eds., *Caribbean Life in New York City: Sociocultural Dimensions*. New York: Center for Migration Studies.

Katznelson, I. 1981. *City Trenches: Urban Politics and the Patterning of Class in the United States*. New York: Pantheon.

Little, K. 1967. "Voluntary Associations in Urban Life: A Case Study in Differential Adaptation." In M. Freedman, ed., *Social Organization: Essays Presented to Raymond Firth*. Chicago: Aldine.

—— 1973. "Urbanization and Regional Associations: Their Paradoxical Function." In A. Southall, ed., *Urban Anthropology*. New York: Oxford University Press.

Makiesky-Barrow, S. 1976. *Class, Culture and Politics in a Barbadian Community*. Ann Arbor: University Microfilms International.

Mangin, W. 1959. "The Role of Regional Associations in the Adaptation of Rural Migrants to Cities in Peru." In R. Adams and D. Heath, eds., *Contemporary Cultures and Societies of Latin America*. New York: Random House.

Manning, F. E. 1973. *Black Clubs in Bermuda: Ethnography of a Play World*. Ithaca: Cornell University Press.

Marshall, P. 1981. *Brown Girl, Brownstones*. Old Westbury, N.Y.: Feminist Press.

Meillassoux, C. 1968. *Urbanization in an African Community: Voluntary Associations in Bamako*. Seattle: University of Washington Press.

Mitchell, J. C. 1959. "The Kalela Dance." *Rhodes-Livingston Paper No. 27*. Manchester: Manchester University Press.

Moore, C. A. 1984. "It's Archie Bunker Time Again." *Carib News*. August 15, p. 13.

Parkin, D. 1966. "Urban Voluntary Associations as Institutions of Adaptation." *Man* 1:90–94.

Pessar, P. 1982. "Kinship Relations of Production in the Migration Process: The Case of Dominican Migration to the United States." *Occasional Paper No. 32.* Center for Latin American and Caribbean Studies, New York University.

Roberts, B. 1979. *Cities of Peasants: The Political Economy of Urbanization in the Third World.* Beverly Hills, Ca.: Sage.

Rogler, L. H. 1972. *Migrant in the City: The Life of a Puerto Rican Action Group.* New York: Basic Books.

Rubenstein, H. 1976. "Incest, Effigy Hanging, and Biculturation in a West Indian Village." *American Ethnologist* 3:765–781.

Sassen-Koob, S. 1979. "Formal and Informal Associations: Dominicans and Colombians in New York." *International Migration Review* 13:314–332.

—— 1984. "The New Labor Demand in Global Cities." In M. Smith, ed., *Cities in Transformation.* Beverly Hills, Ca.: Sage.

—— 1985. "Changing Composition and Labor Market Location of Hispanic Immigrants in New York City, 1960–1980." In M. Tienda and G. Borjas, eds., *Hispanics in the U.S. Economy.* New York: Academic Press.

Schildkrout, E. 1975. "Ethnicity, Kinship and Joking Among Urban Immigrants in Ghana." In B. Du Toit and H. Safa, eds., *Migration and Urbanization.* The Hague: Mouton.

Schiller, N. G. 1977. "Ethnic Groups Are Made, Not Born: The Haitian Immigrant in American Politics." In G. L. Hicks and P. E. Leis, eds., *Ethnic Encounters: Identities and Contexts.* North Scituate, Mass.: Duxbury Press.

Sciolino, E. 1985. "A Brooklyn Dentist Goes to the U.N." *New York Times.* October 16, p. A13.

Smock, A. 1971. *Ibo Politics: The Role of Ethnic Unions in Eastern Nigeria.* Cambridge: Harvard University Press.

Smock, D. 1969. *Conflict and Control in an African Trade Union: A Study of the Nigerian Coal Miner's Union.* Stanford: Hoover Institution Press.

Soto, I. 1987. "Child Fostering: Its Role in Migrant Exchanges." In C. Sutton and E. Chaney, eds., *Caribbean Life in New York City: Sociocultural Dimensions.* New York: Center for Migration Studies.

St. Vincent and the Grenadines Ex-Teachers Association. 1985. *Newsletter 1.*

Sutton, C. 1969. "The Scene of the Action: A Wildcat Strike in Barbados." Unpublished doctoral dissertation, Columbia University.

—— 1975. "Comments." in H. Safa and B. Du Toit, eds., *Migration and Development: Implications for Ethnic Identity and Political Conflict.* The Hague: Mouton.

Sutton, C. and S. Makiesky-Barrow. 1987. "Migration and West Indian Racial and Ethnic Consciousness." In C. Sutton and E. Chaney, eds., *Caribbean Life in New York City: Sociocultural Dimensions.* New York: Center for Migration Studies.

Toney, J. 1985. "Emigration from St. Vincent and the Grenadines: Contextual Background." New York: United Nations Institute for Training and Research.

—— 1986. *The Development of a Culture of Migration Among a Caribbean People: St. Vincent and New York, 1838–1979.* Ann Arbor: University Microfilms International.

U.S. Department of Commerce. 1983. *Ancestry of the Population by State.* Washington, D.C.: Bureau of the Census.

Wilson, P. 1973. *Crab Antics: A Social Anthropology of the English-Speaking Negro Societies of the Caribbean.* New Haven: Yale University Press.

Wiltshire-Brodber, R. and W. Wiltshire. 1985. "Caribbean Regional Migration." Final report. Trinidad and Tobago: Institute of International Relations, University of the West Indies.

7. The Jamaicans: Race and Ethnicity Among Migrants in New York City

Nancy Foner

In the past two decades, many thousands of Jamaicans have moved to the United States, large numbers settling in the New York metropolitan area. Jamaicans, as well as other West Indians, are, as one journalist puts it, "flavoring" many areas of New York City (Fraser 1970). Certain streets in the heart of Brooklyn, another journalist observes, have been "transformed . . . into bustling extensions of Port of Spain [Trinidad] and Kingston [Jamaica]" (Buckley 1974).

The new Jamaican immigrants have had a definite impact on New York City life. By the same token, their own lives have been deeply influenced by the move to New York. This essay, based on my 1982 research among first-generation Jamaicans in New York,[1] is concerned with both of these issues. The focus here is on race and ethnic relations—race being defined by perceived physical characteristics, ethnicity by real or putative ancestry and cultural heritage. The central questions have to do with the way Jamaican migrants have been affected by, and affect, race and ethnic relations in their new home. What impact does the racial and ethnic context have on the attitudes, aspirations, disappointments, and achievements of Jamaican migrants? And, conversely, how has the massive influx of Jamaicans influenced the nature of race and ethnic relations in the city?

This analysis has implications for the general study of race relations and immigration. The examination of ethnicity among Jamaicans in

New York highlights the ethnic diversity within the black population, something that is too often overlooked in the race relations literature. And while this essay points to the importance of ethnic differences among blacks, it also makes clear that studies of black immigrants cannot ignore race relations. Indeed, to focus only on ethnicity, as is common in much recent work on immigration, is to give a one-sided and distorted view of Jamaican migrants. The fact that Jamaicans are identified as "blacks" by white New Yorkers and that Jamaicans themselves share a racial identification with black Americans is, as we shall see, crucial for understanding the Jamaican migration experience.

JAMAICAN MIGRATION TO
THE UNITED STATES

Some preliminary comments are in order about why Jamaicans have moved to the United States in such large numbers in recent years—and how many and what sorts have come. I also look briefly at Jamaican occupational and settlement patterns in New York City and say a few words about the methods used in my study.

Reasons for Migration

A variety of social, economic, and political factors, in Jamaica as well as in the United States, explain the recent mass migration to this country.

Like earlier large-scale movements of Jamaicans abroad, the recent flow to this country is rooted in the harsh realities of the Jamaican economy (for a history of Jamaican emigration patterns see Eisner 1961; Marshall 1982; Roberts 1979). Since the end of the nineteenth century, there have simply been too many Jamaicans with too few opportunities to earn what they consider a decent living. The underdeveloped state of Jamaica's economy stems from the distorting effects of colonial rule and the domination of the island's economy by plantation agriculture for so long and, since independence in 1962, Jamaica's continued dependence on neocolonial powers and multinational corporations (see, for example, Beckford 1972; Girvan 1972; Jefferson 1972).

Markedly unequal land distribution patterns, for example, mean that small farmers do not have enough land. When Jamaicans look to other, or additional, ways to make a living (and increasing numbers of young people have left the rural parishes for Kingston in recent years), they are very often disappointed. The big growth industries of the post-World War II period in the nonagricultural sector—bauxite, manufacturing, construction, and tourism—have not created many new jobs. Unemployment and underemployment have been staggeringly high—with unemployment for the years 1973 and 1976 at, respectively, 22 and 24 percent. Even though most migrants to this country had jobs before they left, employment was many times not steady or only part-time. And, all too frequently, earnings were very low and prospects for advancement dim.

The problem of finding decent jobs has been compounded in the last few decades by rising aspirations as people at all levels of the society want to achieve a standard of living similar to that of the North American middle classes and to consume imported American goods. These aspirations themselves have been fueled by reports and visits from migrants but also by such changes as improved communications, promises of new political elites, and expansion of educational opportunities. Members of the lower class, however, usually cannot obtain the kinds of jobs or afford the life-styles they desire. The better off often find their longings for more amenities and higher wages unfulfilled at home.

During the 1970s, living conditions in Jamaica deteriorated as the pressures of international inflation caused sharply rising prices for consumer goods and foodstuffs. The situation worsened in the late 1970s when Michael Manley's democratic socialist government was forced to implement policies that drastically reduced real wages and living standards in order to qualify for loans from the International Monetary Fund (see Girvan et al. 1980; Koslovsky, 1981). According to a 1977 national opinion survey done by Carl Stone (1982:64), 60 percent of the population of Jamaica would move to the United States if given the chance. The economic crisis and high unemployment rates have not abated in the 1980s under conservative Prime Minister Edward Seaga—nor, it would seem, has the desire to emigrate to the United States.

It was not just that "money was hard" in Jamaica, as one Brooklyn

migrant said. There was also the lure of the United States: the availability of jobs; the higher wages; and the promise of amenities, including, most importantly, higher levels of living and more consumer
goods ("the type of life you would like to get in touch with," as one
man in New York put it). The prospect of more widely available
higher education was an additional attraction, especially among
middle-class Jamaicans who came here. And there was the critical
factor of immigration policy. The passage of the 1965 Immigration
and Nationality Act opened the door to mass migration by eliminat-
ing the small quota Jamaica had been subject to since the 1952 legislation.

Once the movement got underway, it had a snowball effect. People
in Jamaica learned of the benefits to be had abroad not only through
the mass media but from letters and visits from migrants. "People
telling you all the while," said one woman, "so you say you would
like to know New York." Many learned of the opportunities here
first-hand during their own visits; over one-third of the migrants in
my sample had visited the United States, usually New York, before
moving to the city. Moving to New York became, as one woman put
it, "the thing to do. Most of my friends were here."

In addition to spreading the news that encouraged relatives and
friends to come, migrants sometimes exerted pressure on spouses or
dependents to join them. They frequently sent back funds to finance
the trip, served as sponsors or helped prospective newcomers meet
requirements for entry or immigration, and offered accommodation
and showed the ropes to new arrivals. Indeed, the presence of relatives and friends and a large Jamaican community in New York were
important factors (in addition to the availability of jobs) making this
city a logical place in which to settle. About half of the Jamaican-born
population in the United States, in fact, lives in the New York metropolitan area—nearly all in New York City itself (see Kraly, this
volume, tables 2.3 and 2.10).

Migration Trends

The 1965 legislation that ushered in the recent mass migration of
Jamaicans affected the volume as well as other trends that have characterized the movement.[2]

Jamaican immigration skyrocketed as soon as the new law went into effect, going from 2,743 in 1966 to 10,483 in 1967. From then on, Jamaican legal immigration to the United States has kept up at a fairly steady pace, reaching nearly 20,000 in several recent years and going as high as 23,569 in 1981. The total count of legal Jamaican immigrants from 1967 through 1984, according to Immigration and Naturalization Service reports, was approximately 280,000.

Legal immigration, of course, is only part of the story. Large numbers of Jamaicans have entered this country with temporary visitor's visas and have stayed, often for many years, without the proper documents. Because so many Jamaicans are, at any one time, not legally registered—and because undocumented Jamaicans were doubtless undercounted in the 1980 census—it is impossible to say exactly how many Jamaican immigrants live in the United States. Nor are published figures available on the large numbers of second-generation Jamaicans. After all, many thousands of Jamaicans came to the United States in the early part of the century before the restrictive 1924 immigration act. Between 1911 and 1921 alone, net Jamaican emigration to this country amounted to 30,000 (Roberts 1979:139–140). Census reports on first-generation immigrants show that by 1980, 196,800 people of Jamaican birth lived in the United States, with 98,800 in the New York metropolitan area. Almost 85 percent of these 98,800 had immigrated to the United States since 1965 (see Kraly, this volume, tables 2.3 and 2.12).

In addition to making the massive inflow of Jamaicans possible, the new immigration legislation affected the sex ratio among the migrants. Jamaican women have dominated the movement, and women frequently came on their own, later followed by their children and spouses. Between 1967 and 1979, with the exception of two years, women in the legal stream always outnumbered men (U.S. Immigration and Naturalization Service 1967–1979). The proportion of women was particularly high in the early years of the "new immigration," as high as 76 and 73 percent for 1967 and 1968 (and leveling off after 1970 to between 50 and 53 percent). It was easier for women than men to get labor certification, largely due to the demand for domestic labor in American cities. Not surprisingly, the percentage of total immigrant workers who were classified as private household workers peaked in the very same years that the percentage of women migrants was so high: in 1968, 50 percent, and in 1967, 48 percent of total workers were listed as private household workers. Women could also easily obtain immigrant visas as nurses, and indeed about a third of the legal Jamaican immigrants classified as professionals between 1962 and 1972 were nurses (Palmer 1974:576). As the migration progressed, and as a larger percentage of Jamaicans qualified for immigrant status on the basis of family ties rather than occupation, women were probably as likely as men to have relatives here to sponsor them—a reason why the sex ratios began to even out after the first three years of the new immigration. My guess is that women make up a very high proportion of the illegal stream as well, partly because they can readily find jobs in private households as domestics, attendants to the elderly, and child care workers (see Foner 1986).

United States immigration laws, which have favored professionals and skilled workers, are also mainly responsible for the relatively high percentage of professionals and other highly trained Jamaicans in the migrant stream. Of the approximately 86,000 legal Jamaican immigrants to the United States between 1967 and 1978 who were listed as workers in Immigration and Naturalization Service annual reports, about 14 percent were classified as professional, technical, and kindred workers and about 13 percent as clerical and kindred workers.[3]

Occupational and Settlement Patterns

In New York, Jamaicans are concentrated in certain economic sectors. Large numbers of women in New York are employed in the lower ranks of the nursing and health care occupations and in private households as child care workers and attendants to the elderly. Many women, in addition, are found in the clerical, retail sales, and communications fields. Men hold jobs of varying skill levels in such areas as cleaning, maintenance and security, health services, clerical and retail sales, transportation and communication, and manufacturing (Petras 1983).

As for settlement patterns, nearly half of the Jamaican-born population in New York City, according to the 1980 census, lives in Brooklyn, with almost 30 percent in the Bronx and about 20 percent in Queens (Kraly, this volume, table 2.9). In these boroughs, Jamaicans cluster in certain areas: in the Crown Heights and East Flatbush sections of Brooklyn; in the northeast Bronx; and in southeast Queens (mainly St. Albans, Springfield Gardens, and Laurelton).

The New York Study

My research in 1982 took me to all of these areas of Jamaican settlement. The main research technique was structured in-depth interviews with forty first-generation Jamaican migrants. Half were men and half women, and all had migrated when they were eighteen or older, moving to the United States between 1962 and 1975. Most of the men and women interviewed lived in neighborhoods with large concentrations of Jamaicans in Brooklyn (mainly Crown Heights and East Flatbush), with a good number in southeast Queens and several in the northeast Bronx. I located respondents mainly through personal contacts. As it turned out, the sample was fairly typical of the wider recent adult Jamaican migrant population in the United States in terms of occupation and education (see Foner 1983).

Important as the initial structured interview was, I also learned about the Jamaican migrant experience in other ways. Informal talks, after the lengthy interview ended, gave people a chance to speak about topics that interested them and to tell me more about their lives. Particularly since I already knew many respondents or their close friends from my previous field work in Jamaica (Foner 1973), these informal talks sometimes lasted all afternoon or late into the evening. On several occasions I went to weddings and other social functions with people I had interviewed, and attended church and association meetings. While the formal study was conducted in 1982, since then I have maintained contact with many Jamaicans in New York in their homes and on the job. Indeed, my close relations with a number of people I knew in rural Jamaica, now in New York, have significantly deepened my understanding of what the migrants' lives are like and what the move to New York has meant to them.

THE IMPACT OF THE RACIAL
AND ETHNIC CONTEXT

Being Black in New York City

Once Jamaicans arrived in New York, found a place to live, got settled in a job, and developed friends and associates, their lives began to change in innumerable ways. Perhaps the most jarring change was that being black took on a new, and more painful, meaning. As part of the larger black population in a racially divided America, blackness became more of a stigma than it had been in Jamaica.

This does not mean, of course, that black skin was not a stigma back home. Black skin has long been devalued in Jamaica. This stems from Jamaica's history as a plantation colony based on African slavery. Whites, in the days of slavery, were masters and, throughout the colonial period, rulers. Indeed, a white bias has permeated the entire society since the eighteenth century: in the eyes of most Jamaicans, white stands for wealth, privilege, and power. To most lower-class Jamaicans—who comprise the majority of the population—being black is another symbol, along with their poverty, of their low social position.[4]

Blackness in Jamaica, however, is not, in itself—and has not been for the past few decades—a barrier to upward mobility or to social acceptance "at the top." For one thing, blacks are a majority on the island. According to the 1960 census, some 91 out of every 100 Jamacians were, in Rex Nettleford's (1972:27) words, touched by the tarbrush: 76 percent were classified as pure African and less than 1 percent as pure white or European. Furthermore, culture, occupation, and wealth can override skin color in importance so that one can, in a sense, "change" color in Jamaica. Education, manners, wealth, and associates—not just fair skin or such European features as straight hair, thin lips, and a narrow nose—are crucial. "In Jamaica," one Brooklyn migrant said, "we didn't have color prejudice, we had class prejudice." Black or colored Jamaicans who become doctors or lawyers, for instance, or high-level civil servants, who acquire the cultural characteristics associated with white Europeans, and who maintain a "respectable" standard of living are often thought of "as if" they were white.

Black and colored Jamaicans in influential and important jobs are hardly "token representatives" of their race. Colored Jamaicans, in fact, have long predominated in middle-class occupations on the island—a legacy from the days of slavery when free people of color (the product of unions between white men and slave women) had economic and other privileges denied to slaves. While after emancipation in 1838 whites virtually monopolized the highest-ranking positions on the island, and blacks, the lowest positions, colored Jamaicans were preferred for prestigious and well-paid occupations, partly because of prejudice and partly because they had prior access to education (Smith 1970). The days of white rule are gone, of course, and middle-class Jamaicans are now less likely to be light-skinned. Since the end of World War II, and especially since independence in 1962, black as well as colored Jamaicans have dominated public affairs, and it is they who fill prestigious and professional positions in the island. This is obviously quite different from the situation in the United States.

"I wasn't aware of my color till I got here, honestly," said Mr. E., a Queens resident. Mr. E., of course, knew he had black skin when he lived in Jamaica. He was also aware of American racism before he moved here. Like most other migrants, he had learned about the racial situation in the papers and on the radio as well as from friends and relatives. And like a number of migrants, he had even seen it first-hand on a previous visit to New York. But it is one thing to hear about racial prejudice or to even experience it on a short visit. It is quite another to live with it as a fixed part of one's daily existence. At home, after all, Mr. E. had a good job as a policeman and he was a respected person in his community. In New York, as a black man, he is a member of a definite minority. Education, income, and culture do not, as in Jamaica, partially "erase" one's blackness. Nor are whites sensitive to shade differences, as people were back home. Whatever their achievements or their shade, Jamaicans, as blacks, are victims of racial discrimination in housing, employment, and education, and of hostility from sections of the white population. Thus, Mr. E., like so many other Jamaicans I met in New York, became for the first time acutely and painfully aware that black skin was a significant status marker.

Among the various disabilities Jamaicans face as blacks in New York are informal limitations on where they can rent or buy housing.

One reason, in fact, that many Jamaicans prefer to live in black neighborhoods is the likelihood of encountering racial prejudice and discrimination in other areas. As for work, many Jamaicans gravitated
to various low-status occupations associated with racial minorities—
for example, private household work and unskilled or semi-skilled
hospital labor. Not only were jobs open in these fields but skin color
was not an obstacle to employment. Those who entered, or who tried
to enter, "white" occupational spheres—high-level white-collar work
and skilled construction trades, in particular—often found race a barrier. Many people I interviewed in these positions spoke of the problems they encountered, as blacks, in getting employment and in
advancing on the job. "If you're qualified for a job," one man said,
"you have to fight to get it because of your color." A few others
complained of the difficulty in keeping jobs they had obtained—and
of their greater chance of being laid off than whites when cutbacks
were effected.

Being black in New York also means that Jamaicans are often invisible as immigrants and thus, as Bryce-Laporte (1973, 1979) points
out, that their "distinctive problems and unique proclivities" are generally overlooked. Their demands and protests as blacks are also neglected by whites.

Jamaican Identity

While to most white New Yorkers Jamaican migrants are largely invisible in a sea of anonymous black faces, Jamaicans themselves are
highly sensitive to their differences from "native" blacks. Indeed, the
movement from a society where being Jamaican was taken for
granted to one where they are a definite minority and where they
find themselves lumped with American blacks has sharply heightened Jamaicans' consciousness of their ethnic identity.

Jamaican migrants' sense of ethnic distinctiveness is expressed in
and reinforced by their social networks. Most Jamaicans in New York
move, outside of work, in a Jamaican social world. They settle near
kin and friends in neighborhoods that offer such "trappings of home"
as West Indian[5] food stores, bakeries, record shops, barber shops,
travel agents, and restaurants (see McLaughlin 1981:131). And they
maintain their closest contacts with other Jamaicans. In my study,

for example, 80 percent of the forty respondents saw or phoned relatives in New York once a week or more. Of this group, most (69 percent) had relatives living in the same neighborhood. On the whole, friends, too, were Jamaican. All but one person included Jamaicans on their list of the three people they had seen socially most often in the last month. In fact, 70 percent of the total sample only gave the names of Jamaicans—mainly people they knew from home, but also friends from work in New York. If faced with a serious problem or crisis, almost all said they would call on other Jamaicans in New York, usually relatives but sometimes in-laws and friends. The majority of regular churchgoers worshiped in congregations composed predominantly of other Jamaicans and West Indians. And when respondents rented out rooms in their homes or rented rooms from others, it was Jamaicans who tended to be the tenants and landlords.

Contacts with Jamaicans back home also fortify the migrants' identity as Jamaicans. Migrants frequently phone relatives and friends on the island. And they visit Jamaica with fair regularity. In fact, all but one man in the sample (who had obtained a green card only the week before the interview and had previously been afraid to "chance" a trip home) had visited Jamaica since moving to New York. The overwhelming majority had been to Jamaica in the last three years. A few went back every year; some visited every other year; and most had returned to visit several times since they had moved to New York. Relatives and friends also often came up from Jamaica to visit the migrants in New York.

Quite apart from close and continued contacts with other Jamaicans at home and in New York, the fact is that stressing their "Jamaicanness" or "West Indianness" is a way to distinguish themselves from black Americans. Jamaicans came to New York to get on and although there are, as Orde Coombs (1970:31) writes, "no guarantees that identification with the white ruling class assures upward mobility, it is certain, they feel, that affiliation with the black underclass does not."

Setting themselves apart from black Americans on the basis of ethnicity, many migrants believe, brings tangible benefits. Most of the people I interviewed felt they received better treatment from whites than do black Americans. True, a few insisted, like one Brooklyn man, that "the bottom line is whether you are black or white—not whether you are Jamaican." Many more, however, stressed that Jamaicans are more respected and more readily accepted than black Americans. "You're black, but you're not black," said a nurse who felt it was easier for a Jamaican than a black American to get a job. The difficulty, as several people noted, is that whites do not always know "which black is which." Until they find out, one woman told me, "I am handled with kid gloves." Once "you say something," however, one man explained, "and they recognize you're not from this country, they treat you a little different."[6]

Emphasizing their distinct Jamaican or West Indian character is also a matter of ethnic pride. All the respondents felt that Jamaicans were different from black Americans. By different what most meant was superior. A few people, sympathetic to black Americans' plight, explained the differences in terms of the more severe racial conditions— "the wholesale prejudice and segregation"—that black Americans have had to endure. Sympathetic or not, the majority emphasized that Jamaicans and other West Indians were "more ambitious, harder workers, and greater achievers." Many told me that Jamaicans save more and are more likely to buy homes than American blacks. Unlike American blacks, Jamaicans, a number said, do not go on welfare or live off government benefits. Still others said that Jamaicans were less hostile to whites—"don't have chips on their shoulders"—but at the same time have more dignity and greater self-assurance in dealing with whites. "Jamaicans are more conscious of what they can do," said one man. "We believe we can overcome obstacles."

JAMAICANS' EFFECT ON RACE
AND ETHNIC RELATIONS

Jamaican migrants' experiences are thus molded by the structure of racial and ethnic relations in New York City. At the same time, their very presence in such large numbers in the city has had important effects on ethnic relations within the black population as well as on race relations between blacks and whites.

Jamaican migration to the city, of course, is not a new phenomenon and there are many long-term Jamaican-born residents who came to New York during the mass movement in the early part of the century.

But the recent migrant stream has replenished the Jamaican, and indeed the general West Indian, community in New York with thousands upon thousands of new members. This movement has meant that more and more Jamaicans now live among and work with "native" black Americans; that large numbers of West Indians from different countries are coming into close contact for the first time; and that whites are confronted by an increasingly large, ethnically diverse black population with an ever-growing percentage of foreign-born individuals.

Relations with Black Americans

Let us first look at how the Jamaican migration has influenced ethnic relations within the black population, beginning with relations between "native" and Jamaican blacks.

Much as Jamaicans move in largely Jamaican social circles, they cannot avoid contact with black Americans. After all, Jamaicans live mainly in areas of black residence in Brooklyn, Queens, and the Bronx; their children are at school with black Americans; and they often find themselves working beside black Americans.

What has been written about West Indian-black American relations has emphasized the sources of conflict and division between them. One problem is the different sets of norms, values, and attitudes of each group. Jamaicans, like other West Indians, emphasize "discipline, drive, and dedication" in the quest to make it in America. As a group, West Indians in New York, in fact, appear to do better occupationally than black Americans. This comparative success as well as their achievement-oriented values are due to several factors (see Foner 1979).[7] Because of the relatively high percentage of highly trained workers in the West Indian migrant stream, many West Indians brought technical and professional skills with them to New York. As immigrants, they are willing to scrimp and save in low-status jobs to advance themselves. By West Indian standards, wages in the United States are good. Coming from poor countries, they are "accustomed to unemployment without welfare, hard work, low pay, and thus relative deprivation from many of the things Americans consider basic necessities" (Bryce-Laporte 1973:58). West Indians also have an assurance and confidence that come from having belonged to the black majority in societies with a relatively wide occupational range open to blacks and, in the case of many migrants, from having held fairly high-status jobs back home.

With their emphasis on and practice of the Protestant work ethic, Jamaicans turn to black Americans in their midst and look, as I noted earlier, with criticism and disapproval. The stereotype of black Americans that most hold is summed up well by Bryce-Laporte:

They are appalled by the failure of native blacks to take advantage of "opportunities," their tendencies to spend money on big cars and fancy clothes rather than on homes, their predilection for conning each other rather than cooperating to do something constructive, their penchant for buying on credit rather than saving . . . their attitudes of envy and ridicule toward black foreigners rather than emulation of their serious pursuit of education and investment, their tendency to take their jobs for granted and be irresponsible rather than aggressive and competitive. . . . (1973:59)

Jamaicans thus feel themselves to be morally superior to black Americans. They have contempt for indigenous blacks who get "handouts" from the government and who spend their money on the numbers, rather than saving and buying homes. "They will just sit down and get welfare," is how one woman put it. "Jamaicans will work in a house, even if it's menial, just to get the money."

This air of superiority and intolerance, needless to say, communicates itself to black Americans who, in turn, have their own axes to grind against the newcomers. "New York blacks," Orde Coombs writes, "are fully aware of what West Indians feel, and they retaliate by speaking of the West Indian's pushiness, his braggadocio, his delusion of how pleasant life is in the West Indies: 'If it's so good there, why are you here?'" (1970:30; see also Walter 1981–82). Jamaican migrants compete with black Americans for housing and jobs, and black Americans often resent these new, and increasingly numerous, rivals. Several migrants in my sample said that American blacks blamed them, West Indians, for taking away their jobs. "I have had it in my face," said one woman, "you come and take my job." Another put it this way: "Black Americans seem to think we come here and we took something from them. And they have this deep resentment. Even though they will be friendly with us, it comes out in little things they say and do." A number of respondents even cited black Americans' resentment and jealousy as further evidence of

West Indian superiority. "They have a little prejudice for West Indian people," one man explained, "knowing that West Indian people would come here and try to build their living standard. And they here so long and can't really get to that standard. They're always saying, 'how you do that?' That's where the rejection is. When you make it and they don't. And they wondering how you come here and do it over them."

Negative as the caricatures are that so many Jamaicans and black Americans have about each other, it is important to bear in mind that there are some bases of cooperation and amity between them.

The extent to which members of the two groups do come together—and the situations in which cooperation arises—are topics that clearly call for careful research. Black Americans and Jamaicans have common interests on the basis of their occupation or class, and there are occasions—trade union struggles, for example—when they unite over specific economic issues. In the world of politics, race is a unifying factor in some situations. There are times when Jamaican and American blacks join together in a common political cause. And Jamaican politicians, for instance, often stress their kinship with black Americans in an effort to gain support.

Moreover, friendships do arise between some Jamaican migrants and black Americans. Although Jamaicans' closest friends are nearly always other Jamaicans, some migrants develop close ties with American blacks at work, for example, or in the classroom. Informal links also develop through children. Many migrants' children have close friendships with—and some have married—black Americans. These friendships of the migrants and their children do not necessarily undermine the migrants' stereotypic views of black Americans (or vice versa). But many Jamaican migrants are aware that there are exceptions to the stereotypes. "You have some very decent black American," one female hospital worker told me. "Because I went to South Carolina—my cousin is married to an American and we went to visit—and it was just like back home. I was shocked. Some of these black American don't like to work, but you have some very nice black American. You go to their house and it is like a palace." Another woman referred to "colored Americans" with disapproval, but she had nothing but praise for and warm feelings toward the middle-class American black family ("not like most of these colored Americans") she had worked for and with whom she had a very close friendship.

It seems likely that many migrants will develop more extensive ties with black Americans the longer they remain in New York City. Undoubtedly, migrants' children, born and raised in this country, will have even closer relations with black Americans than their parents do. My own research did not include the second generation and, as far as I know, there are to date no studies of second-generation Jamaicans or West Indians in New York. Some tantalizing questions await study. In what ways do second-generation Jamaicans remain apart from, or become integrated into, the larger American black population? Do they become involved in the larger black cause? Do they begin to identify themselves as black Americans? Do they still regard themselves in some ways as Jamaican or West Indian? And do they capitalize in any way on their distinctive cultural background?

Relations with Other West Indians

The immigration of Jamaicans and other West Indians to New York also has consequences for ethnic relations among West Indians from different societies. Various ties have sprung up, and a common West Indian identity has taken root, among West Indian migrants from the Commonwealth Caribbean.

The most significant relations Jamaicans have with other Caribbean people in New York are with West Indians from the English-speaking areas. Despite island rivalries and jealousies, Jamaicans share with these West Indians a broadly similar cultural and linguistic background. Indeed, when asked whether Jamaicans in New York were the same or different in any way from other West Indians, only a third in my sample categorically stated that there were differences. The differences usually mentioned were life-styles, food habits, or accents rather than traits that were thought to be undesirable.

Certainly, Jamaican migrants identify themselves as Jamaican, but a generalized West Indian identity also becomes important in New York. This is especially so in interactions with other West Indians, when the category "West Indian" serves as a common basis for identification, and in interactions with black and white Americans, who often ascribe the label "West Indian" to Jamaicans (McLaughlin 1981; see Midgett 1975 for an analysis of the contextual basis for choice of ethnic identity among St. Lucians in London). In my interviews with migrants in New York, many used the term "West Indian" and "Jamaican" interchangeably, even though the interview questions always used the category Jamaican.

Bonds develop between Jamaicans and other West Indians in a variety of settings. "Encounters with other West Indians," Sutton and Makiesky (1975:130) note in their analysis of Barbadians in New York, "in the neighborhood, classroom, and workplace provide a context for building relations between them. On one construction site in the Bronx, Barbadian and Jamaican workers observe, provoke, and antagonize each other but vis-à-vis white workers on the job and in the bar on the corner after work, they form a united West Indian front. It seems that New York offers more opportunities to build common understandings among West Indians than all the pro-Federation pronouncements of West Indian leaders at home."

Jamaicans and other West Indians also come together in work-related and neighborhood associations. My own observations indicate that church is a primary meeting ground for West Indians from different territories. The main West Indian Seventh Day Adventist Church in Brooklyn, for example, boasts over 1500 members (about 800 were in attendance on the Saturdays I went to services), with large numbers from Jamaica as well as many from such countries as Trinidad and Guyana. Participation in the church fostered a sense of "West Indianness" as opposed to "Jamaicanness" (or other national identity) among the faithful. Many Jamaican Seventh Day Adventists had developed warm friendships with other West Indians in an atmosphere of "churchly love." Church brethren and sisters from various parts of the West Indies met regularly in church services, went on church-sponsored trips, and paid visits to sick members. Many sent their children to the private school sponsored by the church (headed by a Guyanese principal in 1982). And members sought out ministers and elders, often from a country other than their own (the minister in 1982 was from Belize), for advice on spiritual as well as practical matters.

Race Relations

By adding diversity and sheer numbers to the black population, the recent mass immigration of Jamaicans and other West Indians has had an impact on race relations in New York.

One effect has been to permit and indeed to encourage behavior among whites that serves, as it were, to "divide and rule." When West Indians do come to their attention, white New Yorkers often compare West Indians favorably to American blacks. "The white landlord, the white shopkeeper, the white 'boss,'" Bryce-Laporte (1973:56) notes, "will . . . tell them of their moral superiority over the American black and the distinctiveness of their accent—leaving them to believe that they are the recipients of exceptional favors, when in fact they are being exploited no less than black Americans." Such invidious comparisons by whites promote the already deep divisions between American and West Indian blacks—and consequently discourage, or at least make more difficult, attempts at black unity across ethnic boundaries.

Moreover, to the extent that many West Indians are traditionalists in favor of the status quo—"convinced on the one hand that other blacks can do it too if they try, and on the other hand unable and unwilling to support any position of change which will seemingly threaten [their] newly acquired interest or status" (Bryce-Laporte 1973:58)—they provide a conservative core among the black population. And whatever the attitudes of West Indians, the fact is that their greater occupational success relative to that of black Americans is often used by those opposed to affirmative action programs to argue that race is not a barrier to achievement in America. These opponents of affirmative action often stress that if American blacks would only adopt the cultural values West Indians hold, they, too, could make it in the society—and they forget, or minimize, the influence of West Indians' immigrant status, occupational or class background, and roots in black-dominated societies in shaping West Indians' work habits and achievements.

The West Indian immigration has also affected racial strains and conflicts. As the ever-expanding number of Jamaicans and other West Indians continue to push out of black neighborhoods in the search for housing, into "white" areas of Brooklyn, Queens, and the Bronx, white resistance and discrimination undoubtedly spark racial conflicts.

And while ethnic divisions among the black population may impede attempts at unity, there are occasions when West Indians join with native blacks in struggles to improve their position as blacks. West Indians, after all, are acutely aware of the difficulties they face as blacks in America and thus they may add needed numbers to black protests—and, as many become citizens, to support for black candidates. As several academic commentators note, first- and second-generation West Indians have long been actively involved, often as leaders, in black political causes in this country—from the civil rights movement to local black community organizations (see, for example, Bryce-Laporte 1973; Forsythe 1976). It is likely that many West Indian immigrants and their children will, in the future, also sympathize with and swell the ranks of those participating in "the domestic struggle for black liberation and community development" (Bryce-Laporte 1973:60).

CONCLUSION

This essay has looked at Jamaican migrants from a dual perspective. Focusing on ethnicity and race, it has explored what moving to the city has meant to the migrants themselves. It has also viewed Jamaican migration from the perspective of the receiving area, probing how the migration has influenced race and ethnic relations in New York City.

This two-pronged approach has pointed to the way ethnicity operates as a source of conflict and race as a basis of cohesion between Jamaican and black Americans. The move to New York has given Jamaicans a new awareness of being black—as Sutton and Makiesky (1975:130) put it, "a heightened consciousness of themselves as a black minority enclosed within a sometimes menacing, sometimes friendly, world of more powerful whites." This racial consciousness provides a potential bond with both native and other immigrant blacks in political and social movements and, at the individual level, in interpersonal relations on the job, in the neighborhood, and at school. But if race unites Jamaicans with American blacks, ethnicity divides them. Jamaicans, we saw, feel they are different than, indeed superior to, indigenous blacks and they conduct their social life mainly with other Jamaicans. Ethnicity, in fact, is key in shaping Jamaicans' sense of identity in New York, and while it draws them together with their fellow Jamaicans (and often other West Indians), it drives a deep wedge between them and American blacks.

What is clear, then, is that ethnicity and race are of central importance in shaping Jamaican migrants' sense of identity, in structuring individual and collective actions among the migrants, and in generating strains and conflicts with American blacks and whites. Additional research is needed to further probe the contexts in which Jamaican migrants' ethnicity structures their attitudes and behavior—as well as to consider the way ethnicity interacts with, and can be set aside in favor of, migrants' racial identity. Our research agenda for the future must also include the migrants' children so we can begin to understand the role ethnicity and race play in their lives, as well as in the lives of their parents, and so we can identify the bases of cooperation and conflict between second-generation Jamaicans and the wider black population.

NOTES

1. This research, carried out between February and July 1982, was made possible by a grant from New York University's New York Research Program in Inter-American Affairs. I am grateful to the Director of the Program, Christopher Mitchell, as well as to Neva Wartell, my research assistant who did ten of the forty in-depth interviews. For a full analysis of the research, including a discussion of the methods and characteristics of the sample, see Foner (1983). The New York study was conducted to provide a comparison with my earlier research on Jamaicans in London and, in fact, I have compared the significance and effects of race among Jamaicans in New York and London in Foner (1985).

2. The 1965 legislation included Jamaica in the newly introduced hemispheric ceiling of 120,000 per year (with no per country limit). The law also introduced labor certification for all but parents, spouses, and children of U.S. citizens and permanent resident aliens. Applicants for immigrant visas had to show that the Secretary of Labor had certified that there were insufficient workers at the place where they were destined to move; that they were able and qualified to fill the position specified in their application; and that they would not adversely affect wages and working conditions (Dominguez 1975:9). Subsequent legislation in 1976 imposed a 20,000 per country limit for the Western hemisphere and

established preference categories that favored certain close relatives of U.S. citizens and residents as well as professionals. Spouses, children, and parents of adult U.S. citizens received immigrant status outside of the 20,000 per country ceiling (see Keely 1980; Keely and Elwell 1981).

3. How many of these highly trained migrants obtained white-collar jobs after they settled in the United States is unclear. Occupation in the INS annual reports can indicate the job held in Jamaica, job intended in the United States but not yet secured, or job in the United States for which labor certification has been granted (Keely and Elwell 1981:191).

4. See Foner (1978) and Lowenthal (1972) for a more detailed discussion of the Jamaican color-class hierarchy and the symbolic meaning of color in Jamaican society.

5. In this essay, the term West Indian refers only to those with origins in the English-speaking Caribbean, including Guyana and Belize.

6. Forty-two percent of the recent Jamaican migrants in Monica Gordon's (1979) sample said that Americans were more friendly when they knew you were Jamaican, and a majority said they always let others know they were Jamaican.

7. An analysis of 1970 census data shows that West Indians in the New York metropolitan area achieve higher occupational status than American blacks (Sowell 1978). A considerable literature explores why West Indian migrants are more successful than native black Americans. In addition to my own article (Foner 1979), see, for example, Bryce-Laporte (1973), Forsythe (1976), Glantz (1978), Glazer and Moynihan (1970), Lowenthal (1972), and Sowell (1978, 1981). Also see Foner and Napoli (1978) for a comparison of work attitudes and behavior among Jamaican migrants and black Americans on a New York State apple farm.

REFERENCES

Beckford, George. 1972. *Persistent Poverty: Underdevelopment in Plantation Economies of the Third World.* London: Oxford University Press.

Bryce-Laporte, Roy S. 1973. "Black Immigrants." In Peter I. Rose, Stanley Rothman, and William J. Wilson, eds. *Through Different Eyes.* New York: Oxford University Press.

—— 1979. "New York City and the New Caribbean Immigrant: A Contextual Statement." *International Migration Review* 13:214–234.

Buckley, Tom. 1974. "Calypso Finds Brooklyn a Home Away from Home." *New York Times,* June 12.

Coombs, Orde. 1970. "West Indians in New York: Moving Beyond the Limbo Pole." *New York Magazine* 13:28–32.

Dominguez, Virginia. 1975. *From Neighbor to Stranger: The Dilemma of Caribbean Peoples in the United States.* New Haven: Antilles Research Program, Yale University.

Eisner, Gisela. 1961. *Jamaica 1830–1930: A Study in Economic Growth*. Manchester: Manchester University Press.

Foner, Nancy. 1973. *Status and Power in Rural Jamaica: A Study of Educational and Political Change*. New York: Teachers College Press, Columbia University.

—— 1978. *Jamaica Farewell: Jamaican Migrants in London*. Berkeley: University of California Press.

—— 1979. "West Indians in New York City and London: A Comparative Analysis." *International Migration Review* 13:284–297.

—— 1983. "Jamaican Migrants: A Comparative Analysis of the New York and London Experience." *Occasional Paper No. 36*. New York Research Program in Inter-American Affairs, New York University.

—— 1985. "Race and Color: Jamaican Migrants in London and New York City." *International Migration Review* 19:708–727.

—— 1986. "Sex Roles and Sensibilities: Jamaican Women in New York and London." In Rita Simon and Caroline Brettell, eds., *International Migration: The Female Experience*. Totowa, N.J.: Rowman and Allanheld.

Foner, Nancy and Richard Napoli. 1978. "Jamaican and Black-American Migrant Farm Workers: A Comparative Analysis." *Social Problems* 25:491–503.

Forsythe, Dennis. 1976. "Black Immigrants and the American Ethos: Theories and Observation." In R. S. Bryce-Laporte and D. M. Mortimer, eds., *Caribbean Immigration to the United States*. Washington, D.C.: Research Institute on Immigration and Ethnic Studies, Smithsonian Institution.

Fraser, Gerald. 1970. "Neighborhoods: West Indies Flavor Bedford-Stuyvesant." *New York Times*, October 28.

Girvan, Norman. 1972. *Foreign Capital and Economic Underdevelopment in Jamaica*. Kingston: Institute of Social and Economic Research, University of the West Indies.

Girvan, Norman, Richard Bernal, and Wesley Hughes. 1980. "The IMF and the Third World: The Case of Jamaica, 1974–80." *Development Dialogue* 2:113–155.

Glantz, Oscar. 1978. "Native Sons and Immigrants: Some Beliefs and Values of American-Born and West Indian Blacks at Brooklyn College." *Ethnicity* 5:189–202.

Glazer, Nathan and Daniel Moynihan. 1970. *Beyond the Melting Pot*. Cambridge: MIT Press.

Gordon, Monica. 1979. "Identification and Adaptation: A Study of Two Groups of Jamaican Immigrants in New York City." Unpublished doctoral dissertation, City University of New York.

Jefferson, Owen. 1972. *The Post-War Economic Development of Jamaica*. Kingston: Institute of Social and Economic Research, University of the West Indies.

Keely, Charles. 1980. "Immigration Policy and the New Immigrants, 1965–1975." In R. S. Bryce-Laporte, ed., *Sourcebook on the New Immigration*. New Brunswick, N.J.: Transaction Books.

Keely, Charles and Patricia Elwell. 1981. "International Migration: Canada and the United States." In Mary Kritz, Charles Keely, and Silvano Tomasi, eds., *Global Trends in Migration*. New York: Center for Migration Studies.

Koslovsky, Joanne. 1981. "'Going Foreign'—Causes of Jamaican Migration." *NACLA Report on the Americas* 15:1–31.

Lowenthal, David. 1972. *West Indian Societies*. London: Oxford University Press.

Marshall, Dawn I. 1982. "The History of Caribbean Migrations: The Case of the West Indies." *Caribbean Review* 11:6–9, 52–53.

McLaughlin, Megan. 1981. "West Indian Immigrants: Their Social Networks and Ethnic Identification." Unpublished doctoral dissertation, Columbia University.

Midgett, Douglas. 1975. "West Indian Ethnicity in Britain." In Helen Safa and Brian Du Toit, eds., *Migration and Development*. The Hague: Mouton.

Nettleford, Rex. 1972. *Identity, Race and Protest in Jamaica*. New York: William Morrow.

Palmer, R. W. 1974. "A Decade of West Indian Migration to the United States, 1962–1972: An Economic Analysis." *Social and Economic Studies* 23:571–588.

Petras, Elizabeth McLean. 1983. "Competition or Cooperation: Nationality, Race and Gender in the Health Industry." Paper presented at the Conference on Immigration and the Changing Black Population in the United States, University of Michigan.

Roberts, George. 1979. *The Population of Jamaica*. (1957.) Millwood, N.Y.: Kraus Reprint.

Smith, Raymond T. 1970. "Social Stratification in the Caribbean." In Leonard Plotnicov and Arthur Tuden, eds., *Essays in Comparative Social Stratification*. Pittsburgh: University of Pittsburgh Press.

Sowell, Thomas. 1978. *Essays and Data on American Ethnic Groups*. Washington, D.C.: The Urban Institute.

—— 1981. *Ethnic America*. New York: Basic Books.

Stone, Carl. 1982. *The Political Opinions of the Jamaican People, 1976–81*. Kingston: Blackett Publishers.

Sutton, Constance and Susan Makiesky. 1975. "Migration and West Indian Racial and Ethnic Consciousness." In Helen Safa and Brian Du Toit, eds., *Migration and Development*. The Hague: Mouton.

U.S. Immigration and Naturalization Service. 1967–1979. *Annual Reports*. Washington, D.C.: U.S. Government Printing Office.

Walter, John C. 1981–82. "West Indian Immigrants: Those Arrogant Bastards." *New England Journal of Black Studies* 2:17–27.

8. The Koreans: Small Business in an Urban Frontier

Illsoo Kim

A high proportion of Korean immigrants across the nation have chosen small business as the means for pursuing the American dream in postindustrial America. As in the case of Jewish immigrants at the turn of the century, post-1965 Korean immigrants have developed small businesses as an economic beachhead for their own and their children's further advancement in American society. In fact, Korean immigrants have earned a new racial epithet—"Kew" or "Korean Jew." In the New York metropolitan area alone, Korean immigrants, as of 1985, ran some 9,000 small business enterprises, certainly contributing to the recent vitality of the New York economy.

Given the structural changes in the American, and especially the New York, economy in which small businesses have declined in number (Freedman 1983:103), why have Korean immigrants "inundated" small businesses and reactivated a traditional immigrant path to the American dream? The massive Korean entry into small businesses may be welcomed as a revival of old patterns by those who lament the loss of "rugged individualism" and entrepreneurship in the United States and the dominant trend toward business concentration, centralization, and bureaucratization. But Korean involvement in small business is not a duplication of patterns found among "old" European immigrants earlier in the century. Rather, it must be understood on its own terms—a product of Korean immigrants'

homeland-derived socioeconomic and cultural characteristics or resources as well as broader socioeconomic conditions in their new
land.

This essay departs from existing theoretical approaches to immigrant enterprises in the United States that tend to treat these enterprises—including markets, labor, and networks—as self-contained,
"traditional" subsystems somewhat independent of external, "modernized" forces (Light 1972; Wilson and Portes 1980; Cummings 1980;
Bonacich and Modell 1980). While I do note that traditional family
values have played a role in Korean business activity, my analysis in
this essay focuses on three modern, structural factors that have supported or been conducive to the proliferation of Korean small businesses in New York. The first factor is the utilization of modern
"ethnic class resources" which Koreans brought with them from their
home country. These ethnic class resources include advanced education, economic motivation or "success ideology," and money. The
second factor is the economic opportunities available in New York
where limited employment possibilities in the mainstream economy
coincided with opportunities that opened up in New York's economic
structure due to demographic, residential, and ethnic changes in the
city. Finally, the third factor is the role of such "modern" ethnic
institutions as the mass media, churches, and businessmen's associations in the New York Korean community.

This essay is mainly based on my lengthy, unstructured interviews
with some fifty Korean businessmen and community business leaders during 1985.[1] This research is a continuation of a larger project
on the New York Korean community that I carried out between 1974
and 1979 (see Illsoo Kim 1981a). During the two separate research
periods, I spoke to businessmen, as well as hundreds of other immigrants, about their careers, life histories, and particular problems.
As an immigrant from South Korea—I came to New York City from
Seoul in 1970—I had a tremendous research advantage since it was
easy for me to conduct interviews or just talk with immigrants in a
natural or informal manner. The interviews and conversations took
place in such settings as ethnic churches, picnics, alumni association
meetings, and shops. Participant observation, in fact, was a key part
of the study, and I attended countless association meetings, church

services, and other collective activities. The figures on Korean enterprises, unless otherwise indicated, are estimates provided by community business leaders.

THE BACKGROUND OF
NEW KOREAN IMMIGRANTS

Migration and Settlement Patterns

The Korean community in the New York metropolitan area is the result of the 1965 Immigration and Nationality Act which ended the severe numerical limits on immigration from Asian countries. According to the 1980 census, 94 percent of the Korean-born population in the New York metropolitan area arrived since 1965 (Kraly, this volume).

The reason most Koreans give for emigrating to America is basically "to find a better life." Behind this rather simple answer are a number of complex push factors, including Korean population pressure and political instability. The political uncertainty in South Korea, caused mainly by the military tension between South and North Korea since the Korean War (1950–53), led many middle- and upper-middle-class Koreans to leave for the United States in fear of another Korean war, especially in the 1970s (see Illsoo Kim 1984). Population pressures have also driven South Koreans from their homeland. In a nation roughly the size of the state of Maine, the number of people has grown from 25 million in 1960 to 40 million in 1984. The population density of South Korea is the third highest in the world. This population explosion, along with rapid industrialization and urbanization, has led to typical Third World urban problems—severe crowding, pollution, and intense economic competition for limited resources and opportunities.

South Korea has also witnessed a revolution of rising expectations, a result of the country's rapid economic development through increasing international trade as well as the population's encounters with Western, especially American, mass culture. Koreans are now fascinated by American life-styles, which the vast majority cannot hope to obtain in South Korea. The disparity between their desires and their limited resources and opportunities has tended to make urban, especially college-educated, Koreans restless and dissatisfied and to intensify their conviction that South Korea is not a good place to live. As I will discuss later, the majority of Korean immigrants are drawn from this urban middle class in South Korea.

There is considerable disagreement as to the number of Koreans in the United States. According to an estimate of the Korean Ministry of Foreign Affairs, in 1985 there were 920,533 Koreans in the United States (*Hankook Ilbo*, December 26, 1985). Census figures are much lower. According to the 1980 census, 377,000 Koreans, including all those of Korean ancestry, lived in the United States, with 37,399, or 10 percent, in the New York metropolitan area and 22,073 in New York City alone (U.S. Department of Commerce 1984). The census, however, is already out of date, given that over 30,000 Korean immigrants have been admitted to the United States each year since 1980 and that there is an estimated annual natural increase rate of 3 percent for the Korean population in the United States (Koo and Yu 1981). In addition, the census did not count most undocumented Koreans or most nonimmigrant Koreans such as businessmen, government officials, and students. Based upon the figures available from the "Korean" sources, I roughly estimate that there are, as of 1986, more than 100,000 Koreans—including all those of Korean ancestry—in the New York metropolitan area.

Korean immigrants have predominantly settled in large metropolitan areas in the United States. The largest Korean community is in the Los Angeles metropolitan area, followed by New York, and then Chicago. Within the New York metropolitan area, Koreans have not formed one single territorial community, although there are heavy concentrations in the white lower-middle-class sections of Flushing, Jackson Heights, Corona, and Elmhurst in Queens. Even in these neighborhoods, Korean immigrants have not established single-block residential enclaves and they live among members of the second or third generation of old European immigrants as well as such new immigrants as Cubans and other Asians (see Illsoo Kim 1981a:181–86 for characteristics of the Korean nonterritorial community). Once Koreans make it in New York City—as doctors, engineers, or successful businessmen—they nearly always move to the suburbs.

Socioeconomic Characteristics

The recent Korean immigration is selective and includes a high proportion of well-educated urban middle-class people. A majority of Korean immigrants are drawn from the upper middle or middle classes in the major cities of South Korea such as Seoul, Pusan, and Taegue (Illsoo Kim 1981a:38) and thus had experience of living in large modern urban centers before moving to the United States. Consider some of the available figures. Forty percent of the Koreans who came to the United States between 1974 and 1977 had previously engaged in professional and technical occupations in South Korea (Yu 1983:475). According to a sample survey conducted by Jae T. Kim in the New York metropolitan area in 1975, 67 percent of the 560 Korean householders reported that they had finished college in their homeland (cited in Illsoo Kim 1981a:40). In the Los Angeles metropolitan area, according to another sample survey conducted in 1979, 61 percent of the male and 53 percent of the female respondents said they had completed college in South Korea (Hurh and Kim 1984:58). Korean immigration is also selective in terms of religious affiliation. Whereas Korean Christians represented only 24 percent of the total South Korean population in 1984, in the Los Angeles survey 51 percent of the respondents were affiliated with Christian, especially Protestant, churches in South Korea (Hurh and Kim 1984:129). A high proportion of Koreans in New York also have a Protestant background.

Despite the fact that so many Korean immigrants come to New York with high levels of education, professional experience, and an urban middle-class background, most are not able to obtain well-paid professional, white-collar work in the mainstream American occupational structure. Such work requires proficiency in English and a long period of training in large-scale American organizations—insuperable barriers to most Korean immigrants. In urban America, especially in New York, the center of economic activities has shifted to white-collar, service industries; lacking professional service skills, Koreans are handicapped.

Under these circumstances, Korean immigrants, who generally had little propensity for commercial activity in South Korea, often turn to small business in New York. In so doing, they utilize the very ethnic class resources they bring with them—money, advanced education, high economic motivation, a work ethic, and professional or sometimes business skills. I refer to these resources as "ethnic class resources" since they are mainly derived form the social class circumstances of the immigrants in South Korea, a homogeneous ethnic state. Many Korean immigrants in New York come with money they can use to set up small businesses. Their educational background means they have skills relevant to running businesses. And the fact that large numbers held high-level and prestigious jobs in South Korea gives them the confidence and motivation to work hard to succeed.

The Immigrant Family

Koreans have generally come to New York with members of their nuclear family, their basic social unit, although frequently a family is temporarily separated so that a pioneer member can establish an economic base or because of a bureaucratic delay under United States immigration laws. The immigration of families has been made possible by the humane nature of the 1965 U.S. immigration law, which emphasized the reunion of immediate relatives. According to a 1975 sample survey in the New York metropolitan area, 86 percent of the 560 Korean householders were married and living with their spouses (Jae T. Kim, cited in Illsoo Kim 1981a:45).

The continuation of two- and often three-generation families in New York is another key factor in the proliferation of small businesses among Korean immigrants. First, family members who have come to New York are a major source of capital for small businesses. Some families bring considerable amounts of money from South Korea; others rely heavily on savings accumulated and pooled in New York for their first businesses (compare Kim and Hurh 1985:101–102 on Korean businesses in the Chicago area). The South Korean government allows each emigrant family to take a maximum of $100,000 to the United States in the form of settlement money. Family members planning to emigrate frequently gather a significant sum by combining their savings or by selling personal property. This settlement money represents one of the few ways a Korean family can enter the United States prepared to buy a small business or to pay initial living expenses. Second, many immigrants can rely on family labor in their enterprises in New York. Largely owing to the cultural legacy of Confucian familism, Korean immigrants subscribe to a family-centered success ethic that leads family members to be willing to devote themselves to the family business. That family members are willing to work long hours has been especially important in the greengrocer business, enabling Korean enterprises in New York to compete with supermarket chains (Illsoo Kim 1981a:115–116). Here is one family story:

Mr. Yun, his wife, and their two teenage children entered the United States in 1974 after Mr. Yun's brother, a naturalized American citizen, had petitioned the U.S. Immigration and Naturalization Service on their behalf. Upon arrival, Mrs. Yun immediately sent for her parents on a tourist visa, and consequently a three-generation family was established at Mr. Yun's residence. Mr. Yun, a college graduate with a major in business management, had worked for the U.S. Army in South Korea. He had a good command of colloquial English and, when he arrived, was able to get a low-level clerical job in a New York City government agency. His wife and mother-in-law did piecework for New York garment factories. In two years they had saved $20,000, which they used to buy a fruit and vegetable store from another Korean who, in turn, had purchased it from an old Italian.

Thereafter, Mr. Yun arose at 4 A.M. every morning and drove to the Hunt's Point wholesale market in the Bronx to purchase the day's goods. His wife worked from 7 A.M. to 7 P.M. as the store's cashier. Mrs. Yun's mother washed, clipped, and sorted vegetables; her father, who was too old to engage in physical labor, regularly stationed himself on a chair at the store's entrance to help deter shoplifters. The teenagers, too, were part-time but regular workers, helping in the store before and after school. In Mr. Yun's words, "We worked and worked like hell." But he and and his family were successful. Mr. Yun found a Korean partner and in 1980 they bought a gas station on Route 4 in New Jersey. Mr. Yun continued to run the greengrocery business while leaving the management of the gas station to his partner, an auto mechanic.

SMALL BUSINESS AS AN ECONOMIC
BASIS OF THE KOREAN COMMUNITY

The extent of Korean immigrants' involvement in small business in New York is striking. It is true, of course, that Koreans are found in other occupational spheres in New York—many as medical professionals (doctors, nurses, pharmacists, and technicians) and as engineers, mechanics, and operatives (see Illsoo Kim 1981a:40). Nonetheless, small businesses can be said to be the economic foundation of the Korean community in New York and in the United States in general.

According to an estimate by the Korean Produce Retailers Association, as of 1985 there were some 9,000 Korean small businesses in the New York metropolitan area, most in New York City. In my estimate based on the 1985 Korean Directory of Greater New York, 41 percent of the Korean families in the New York metropolitan area run small businesses. The percentage is much higher when Korean employees are also included. Sung Soo Kim, former executive director of the Korean Produce Retailers Association, estimated that in 1986 some 70 percent of employed Koreans in the New York metropolitan area found employment in Korean businesses (Sung Soo Kim 1986). The involvement in small businesses is even more remarkable in Los Angeles County where, according to Ivan Light, 80 percent of employed Koreans worked in Korean-owned firms in 1982 (1985:162).

Most Korean businesses, especially labor-intensive retail shops such as greengrocery businesses, fish stores, and discount stores want to hire, and actively recruit, Korean immigrants or *kyopo* (fellow countrymen). In the New York Korean community small businesses are the primary source of employment for newcomers or greenhorns who lack proficiency in English and skills that are marketable in the wider economy. These newcomers have no choice but to take jobs with Korean employers, working long hours without such benefits as medical insurance and overtime pay. The availability of this kind of labor is beneficial to business owners who, at the same time, can feel they are helping their compatriots. One Korean business leader, for example, boasted of the small business contribution to the community: "In our *kyopo* (fellow countrymen) society there is no unemployment problem thanks to the jobs created by *kyopo* businessmen. I have never seen unemployed Koreans." Indeed, it is also my observation that unemployed Korean immigrants are few in number.

The very proliferation and success of Korean small businesses has, in itself, had an independent effect in stimulating further business activity in the Korean community. Setting up a small business has become, in a sense, a "cultural fashion" among Koreans, a point that has not received sufficient attention in the literature on immigrant enterprises. A Korean aphorism has it that "running a *jangsa* (commercial business) is the fastest way to get ahead in America," and this saying is widespread among Korean immigrants, including those who have just arrived. In Korean gatherings such as church meetings, alumni meetings and picnics, Koreans devote much of their time to talk about *jangsa*. At one church meeting, a Korean immigrant, who had just opened a fine jewelry store in midtown Manhattan, talked to church members about his business: "Making money is a mysterious magic to me. I never expected such a good profit." Many Korean immigrants have been susceptible to this kind of glorification of small business and, impressed by the success of others, have entered small business. In addition, the ethnic media, especially Korean daily newspapers, frequently present stories about Korean Horatio Algers who have "made it" through small business and this, too, encourages Korean entry into small business.

CLASSIFICATION OF
BUSINESS ENTERPRISES

Korean businesses in the New York metropolitan area can be classified into four categories by considering the following two factors: (1) whether the customers they cater to are Koreans or members of other ethnic groups; and (2) whether the goods or services are produced and sold within the United States market or depend on economic relations with South Korea.

The businesses in the first cell in table 8.1 deal with goods or services specifically geared to Korean ethnic tastes and cultural or economic needs that can be satisfied by commercial interaction between the two countries. Korean food and gift stores and book shops sell

Table 8.1. Types of Korean Business Enterprises

	Ethnic Origin of Customers	
Supply and Demand Mechanism	Korean	Other
Originating in the interaction between the United States and Korea	1. Korean food and gift stores, book stores, newspaper branches, bank branches, travel agencies, emigration agencies, etc.	3. Retailers or wholesalers of wigs and other imported goods, Korean karate gyms, etc.
Originating within the U.S. market	2. Accounting and legal services, real estate and insurance brokers, restaurants and bars, beauty salons, carpenters, moving companies, etc.	4. Greengrocery businesses and fish stores, liquor stores, hardware and furniture stores, dry cleaners, garment subcontractors, etc.

South Korean products to Korean immigrants. Items such as books, gifts, magazines, cassette and video tapes, and records are directly imported from South Korea. Travel agencies provide services to Koreans who wish to visit their homeland. A total of twelve South Korean commercial banks maintain branches in New York City, serving the economic needs of Korean immigrants. In New York City, as of 1986, there were six daily Korean language newspapers and one in English, all but two published in and imported from South Korea. The New York branches of the imported newspapers add local news and advertisements to the Korean editions and distribute the newspapers to Koreans in the Northeast. There are also one television and three radio companies; most of the television programs are imported from South Korea. As I will discuss later on, the ethnic media play a key role in the development of Korean business enterprises in New York.

The enterprises in the second cell do not have a commercial tie with the homeland, although they mainly cater to Korean immigrants. Businesses that provide such services as accounting, legal counseling, and real estate and insurance brokerage help Koreans adjust to the institutions of the larger American society. In addition, there are eight "ethnic" medical centers where a group of Korean physicians provide medical services to their fellow immigrants. In response to immigrants' ethnic tastes and desire to be with other Koreans, Korean restaurants, bars, *giseng* (female entertainer) salons,[2] and beauty and barber shops have emerged. There are some ninety Korean restaurants in the New York metropolitan area that not only serve ethnic foods to Koreans but also provide space for all major community affairs such as business luncheons and speeches, welcoming parties for South Korean celebrities, and alumni meetings.

Since the enterprises in both the first and second cells mainly cater to Korean customers, their further growth depends as much upon an increase in the number of Koreans in the New York metropolitan area as on their own success in the new economic environment. Keen competition has arisen among these businesses as they try to attract ethnic customers from a limited population.

The enterprises in the third cell have been established and have expanded due to the ever-growing trade between the United States and East Asia, including South Korea, Taiwan, Hong Kong, and mainland China. Korean immigrants import such cheap consumer goods as wigs, jewelry, clothing, handbags, and gloves from South Korea and other Asian nations and "dump" them in large American inner cities, primarily in non-Korean ethnic minority neighborhoods. Since New York City is a center of international trade as well as the largest inner city, with an enormous minority population, Korean importers (or wholesalers) and retailers dealing with such items have flourished. Most of the Korean retail stores in the third cell—discount and clothing stores, for example—are, in fact, located in the commercial districts of minority communities. Blacks and Hispanics are their typical customers, and the business enterprises presuppose a dominant mass consumption trend among these minorities. These minority-oriented business enterprises constitute a large portion of Korean retail and wholesale businesses, and a number of millionaires have come out of such enterprises.

Korean shopowners who sell imported Asian goods maintain close commercial ties with various Korean importers or wholesalers in New York's "Koreatown" in Manhattan, on Broadway between 23d and 31st Streets. A Korean gift shop owner in the South Bronx, who bought his store in 1985 from another Korean for $40,000 in key money, said: "I drive to Koreatown three or four times a week to buy new items." By 1985, "Koreatown" had greatly expanded, completely renovating the old business district. Strictly speaking, "Koreatown" is a racially mixed commercial district where Jewish landlords and Indian, Pakistani, Chinese, and Korean businessmen and other non-Asian merchants intermingle to do business. Yet, of all the Asian groups, Koreans were the first to "invade" that area and they now dominate it. There are some 350 Korean wholesale (or import) businesses and South Korean corporation branches, three South Korean bank branches, offices of three branches of Korean daily newspapers, about twenty Korean restaurants and *giseng* (female entertainer) salons and countless other Korean commercial establishments. Since the Korean invasion in the early 1970s, commercial rents have risen so high that several Korean-owned shops have gone out of business. A number of Korean merchants once even tried to move "Koreatown" to a low-rent area, but this attempt was in vain.

Korean enterprises in the fourth cell are typical American small businesses. The goods they sell are supplied by the U.S. market— and the demand for the goods and services they provide is also generated in this country. They cater to all ethnic and racial groups in the New York area, although a high proportion are located in black and Hispanic neighborhoods of the city. Ethnic succession is typical of these small businesses in the fourth cell. Koreans have almost succeeded Jews and Italians in such lines as greengrocery businesses, retail fish stores, and dry cleaning establishments. As of 1985, Koreans owned and ran some 950 greengroceries, 350 retail fish stores, and some 1,000 dry cleaning establishments throughout the New York metropolitan area. Koreans' penetration of the greengrocery business is perhaps the most apparent to New Yorkers, and, according to an estimate by the Korean Produce Retailers Association, they account for about 85 percent of the independent fruit and vegetable stores in the city. In the process of taking over so much of the greengrocery business, they have also changed it—offering a wider variety of fresh produce in many stores, for example. According to the chairman of one of the city's supermarket chains, Korean greengroceries are taking a bite out of the supermarket business and forcing supermarkets to sell better quality produce and display it more attractively (quoted in *Time*, July 8, 1985:73).

Korean immigrants have been able to establish so many businesses of the type listed in the third and fourth cells, especially those catering to urban minorities, partly because of the opportunities available. In focusing their sales efforts on urban minorities, Korean immigrants have responded to racial and ethnic changes in New York. Blacks and Hispanics have become an increasingly large proportion of the city's population. In 1980, according to census reports, blacks and Hispanics represented 45 percent of the city's population, up from about 22 percent in 1960 and 34 percent in 1970. This fundamental shift is an important factor determining the way Korean immigrants have established small business niches in the New York economy. A very high proportion of Korean retail shops in both the third and fourth cells cater to blacks and Hispanics, usually in increasingly minority or "transitional" areas (see Min 1984 on the effect of urban racial segregation on Korean businesses in Atlanta).

It is not simply that the minority population—and the potential minority clientele—has expanded in the city. It is also that old Jewish, Italian, and other white shopkeepers in minority and especially transitional areas have been moving out or dying out, creating a business vacuum that is being filled by Korean and other immigrants. Korean immigrants have been able to buy shops from these whites, particularly Jews who are old or about to retire. The children of these Jewish shopkeepers have already moved into occupations in the mainstream American economy and do not want to take over their parents' businesses. For instance, some fifty Korean businesses such as furniture, liquor, toy, wig, hardware, gift, Korean food, fruit and vegetable, and "discount" stores have emerged since 1973 along the Fordham Road shopping area in the Bronx.

Gone, by the tens of thousands, are the middle-class Jews, Irish and Italians who used to come to Fordham Road to trade up to $200 suits and $1,000 bedroom suites. But in their place have come tens of thousands of generally poorer Spanish-speaking people and blacks who have less to spend individually, but who collectively are spending heavily enough on moderately priced goods to keep Fordham Road the sixth biggest shopping center in the Metropolitan area. (*New York Times*, December 24, 1976)

On Fordham Road, as in other commercial districts in minority areas, Koreans have thus found business possibilities. In taking advantage of them, Koreans have changed the ethnic flavor of small businesses—and played a role in reviving these commercial districts in the wake of the exodus of "old immigrant" shopkeepers.

COMMUNITY INSTITUTIONS AND BUSINESS ENTERPRISES

Korean community institutions play an important role in the proliferation and success of Korean small businesses in New York City, but these differ from the traditional ethnic associations that several works on immigrant enterprises in the United States have emphasized.

A number of studies of immigrant enterprises in this country stress the role of traditional ethnic or communal organizations in tapping ethnic resources for minority business development (see Cummings 1980; Fratoe 1984)—what I call the traditional organization approach. Thus, studies have shown that Chinese and Japanese immigrants at the turn of the century—barred from the mainstream economy and politically disenfranchised—organized ethnic associations based on regional or clan ties to provide each other with jobs, mutual aid, and business capital (Light 1972; Lyman 1974). Ivan Light, in his study of ethnic enterprises in America, stresses, in particular, the decisive role of traditional rotating credit associations among the Chinese and Japanese in the capitalization of their business enterprises (Light 1972; see also Bonnett 1980 on rotating credit associations among West Indian immigrants and Lovell-Troy 1980 on clan ties among Greeks). Important as traditional ethnic associations may be, too often the role of more modern institutions is overlooked. Moreover, traditional ethnic institutions themselves tend to be treated as self-contained, ethnic shells that are isolated from external forces.

In the case of Korean immigrants in New York, it is modern ethnic institutions, many derived from South Korea but all influenced by external forces in New York, that are crucial. These institutions serve many important functions for Korean enterpreneurs and stimulate Korean business activity in New York. The modern, ethnic institutions that support Korean enterprises in the New York metropolitan area include churches, the mass media, and business associations. The analysis below considers the extent to which each contributes to Korean business development.

The Protestant Church as a Community

Protestant churches have flourished among Koreans in New York partly because so many immigrants are drawn from the Christian, especially Protestant, population in South Korea. In addition, the churches have become important community centers for immigrants in the absence of discrete, residential enclaves among them. Indeed, at least for members, church communities have become the substitute for ethnic neighborhoods.

The fact that Korean Protestant churches in the New York metropolitan area have increased from 6 in 1971 to some 285 in 1986 reflects not only the dramatic increase in the number of Korean immigrants but also their desire for communal life and social activities (for an ethnographic treatment of Korean Protestant churches see Illsoo Kim 1981a:187–207; Illsoo Kim 1985). In providing this communal life, the churches, as I will show, also end up contributing to the expansion of Korean enterprises.

Korean churches are much more than sites for religious services. Because they serve multiple, secular functions they are central places for community activities and they have, in fact, opened up membership to all segments of the Korean population. A Korean engineer living in a "white" New Jersey suburb said: "On Sunday I do not want my children watching TV all day long. At least one day a week I want them to intermingle with other Koreans and learn something about Korea. This is the reason why my family and I attend [Protestant] church even though I am a Buddhist. My offerings are nothing but the payment for the services my family has received from the church." Ministers in the churches perform numerous secular roles, and they are mainly judged by their congregations according to how well they do so. The ministers' extrachurch activities include: "matchmaking, presiding over marriage ceremonies, visiting hospitalized members, assisting moving families, making congratulatory visits to families having a new baby, making airport pick-ups of newly arrived family members, interpreting for "no-English" members, administering job referral and housing services, and performing other similar personal services" (Illsoo Kim 1981a:200).

In this context, most Korean Protestants attend churches not only for religious salvation but also for secular—economic and social—reasons. They want to make and meet Korean friends; they are looking for jobs or job information; they want to obtain business information, make business contacts or conduct business negotiations; or they seek private loans or want to organize or participate in *gae*, a Korean rotating credit association. The economic affairs of church life frequently lead to financial or business scandals. In the late summer of 1985, for instance, a deaconness in a Korean church in Flushing ran away to South Korea with a large amount of money she had borrowed from some church members and with the pooled *gae* fund she had been holding for a group in the church.

The formation of Korean personal "economic" networks centered around church life has been facilitated by the class meeting, a Methodist institution which Korean Protestant churches of all denominations in both South Korea and the United States adopt and utilize to create a "family atmosphere" among church members. Church members are grouped according to the residential area in which they live; in every church at least five or six district service areas or "class meetings" are organized in order to extend group activities beyond the location of the church itself. The purpose of the district service area is to promote mutual assistance among nearby members and enhance their faith by holding a religious service at a member's residence on a rotational basis. Food is served, and informal social interactions among members follow the religious service. Members, especially small businessmen, are frequently preoccupied at this time with business talks.

In the process of performing the manifest or intended function of providing religious services, the Korean Protestant churches thus serve various latent or unintended economic functions. Churches, as I described, are places where immigrants can get funds for their enterprises by arranging loans or by participating in *gae* and where they can make business contacts and find out information relating to their businesses. These economic functions are unintended in that the church or minister does not officially become involved in personal business interactions among church members, except in providing job information or job referral service to them. It should be noted, too, that another unintended function of Protestant churches—so important to Korean business success—is to reinforce members' values of self-control and hard work by constantly emphasizing self-abnegation, endurance, hardship, and frugality (see Illsoo Kim 1981a:205–206).

Some of the economic functions of Protestant churches are intended, however. Many Korean churches or ministers of fundamentalist or conservative religious orientation consciously and "officially" promote Korean capitalism among members. One Korean fundamentalist church, with several branch churches throughout the New York metropolitan area, provides its members with start-up capital, with the stipulation that they contribute a proportion of their profits to the church when they are prosperous. A Korean minister said: "It is my theology that economic prosperity is supportive of religious salvation. I always emphasize this to my congregation. I frequently go to banks to help my members get loans for opening shops."

Ethnic Media and the Business Community

The Korean ethnic media also play a decisive role in maintaining the Korean community in the New York metropolitan area. The Korean ethnic media go beyond delivering news. By informing geographically dispersed Korean immigrants of community events and meetings as well as of commercial sales and news, the media are a powerful means of integrating and sustaining the Korean community. What is pertinent here is that the ethnic media have been crucial in the rapid expansion of Korean enterprises.

The Korean ethnic media in the New York metropolitan area, as of 1986, consist of: (1) six daily Korean language newspapers and one in English, of which five are published in South Korea; (2) three weekly or monthly newspapers, all published in New York City; (3) one television and three radio companies. Of all the media, the daily Korean language newspapers—the *Hankook Ilbo*, the *Dong-A Ilbo*, the *Joong Ang Ilbo*, and the *Chosun Ilbo* (the four leading newspapers in South Korea) and the *Mijoo Daily News* and the *Ilgan New York* (two dailies in Korean published in New York City)—provide the primary mass communication, information, and advertising services to Korean immigrants in the New York metropolitan area. Each of the newspapers published in South Korea is sent air mail daily from Kimpo International Airport to Kennedy Airport. The New York branch of each newspaper then photocopies the issue on an electronic copier, also adding local news and advertisements to the original edition. The newspapers are not sold on general newsstands but are sent directly to each Korean subscriber by second-class mail. The majority of Koreans in New York subscribe to one of the newspapers and many well-established Korean businessmen subscribe to two or three.

The contribution of the newspapers to Korean enterprises is twofold. First, they are an influential agency for socializing Korean immigrants into small business capitalism. They provide immigrants with all kinds of commercial information on tax guidelines, accounting, commercial issues, and prospects for new businesses. They carry articles or essays on successful *kyopo* (fellow countrymen) in business, who serve as role models for newcomers to emulate. They also quickly cover events affecting Korean small businessmen. For example, they have alerted Korean businessmen to immigration officials' crackdowns on Korean illegal aliens employed in Korean businesses and they have promptly published news of frequent conflicts between Korean businessmen and blacks. Second, the community media, especially the daily Korean language newspapers, facilitate the expansion of the Korean subeconomy by carrying advertising for ethnic business products, ethnic services, commodity sales, housing sales or rentals, jobs, and so forth. A Korean wholesaler of general merchandise in "Koreatown" described the impact of his commodity advertisement in the *Hankook Ilbo*, the largest newspaper: "I feel it. My office telephones keep ringing all day long." Newcomers are quickly absorbed into the ethnic labor market through the daily advertisements for jobs in Korean enterprises. The *Hankook Ilbo* annually publishes a Directory of Korean Business that is distributed to its readers and Korean business establishments to facilitate business transactions among Koreans.

Businessmen's Associations and Ethnic Solidarity

Korean businessmen's associations, as their name suggests, are clearly involved in Korean business development. They can be classified into two categories: (1) associations based on business type and

(2) associations based on geographical area. Korean businessmen have formed associations of the first type in business lines in which they are active. There are, for example, associations of greengrocers, fish retailers, dry cleaners, garment retailers, garment subcontractors, and gas station operators. As for the second category, Korean businessmen have also established "prosperity associations" in major commercial areas of Korean business concentration. Korean prosperity associations can be found in the following areas of New York City: the South Bronx; Flushing, Sunnyside, and Jamaica in Queens; Church Avenue in Brooklyn; the Lower East Side, Central Harlem, and Washington Heights in Manhattan.

The main organizational goal of both types of associations is to establish friendship among members and to further their common interests. Friendship among members is usually strengthened by picnics and parties in which they and their families participate. Beyond recreational activities, the extent and intensity of organizational activities differ from association to association. Such big associations as the Korean Produce Retailers Association, the Korean Seafood Association, and the Korean Dry Cleaners Association have large annual budgets for delivering all kinds of services to their members—group insurance, tax guides, legal services, and informative seminars. A member of the Korean Dry Cleaners Association, affiliated with its "American" counterpart, the Neighborhood Dry Cleaners Association, said: "My association is greatly helpful to my business. I did not know how to treat (chemical) wastes until they taught me how to do it."

Of all the associations, the Korean Produce Retailers Association has initiated and carried out the most intense and systematic activities for members' common interests. This is partly because it has the largest membership. Also, the operation of greengrocery businesses often leads to conflicts with government officials over laws and regulations such as parking regulations and consumer protection laws as well as hostility from some segments of the native-born American population. Here is an account of how and why the Korean Produce Retailers Association organized and staged a mass demonstration for the first time in the history of New York's Korean community:

Though they are, in many ways, imitating earlier European immigrant groups in their climb up the American economic ladder, Koreans have also been subject to harassment by members of these groups. Especially in their first years of emergence into the fruit and vegetable business, Koreans reported many incidents at the Hunts Point Market. The incidents ranged from unfair pricing and sale of poor-quality produce by the Italian and Jewish wholesalers, to physical threats and beatings administered by competing white retailers.

A prevailing prejudice, held by many Americans, seems to be that New York's Korean greengrocers are somehow associated with or controlled by the Unification Church of the Reverend Sun Myung Moon. In 1977 a remark linking Moon and the Korean greengrocers was rumored to have been made by one of the Hunts Point sales personnel and sparked the first mass demonstration by Koreans, ever, in New York. A hundred or more Korean greengrocers marched through the market carrying posters with such slogans as "We Are Not Moonies" and "We Are Gentlemen. Treat Us That Way."

The demonstration and the confrontation with the salesman in question were resolved peaceably. But the demonstration, in combination with the growing economic clout of Korean retailers, had the desired effect: Reports of anti-Korean acts at Hunts Point are today nonexistent, and Korean greengrocers have become accepted as a powerful part of the retailing community. (Illsoo Kim 1981b:51).

Korean merchants have organized prosperity associations in business districts of Korean business concentration since the late 1970s to ensure prosperity in the face of such serious problems as robbery, shoplifting, burglary, and racial prejudice and resentment. Anti-Korean activities by minority, especially black, residents have been a major factor behind the emergence of the prosperity associations. Since 1979, a small number of blacks have organized and engaged in systematic anti-Korean activities—distributing anti-Korean leaflets and other materials and picketing in front of Korean shops—in many commercial areas where Korean businesses are concentrated. The prosperity associations, which have come into being to deal with this kind of hostility, have somewhat less extensive and intense activities than the major business-line-based associations. One of their major purposes is to improve Korean merchants' relations with local residents or communities. The prosperity association in Brooklyn, for instance, hosted a huge community picnic where Korean foods were served to local residents and leaders. At the same time, most of the prosperity associations maintain informal relations with local police precincts in order to receive adequate police protection for their members' businesses.

CONCLUSION

Moving to New York has, for large numbers of Korean immigrants, meant entering the world of small business ownership. As I have shown, structural forces or factors largely account for this trend. There are, for one thing, the selective characteristics of Korean immigrants associated with certain "ethnic class" resources. A majority of Korean immigrants have come to New York with a middle-class background and a strong "class" motive for upward economic mobility. While they confront enormous barriers in obtaining high-level positions in the mainstream economy, they have found in small business the ideal way toward the American dream. Homeland-derived class resources—advanced education, high economic motivation, professional experience, and dollars—are decisive in supporting their massive entry into and success in small business enterprises.

Koreans accidentally encountered racial and ethnic changes in the New York metropolitan area which have greatly contributed to the proliferation of their businesses. In the face of the growth of racial and ethnic minorities in New York City, white merchants in "transitional" areas have moved out en masse, creating a business vacuum that is being filled by Korean immigrants. I also indicated that intergenerational mobility among "old" European immigrant groups has provided opportunities for Korean immigrants. Because second- and third-generation Jews and Italians have already entered the mainstream American economy, and are not interested in running their parents' or grandparents' businesses, Koreans have been able to step in and take over. That New York City is a center of international trade is another factor conducive to the development of small business enterprises among Koreans. Korean wholesalers import inexpensive consumer goods from South Korea, Hong Kong, and Taiwan and distribute them to Korean and other non-Korean "ghetto" retailers. In this context, Korean immigrants have facilitated the international trade between the United States and the Far East. Korean businesses have had other effects on New York City, giving their own stamp to fruit and vegetable stores, for example, and contributing to the revival of commercial districts in many parts of the city. Less happily, the presence of clusters of Korean merchants in transitional or ghetto areas has, at times, led to conflicts with black residents although, as I have noted, Korean businessmen have formed prosperity associations to help improve community relations.

Since Korean immigrants are "modernized" ethnics, they rely upon modern ethnic institutions—churches, the media, and businessmen's associations—in their development of small business capitalism. The Korean utilization of these modern institutions departs from the old pattern of Chinese and Japanese solidarity for business based upon kinship and regional associations. It is my view that studies of ethnic enterprise in America have not paid sufficient attention to the impact of "modern" ethnic community institutions on immigrant enterprises—or, for that matter, to the effect of homeland-derived class resources and economic opportunities in particular American urban contexts. These structural factors, so critical in Korean enterprises in New York, are, I would argue, bound to be important in understanding the involvement of other new immigrant groups in small businesses as well.

NOTES

1. This research was supported by a small research grant from Drew University.
2. A *giseng* salon is similar in many ways to a Playboy Bunny club. It is a combination of bar and restaurant where food and liquor are "personally" served by young Korean women.

REFERENCES

Bonacich, Edna and John Modell. 1980. *The Economic Basis of Ethnic Solidarity: Small Business in the Japanese American Community.* Berkeley: University of California Press.

Bonnett, Aubrey W. 1980. "An Examination of Rotating Credit Associations Among Black West Indian Immigrants in Brooklyn." In Roy S. Bryce-Laporte, ed., *Sourcebook on the New Immigration.* New Brunswick, N.J.: Transaction Books.

Cummings, Scott. 1980. "Collectivism: The Unique Legacy of Immigrant Economic Development." In Scott Cummings, ed., *Self-Help in America.* Port Washington, N.Y.: Kennikat Press.

Fratoe, Frank A. 1984. "Sociological Perspectives on Minority Ownership: A Synthesis of the Literature with Research and Policy Implications." Research report. Minority Business Development Agency, U.S. Department of Commerce.

Freedman, Marcia. 1983. "The Labor Market for Immigrants in New York City." *New York Affairs* 7:94–110.

Hurh, Won Moo and Kwang Chung Kim. 1984. *Korean Immigrants in America.* Rutherford, N.J.: Fairleigh Dickenson University Press.

Kim, Jung Keun. 1984. "The Trends and Policies of Korean Emigration." Paper presented to the Conference on Asia-Pacific Immigration to the United States, East-West Population Institute, Honolulu, Hawaii.

Kim, Kwang Chung and Won Moo Hurh. 1985. "Ethnic Resources Utilization of Korean Immigrant Entrepreneurs in the Chicago Minority Area." *International Migration Review* 19:82–111.

Kim, Illsoo. 1981a. *New Urban Immigrants: The Korean Community in New York.* Princeton: Princeton University Press.

—— 1981b. "How Korean Immigrants Saved a New York Institution." *Asia* (September/October).

—— 1984. "Korean Emigration Connections to Urban America: A Structural Analysis of Premigration Factors in South Korea." Paper presented at the Conference on Asia-Pacific Immigration to the United States, East-West Population Institute, Honolulu, Hawaii.

—— 1985. "Organizational Patterns of Korean-American Methodist Churches: Denominationalism and Personal Community." In Russell Richey and Kenneth E. Rowe, eds., *Rethinking Methodist History.* Nashville, Tenn.: United Methodist Publishing House.

Kim, Sung Soo. 1986. "Kyopo sogiop" (Korean Immigrants' Small Businesses). *The Joong Ang Ilbo,* January 2.

Koo, Hagen and Eui-Young Yu. 1981. *Korean Immigration to the United States: Its Demographic Pattern and Social Implications for Both Societies.* Honolulu, Hawaii: East-West Population Institute.

Light, Ivan. 1972. *Ethnic Enterprise in America.* Berkeley and Los Angeles: University of California Press.

—— 1985. "Immigrant Entrepreneurs in America: Koreans in Los Angeles." In Nathan Glazer, ed., *Clamor at the Gates.* San Francisco: Institute for Contemporary Studies.

Lovell-Troy, Lawrence A. 1980. "Clan Structure and Economic Activity: The Case of Greeks in Small Business Enterprises." In Scott Cummings, ed., *Self-Help in America.* Port Washington, N.Y.: Kennikat Press.

Lyman, Stanford M. 1974. *Chinese Americans.* New York: Random House.

Min, Pyong-Gap. 1984. "A Structural Analysis of Korean Business in the United States." *Ethnic Groups* 6:1–25.

U.S. Department of Commerce. Bureau of the Census. 1984. *1980 Census of Population* (PC80-1-C1). Washington, D.C.: U.S. Government Printing Office.

U.S. Department of Justice. Immigration and Naturalization Service. 1966–1979. *Annual Reports.* Washington, D.C.: U.S. Government Printing Office.

Wilson, Kenneth L. and Alejandro Portes. 1980. "Immigrant Enclaves: An

Analysis of the Labor Market Experience of Cubans in Miami." *American Journal of Sociology* 86:295–319.

Yu, Eui-Young. 1983. "Migug eui han-in sahoe" (The Korean Society in the United States). In Koo Young-Rok et al., eds., *Hangug gwa migug (Korea and the United States)*. Seoul, Korea: Bak Young Sa.

9. The Chinese: New Immigrants in New York's Chinatown

Bernard Wong

New York City's Chinatown has changed significantly since 1965. The boundaries of Chinatown have been enlarged and demographic characteristics of the community—such as population size, occupational composition, and locality of origin—have been altered. The nature of community organization, social stratification, and attitudes toward the larger society have also changed.[1]

This community in the Lower East Side of Manhattan has always been socially diverse, but it has become even more so in recent years (Wong 1976, 1982, 1985). The population includes old settlers who came before 1965, second- and third-generation American-born Chinese, new immigrants, jumped-ship sailors, and refugees from Vietnam of Chinese descent. Among the new arrivals since 1965 are professionals and unskilled workers, millionaires and paupers. The community is now home to alienated youth gangs as well as rich corporations composed of experienced businessmen from Hong Kong.

One of the most important factors responsible for these population changes was the 1965 Immigration and Nationality Act. In the past 150 years, the United States has implemented several immigration policies affecting the Chinese (Kung 1962). At first, between 1850 and 1882 there was a period of free immigration when the Chinese were welcomed to this country as a source of cheap labor (Rose Hum Lee

1960). However, this period was followed by one of exclusion and restriction. In 1882 the Chinese Exclusion Law was passed by Congress, barring Chinese from admission to the United States, with the exception of certain special categories of people such as spouses and minor children of U.S. citizens, teachers, and ministers. Subsequent modifications of this law over the next sixty years were even more restrictive. It was not until 1965 that significant positive changes in immigration legislation were enacted. The 1965 law abolished the "national origins" quotas and established a system of preferences whereby immediate relatives, skilled and unskilled workers, refugees, scientists, and technical personnel were listed under different categories of preference. For the first time, Chinese immigrants were treated equally with other nationalities by U.S. immigration law, thus ending some eighty-five years of bias against the Chinese. Many Chinese once again flocked to the United States, and New York was a major area of settlement. According to the 1980 census, there were about 82,000 people born in China and Hong Kong living in the New York metropolitan area (Kraly, this volume). When we consider people of Chinese ancestry, not just Chinese birth, the numbers of course are even higher. The population of Chinese ancestry in the New York metropolitan area swelled to a high of 158,588 in 1980 (U.S. Bureau of the Census 1982). Of this number, 80,000 resided in the Chinatown area. Other areas of Chinese concentration are the southern part of Brooklyn and the Jackson Heights, Flushing, and Elmhurst sections of Queens.

The increase of the Chinese population in the Chinatown area has had a direct effect on the boundaries of Chinatown. Today's Chinese population on the Lower East Side has expanded beyond the Mott-Mulberry-Canal area north to Houston Street, south to the piers, east to Allen Street, and west to Broadway. The commercial areas of Chinatown have also branched out from the traditional core area (Mott, Pell, Bayard, Doyer Streets) to include Mulberry, Canal, the Bowery, East Broadway, Catherine, Hester, Elizabeth, and Grand Streets. Thus, both residential and commercial areas of Chinatown have expanded and other ethnic territories have been penetrated. There is an effort to establish another Chinatown in the Flushing area of Queens. All of these expansions are the direct result of population increases attributable to the 1965 immigration law.

The 1965 immigration law and the subsequent Chinese migration to New York City have not only changed the geographical boundaries and population size of Chinatown but also the social and economic characteristics of the people in the community. Chinatown is now mainly occupied by Chinese who intend to stay in the United States permanently, as opposed to the sojourners of the past (see Wong 1982). Before 1965 Chinatown was dominated by people from Kwangtung Province, mostly from the county of Toysan. Not surprisingly, the lingua franca in those years was the Toysan dialect. Today, although people from Kwangtung still make up more than half of the population there are also many people from North China, Shanghai, Hong Kong, Fukien, and Taiwan. Standard Cantonese, as spoken in the cities of Hong Kong, Macao, and Canton, is now the lingua franca of Chinatown. Speakers of other dialects such as Mandarin, Fukienese, Shanghainese, and Hakka have to learn the Cantonese dialect of Chinatown in order to communicate with shopkeepers and coworkers. Mandarin speakers, however, are more likely to be understood in Chinatown today than before 1965 because many young Cantonese also learn the national language (Mandarin) and because Chinatown has many Mandarin-speaking immigrants from Taiwan and mainland China.

Before 1945, there were very few women and children in Chinatown, and the population mainly consisted of male sojourners. The female population in Chinatown has gradually grown since 1945—initially with the influx of Chinese war brides. Only after 1965, however, did the sex ratio narrow significantly. In 1960 the male/female ratio was 2:1. In 1980 it became nearly equal.

The recent migration stream includes some extremely wealthy individuals from Hong Kong who have fled with their capital, due to the uncertain situation in the colony. Hong Kong's lease will expire in 1997, when the People's Republic of China (PRC) will claim sovereignty over Hong Kong. Although an agreement between Great Britain and the PRC has been signed and an extension of the present system of capitalism has been pledged, there is still fear among the very rich in Hong Kong. Many have contemplated abandoning their businesses; some have transferred their major assets to New York City; and others have already migrated. As I will explore later, the availability of "flight capital" has been responsible for the speculative activities in real estate and for various modernization projects in Chinatown.

Most recent immigrants, of course, are not wealthy and most did not move to New York to protect their assets. In fact, most new immigrants came to New York to improve their economic well-being and for the future education of their children. The majority are of urban background; some came with considerable educational and professional attainments. As compared with old settlers, the new immigrants consider themselves to be more "genteel," more literate and more modern as most of them lived in Hong Kong at least for a period of time (having originally come from urban areas in the PRC) and some were born and raised in that international city. They feel that the old settlers are "country bumpkins" with unrefined manners who came from rural areas of the old land. Most old settlers do have peasant origins in China, and their life-styles before emigration were very different from those of the new immigrants. That new immigrants and old settlers have such different social and economic backgrounds helps to explain why their experiences in New York have diverged in so many ways. This essay will show that other factors are also important, including the different resources and opportunities available to the two groups of immigrants in New York and the immigrants' intentions to stay, or eventually leave, the United States.

POLITICAL ADAPTATION OF
NEW IMMIGRANTS

Moving to New York has led to numerous changes in the lives of new immigrants as they adapt to life in their new home. Many newcomers to Chinatown, as I already mentioned, have had to learn Cantonese to get by in the community. Many have also come to rely on American-style social service organizations and have become willing to use American political methods. Some have, on occasion, rallied together through new associations to further the interests of the Chinese community. Such political activities are a new feature of the Chinatown scene and represent a departure from the political behavior and beliefs of old settlers.

One major difference between new immigrants and old settlers is in the types of associations they form and use. The traditional power structure—the Consolidated Chinese Benevolent Association (CCBA) and affiliated associations—simply cannot adequately handle the problems of the new immigrants. These associations, established in the pre-1965 era, principally served the financial, social, and emotional needs of the old settlers who were single males, and they recruited members mainly on the basis of traditional kinship and friendship ties and locality of origin, family name, and dialect similarities. The leaders of the major traditional associations, who sat on the governing board of the CCBA, claimed to speak for the community as a whole. Even in the old days, the CCBA was not an effective organization in representing the community. The leaders were not familiar with U.S. society. Many could not even speak the English language. As sojourners, many old settlers were not interested in any kind of assistance from the American government. They wanted to socialize with people who spoke the same dialect, and they sought mutual financial and emotional support through various family name, hometown, and linguistic associations. Some were primarily interested in having a burial service handled by their hometown or surname associations. In the 1940s, to be buried first in New York City and later exhumed and reburied in China was a concern of many old settlers (Rose Hum Lee 1960). New immigrants have no such wishes, since they intend to make their permanent home in the United States, pursuing the "American dream" (Hsu 1971). Such problems as housing, education, family disputes, teenage gangs, medical assistance, and social security benefits are very much on new immigrants' minds. Realizing the inadequacies of traditional associations, new immigrants have formed new associations and use modern social service organizations. In fact, the community is no longer controlled by the monolithic power structure of the CCBA and its affiliates (James Lee 1972).

The community is coordinated today by three groups of associations: traditional, new, and modern social service organizations. While some new immigrants belong to traditional associations, most depend on new associations and social service organizations to solve problems that they encounter in day-to-day living. In addition to the limitations of traditional associations, several other factors account for this preference. One is the new immigrants' educational background. Many have learned about the workings of the U.S. government as well as the New York Chinatown community from books or newspapers published in Chinese. As I mentioned earlier, the new immigrants tend to be urban and aggressive; they are diligent in seeking information relevant to their new lives. Moreover, modern social service agencies get results. Newly arrived immigrants have learned from kinsmen or friends of the effectiveness of the various social service organizations in Chinatown. Modern social service agencies like the Chinatown Planning Council and Chinatown Health Clinic have the financial resources and connections to help the new immigrants. There is also the language factor. Most of the modern social service organizations and new associations are run by Cantonese-speaking people, many of whom are new immigrants themselves. Similar background and linguistic convenience thus facilitate communication. The new immigrants do not feel at ease in their dealings with the old settlers who speak a different dialect and who migrated from rural China with different sets of social values and habits.

New associations, which recruit members on the basis of common interests, professions, or educational background, have multiplied in size and number in the past two decades, so that by 1980 there were over 200 in Chinatown. Most of these associations—alumni groups, for example—are social and recreational in orientation, although three, including the Organization of Chinese-Americans, are actively concerned with Chinese civil rights. As for modern social service organizations, they have assumed many of the functions that used to be performed by traditional associations. Such organizations include state- or federally funded agencies and nonprofit charitable groups that have appeared in the past two decades. The Chinatown Advisory Council, for example, established in 1970, is made up of representatives from the government and from schools, churches, and hospitals in the Chinatown area. It provides immigrants with help in finding housing and jobs and obtaining health care and also mediates between the immigrants and institutions of the larger society.

Many of the new associations and social service organizations have played an important role in introducing new immigrants to American customs. The leaders of these associations are often new immigrants who are familiar with the workings of U.S. society and who are capable social workers. Some work in Chinatown as career social workers, community developers, or volunteers. In any event, new immigrants who belong to new associations or utilize social service organizations are clearly interested in participating in the resource distribution of the larger society. Unlike their predecessors, who shunned the confrontational approach, a good number of new immigrants are willing to use such American methods as strikes, petitions, and demonstrations to obtain their goals. They have learned these methods in this country through the mass media, especially television and newspapers. Further, instead of using Chinatown as a colony for the transmission of traditional culture as the old settlers did, new immigrants prefer to use Chinese ethnicity as a base for the formation of an interest group (see Wong 1977). Having lived in an era of intense racism against Chinese, old settlers came to feel that any intimate contacts with the larger society would invite trouble and they isolated, and still isolate, themselves from the mainstream of American life. Most of the new immigrants do not want to isolate themselves and the community from the larger society. On the contrary, they would like to see their community as an integral part of the city as well as of the wider U.S. society. Thus, Chinatown is not an "unmeltable" ethnic community (Novak 1972). Rather, it is an assimilable community with an interest in changing its ethnic boundaries (Fredrik Barth 1969).

The new immigrants, of course, are not a homogeneous group. Some are highly educated and sophisticated about the United States; others have little education and are unfamiliar with the politics of American society. As compared to old settlers, however, significantly more new immigrants have become knowledgeable about, and involved in, the American political process and this is in part due to the fact that new immigrants, as a group, are better educated than earlier settlers. Not only do new immigrants know they have to organize as a united front with all co-ethnics, they are also eager to cooperate with other ethnic groups to fight for equal rights and equal justice (Wong 1982). New immigrant leaders have on occasion sought alliances with other minority groups, especially with other Asians, who have similar cultural backgrounds and have encountered similar types of discrimination. Politically ambitious citizens have participated in city and state elections for various offices. Along with second-generation Chinese, some new immigrants have been instrumental in persuading the community to organize collective actions such as the 1983–84 fight against the decision to build a prison near Chinatown. Though this effort failed to change the New York City mayor's decision concerning the prison, the petitioning, picketing, and demonstrations have been important for the community: they indicate a determination to use American methods to obtain political goals. In recent years, moreover, various government institutions in the Chinatown area have been successfully pressured by the modern community organizations in Chinatown to employ more Chinese-Americans.

New immigrant activists have also learned that, to participate in the resource distribution of American society, they must organize their own interest groups to lobby the U.S. Congress for passage of favorable legislation and against enactment of unfavorable bills. Recently, the Organization of Chinese-Americans (OCA), one of the new associations with many new immigrant members, lobbied for passage of the Urban Jobs Enterprise Zone Act (1981) and the Voting Rights Act (1980). In 1983, the OCA also urged a Senate subcommittee to lift restrictive immigration quotas for colonies (Hong Kong was included). The limited quota for Hong Kong means that, apart from spouses, minor children, and parents of U.S. citizens, only 600 people born in Hong Kong may be legally admitted as immigrants each year. Many new immigrants from Hong Kong realize that brothers and sisters of U.S. citizens waiting in Hong Kong may face between six and eleven or more years to be reunited. Some new immigrant activists have formed coalitions with other ethnic groups who have similar incentives for wanting the colonial quota repealed. And on other occasions new Chinese immigrants have allied with Hispanic and West Indian immigrants on immigration-related issues. This kind of political involvement and interest in achieving results through political participation are notable only since the arrival of the new immigrants.

In the pre-1965 era, citizens in the community generally ignored American political life. After the influx of large numbers of educated immigrants, and a changed political climate that gave minority groups more political scope than before, many in the community began to learn the meaning of participatory democracy and to recognize that Chinatown cannot solve all its problems alone. The prison construction issue and the fight against gentrification that I discuss in a later section have made clear to many in the community how important it is for the Chinese population to be involved in city politics. In fact, editorials in various Chinese community newspapers have discussed the painful results of ignoring events of the larger society. The majority of these papers were founded by new immigrants and are alert to any anti-Chinese sentiments around the United States and elsewhere in the world.[2] The newspapers have frequently chastized "isolationists" in the community and stressed the need for developing public consciousness and the importance of political participation in the United States.

NEW IMMIGRANTS AND THE LAW

Recent immigrants also have a new orientation toward the law now that they have moved to the United States—one that differs from the attitudes of the old settlers. In the old country, the Chinese were passive toward law enforcement institutions. In traditional China, as well as in old Chinatown, a saying held that "one does not go to government offices while living, one does not go to hell when dead." Among new immigrants, this saying is no longer valid.

New immigrants are sensitive to social injustices against Chinese-Americans. Cases like the murder of Vincent Chin in Detroit (June 1982), the shooting of Asian-Americans in Davis, California (1984), discrimination against Chinese-American businesses in Washington, D.C., the assault on the Chinese in Grand Ledge, Michigan (January 1984), and the shooting death of a Chinese immigrant by police on Long Island (June 1982) not only aroused indignation in the community, they also made immigrants aware of racism in America. Unlike their forebears, the new immigrants, as I already indicated, have learned that, to participate in American society, they have to fight individually and collectively for their rights, to use litigation, strikes, demonstrations, and other methods of confrontation.

Police harassment and brutality against citizens of Chinatown are reported in Chinese newspapers. Some citizens are not afraid to complain to the police or to civil rights organizations about official harassment. Most recently, in a case of alleged police brutality involving a Chinese immigrant motorist, the police accused the motorist of assault and resisting arrest. The immigrant claimed that he was beaten up by two police officers simply because he was asking questions about the parking ticket they were giving him, and he took his case to court. Disregarding the merits of the case and the outcome of litigation, the motorist's reaction is significant because it shows that some new immigrants are not afraid to go to court to redress grievances.

In the old days, there was a saying in Chinatown that "good son will not be a soldier." This premise is no longer relevant in Chinatown. Chinese-Americans now serve in various branches of the armed forces as well as in the police force. The Fifth Precinct in Chinatown employs Chinese police officers, translators, and civilians. The new immigrants are not hesitant to use the police to solve problems and to fight crime.

While old settlers shunned dealings with the U.S. courts, new immigrants have a desire to use the law enforcement system of the United States to keep the streets safe. Not only will new immigrants assist the police in apprehending criminals, but many also serve as witnesses when called, and some even become involved in cases against Chinese youth gang members. People outside the Chinatown community often believe that Chinese immigrants condone Chinese youth gangs. In fact, the majority in the community despise those *Tongs* (or secret societies) that engage in illicit activities such as extortion for protection, gambling, prostitution, and drugs—and the youth gangs that carry out orders from elders of the *Tongs*. In the old days, old immigrants were afraid to confront assailants, even in court. Several years ago, a leading businessman, who was a new immigrant in the community, gave a speech at a public meeting indicating that he would help put criminals in the youth gangs in prison, regardless of their ages. He was later stabbed. After convalescence, he identified the assailant in court. This kind of cooperation with the law is indeed a new phenomenon. New immigrants have learned the American way in handling criminals.

Although nearly all new immigrants want to rid Chinatown of gangs—and a few are even willing to help fight them—gang problems actually seem to be related to the new immigration. Betty Lee Sung (1979) found that almost all gang members in Chinatown were new immigrants from Hong Kong and all were under eighteen years of age. One reason for the predominance of Hong Kong emigrants among gang members is simply that most Chinatown residents come from Hong Kong (even if they only lived there for a while) and are Cantonese speakers. Children migrating directly from Taiwan or mainland China are fewer in number and many speak no Cantonese, so numerical and linguistic factors delimit gang membership (Sung 1979). While it is difficult to establish direct connections between New York gangs and secret societies in Hong Kong, gang activity is not uncommon in Hong Kong. It may well be that gang members in Chinatown were exposed to certain influences in Hong Kong at a young age that predisposed them to join gangs after they emigrated (Sung 1979). Perhaps some were already gang members in Hong Kong. Gangs are less of a problem in Taiwan and mainland China, where criminals, including young criminals, are severely punished (Sung 1979).

The gangs in Chinatown have a particular appeal to young people experiencing difficulties in adjusting to American life. The change from a Chinese-speaking school in Hong Kong to an English-speaking school in New York City creates many problems for newly arrived immigrant children. Instructional difficulty, alienation, loss of self-esteem because of poor school performance, ethnic conflicts, and confrontation in the public school system impose great pressures on young children, especially those who have no close family members in whom to confide. Socially, the "American dream" becomes an illusion. Many young people join gangs for protection and excitement, and some are under peer group pressure to affiliate with a gang.

Gang membership in New York's Chinatown, despite much publicity, is not large. Police think there are only several (two to three) hundred members. My informants suggested 500, including the inactive ones. Gang membership also fluctuates as gang members inevitably dissociate themselves after age 19 since American courts deal more severely with adults than with juveniles. In the past twenty years, gangs have disbanded and organized with names like Black Eagles, White Eagles, Quon Yings, Ernie's Boys, Fukien, etc. (Sung 1979). In 1984, the major gangs in Chinatown were the Ghost Shadows and the Flying Dragons. The major gangs in 1984 worked for two

Tongs, the On Leong or Hip Sing Associations. The On Leong group controlled Mott Street, while the Hip Sing affiliates controlled Pell Street and the Bowery.

ECONOMIC ADAPTATION OF NEW IMMIGRANTS

The overall economic performance of the Chinese in the United States as compared to other nonwhite ethnic groups is impressive. In New York City, as in the rest of the country, many second-, third-, or fourth-generation Chinese have attended college or professional schools and, after graduation, they usually prefer to work for white American establishments. In fact, the professional Chinese in New York tend not to be Chinatown connected, living instead in middle-class neighborhoods. Although some go to Chinatown to practice their trades, most do not live in the community.

New immigrants who live in Chinatown are heavily concentrated in service and factory work. Indeed, whether they are new or old immigrants, most Chinatown residents depend on the ethnic niche— although, as I will demonstrate, new and old immigrant entrepreneurs differ in terms of the types of businesses they engage in and the management methods they use.

Occupational Patterns

Laundries, restaurants, and grocery stores were traditionally the stereotypical businesses of the Chinese in New York. These businesses are still important, but today the Chinese in the city have also moved into other lines of work.

Census data for 1970 on the occupational distribution of people of Chinese ancestry in New York City indicate that 36 percent of the Chinese men in the labor force were service workers connected with Chinese establishments, while 43 percent of the employed females were operatives, mostly seamstresses. The same census also shows that the second most important occupational group for males was professional and technical, accounting for 19 percent of the Chinese male labor force; for females, it was clerical work, with 25 percent of the Chinese female labor force. The relative importance of these four occupational groups was the same in 1985. The ethnic niche, which is composed of restaurants, garment factories, grocery stores, and other types of Chinese-run businesses, still employs the largest group of Chinese in New York City, including a very high proportion of new immigrants. According to my informants, in 1985, some 50,000 Chinese in the city worked in Chinese garment factories and restaurants. Chinese professionals and other white-collar workers are the second most numerous group. Although the majority of these workers are not connected with Chinatown, some new immigrants who live in Chinatown hold clerical and other white-collar jobs outside the community. Within Chinatown itself, people mainly work in ethnic businesses. Other occupations include a small group of professionals—physicians, accountants, lawyers, and journalists—who serve the Chinese-speaking residents in the community.

The unemployment rate is low in Chinatown. Census data for 1970 indicated a 2.8 percent unemployment rate among Chinese in New York City, and in Chinatown it was perhaps lower than 2 percent. The unemployment situation was similar in 1985. Yet behind these impressive statistics lies a distressing fact, namely, that many new immigrants are not working according to their potential, training, or education. Due to their lack of English proficiency and unfamiliarity with American society, many qualified technicians and professionals have to work at menial jobs and thus function under capacity.

Some of these workers, of course, will eventually improve their positions. In general, new immigrants who are not proficient in English mainly find avenues for mobility in ethnic businesses. Those who begin as workers may end up accumulating enough savings to start their own small restaurant, garment factory, or laundromat.

Business Activity and Family Firms

Business activity among new immigrants in Chinatown differs from that among pre-1965 arrivals in terms of the kinds of businesses entered and methods of management. In addition to traditional Chinese businesses like restaurants, gift shops, grocery stores, and laundries, some new immigrants operate travel agencies and bookkeeping offices. Garment factories now constitute the major ethnic niche in Chinatown and the vast majority of the 500 garment factories in the community in 1985 (actually "assembly plants" for American garment manufacturers) were controlled by new immigrants. Table 9.1 compares the kinds of Chinese businesses new and old immigrants run. New immigrants not only control garment factories but also laundromats, bookstores, and certain types of Chinese restaurants in Chinatown, while old settlers monopolize most branches of the laundry trade and Cantonese restaurants.

Many new immigrants organize and establish their businesses through the use of family members—something that is increasingly

Table 9.1. Relationship Between Types of Chinese Businesses in Chinatown and Types of Chinese (1984)

Type of Chinese Business	Subtypes	Controlled by
Laundries	Washer plants Presser plants Collection and delivery stores Complete service hand laundry	Old settlers
	Laundromats	New immigrants
Restaurants	Chop suey restaurants Snack and coffee shops Cantonese restaurants	Both old settlers and new immigrants
	Shanghai, Peking, Hunan, Szechuan restaurants	New immigrants
Garment factories	Skirts, blouses, and sportswear	New immigrants
Travel agencies, law, accounting and insurance firms		Mostly second-generation Chinese-Americans
Groceries		Both old settlers and new immigrants
Gift stores		Both old settlers and new immigrants
Bookstores		Mostly new immigrants

possible now that so many immigrant families have arrived in recent years. Family firms are much less common among old settlers, and most family firms in New York's Chinatown are run by new immigrant families.

In the pre-1965 era, few men in Chinatown had families with them, save those who sent for their children and wives before the 1924 Quota Act and those who sponsored their war brides shortly after 1945. Thus, for some time Chinatown was labeled a bachelor society (Wu 1958; Rose Hum Lee 1960; Beck 1898). Apart from traditional hand laundries and small-scale chop suey restaurants, there were few family member firms among old settlers. Old settlers who set up businesses often did so through partnerships with kinsmen and friends. Rich old settlers in the pre-1965 period tended to be partners in different businesses at the same time—multiple shareholders, as it were. As for second- and third-generation Chinese, born and raised in the United States, they are not particularly interested in returning to Chinatown to work. Some are college-educated and professionally trained and prefer to work in American establishments. Those second- or third-generation Chinese professionals who have returned to Chinatown tend to run travel agencies and law, accounting, and insurance firms which require fluency in English and Chinese. In fact, some educated new immigrants who have the capital also have become involved in these types of business. Chinatown is reputed to be a gold mine for bilingual lawyers and accountants. I met several American-born lawyers of Chinese descent who are studying Cantonese for the sole purpose of making money from the immigrants. The enterprises that appeal to bilingual members of the second and third generations, however, are not run along family lines. As in the past, family members of second- and third-generation Chinese are seldom involved in business activities in Chinatown; they feel it is more rewarding and more comfortable to work with U.S. firms. Indeed, new immigrants in Chinatown today hope that their children will not be dependent on traditional Chinese businesses and will enter such professions as medicine, engineering, and law.

New immigrants themselves, however, are still firm believers in family businesses. Not all new immigrant businesses, of course, are run by families. Some new immigrants are involved in partnerships and corporations that have been formed by shareholders and partners who are not related to each other. In a number of cases, new immigrants have learned about such business opportunities through notices in local Chinese newspapers inviting people to become shareholders or partners in well-known restaurants and garment factories. However, the majority of new immigrant entrepreneurs prefer to run family firms for the sake of flexibility, independence, and greater control over their workers. Use of family ties in the family firm environment can bring other advantages. Family members can be trained in business operations; they are trustworthy and able to keep trade secrets; they are willing to put in more hours; and they are an important source of financing, many firms having been established through pooling of family members' savings. Kinsmen of the family also constitute an inexpensive labor pool.

Many new immigrants are in the garment industry where flexibility is especially important. Garment factories are highly competitive and business is seasonal. Firms that cannot cope with fluctuating demands in the New York market can easily go bankrupt. However, those Chinese businesses run by the family have greater endurance and flexibility. When business is slow, family members do all the work themselves and thus cut down on outside help. In adverse situations, family members can simply stop their salaries or reduce the profit for every garment. Low profit margins and reduced production costs in the family firm environment have thus enabled many family-run garment factories to survive.

Family firms among new immigrants come into being due to the initial efforts of their founders who are usually heads of the families. Beyond this, however, there are several different ways that such firms are started. One way to set up a firm is for family members, who will work in the business, to pool resources to supply capital and equipment. A second method involves several years of hard work in New York on the part of the family head. After he has accumulated enough savings and has borrowed funds from friends, he sponsors family members so they can come to New York. All family members live under one roof, if possible, or try to live in the same neighborhood so they can eat together during the day, thus saving money, food, and time. A third way many family firms start is by a process of fusion and fission. Initially, a person will cooperate with friends or kinsmen to set up a firm. After some profits are made, one partner will buy the whole firm and the others will get a share of the profits and leave. The person who buys the firm then reorganizes it into one of the kinds of family businesses I discuss below.

Types of Family Firms

In general, there are three types of family firms run by new immigrants. Type 1 firms are owned, managed, and staffed only by family members and kinsmen; type 2 firms are run by a core group of family members with some outside employees; and type 3 firms are run by a core group composed of family members with a labor boss and his staff. In the family firm environment, the family head is often the major decision maker. He plays the role of father, patron, and friend in his relationships with family members, employees, and the labor boss. Thus, relationships among firm members are based on kinship, friendship, and patron-client ties.

Many small-size businesses in Chinatown are of the type 1 variety, run by an entire family group. Benefiting from the 1965 immigration law changes, some new immigrants arrived in this country with entire families—an important economic resource. In the type 1 family firm run by the entire family group, the family head is usually the father or the oldest effective male. The family is an economic unit both in production and consumption. Every family member who can help works in the firm and contributes to the common resources. Wives, parents (normally only one set of parents, either the husband's or wife's), and children usually get only the money they need for daily living. Those who work in the firm take their meals together; food is provided from the common kitchen. Taking meals together saves manpower, since only one person cooks and shops. Communal eating also saves money in that costly equipment is purchased together and food can be bought in bulk. Although family members can bring expenditures up for discussion, the decisions are generally made by the family head. The family firm is also a business training center for family members. Children learn various aspects of business operation from working in the family firm.

Family firms of the type 1 sort are extremely durable, enduring through sagging economic conditions and slow business seasons. They also facilitate the generation of family wealth among new immigrants, since everyone contributes to the family resources through savings. The wealth accumulated in this way is generally spent on family necessities such as houses, cars, and education of the children. The dream of many new immigrants is to send their children to college to train them to be professionals.

The second type of family firm is run by a core group of family members with some assistance from outsiders, who are hired only because the family cannot supply all the needed workers. Usually, this kind of family firm has a sizable group of employees. Many garment factories in Chinatown have thirty to eighty employees, so outsiders must be hired. Likewise, medium-sized Chinese restaurants need outside help. Members of the core group are insiders who are familiar with business operations, and they also make routine day-to-day decisions. Family members usually contribute both capital and expertise to the firm, since, as new immigrants, no one person commands enough capital for a medium-sized business. Thus, many new immigrants in this kind of family firm are both shareholders/ business partners and workers at the same time.

The third kind of family firm, run by the family with assistance from a labor boss and his staff, is commonly found in medium- and large-sized Chinese establishments. What differentiates this type of family firm from the type 2 sort is that here there are two separate groups of personnel in the firm, and an outsider labor boss heads one of these groups, composed of his hired employees. The other group, made up of family members, is supervised by the family head, who is also responsible for the management and operation of the entire firm. In terms of authority structure, the family head is thus the supreme authority, a superpatron for everyone in the firm. The outsider labor boss is a patron for his staff (compare Bennett and Ishino 1963 on the Japanese labor boss system). He may work alongside his subordinates, and a close esprit de corps may develop among them. The labor boss trains his employees and, at times, even assumes the position of foster-father-cum-teacher of his younger staff members. He can hire his own workers, recruiting his relatives, friends, and people with whom he has ties of locality of origin and dialect.

To sum up, then, many firms in the post-1965 era have been established with the help of family members because these people are available. In fact, the use of family members in new immigrant businesses represents a successful economic adaptation in a competitive urban environment. Family firms allow flexibility and can withstand market fluctuations. Moreover, family members are important for capital formation and they also provide labor resources and generate high productivity.

Methods for Obtaining Employment

The discussion of family firms clearly indicates how important family and kinship ties are for new immigrants looking for employment. There are also other ways to obtain employment: through friendship networks; various family and alumni associations; and employment and social service agencies. Although many immigrants have had to accept lower-status jobs than they held before emigration, the fact is that obtaining employment in Chinatown is easy if one is willing to work at a menial job. Indeed, the Chinatown Study Group (1969) found that a major reason why Chinese immigrants moved to Chinatown in the first place was that they had friends and relatives—and knew there were job opportunities—in the area.

Family members, kinsmen, and friends in the New York Chinese community, as in overseas Chinese communities elsewhere (Wong 1984:230), are given priority in employment. The unique aspect of employment in the New York Chinese community today is the special preference given family members and relatives who may not even be in the United States. That is, the cohesiveness of the kinship network is not necessarily diminished by geographical distance. Since 1965, U.S. immigration policy has favored the migration of immediate relatives, and Chinese businessmen, especially after they have their own firms, want to sponsor relatives from Hong Kong or Taiwan who will work for them when they move to New York. Major reasons for this preference are: (1) the belief that family members and kinsmen are more trustworthy than outsiders; (2) the expectation that kinsmen will work harder; (3) the fact that it is cheaper for a businessman to sponsor kinsmen employees from Hong Kong or Taiwan than to hire a Chinese or an American from this country; and (4) the desire to live up to the cultural expectation that successful immigrants will sponsor family members so they can migrate to the United States.

Chinese employers prefer to hire friends as well as kinsmen, and they also give priority to people from their locality back home and those who speak their dialect. No high degree of specialization exists along kinship lines in today's Chinatown so that, for example, Chans or Lees do not dominate any sector of Chinatown's economy. Yet there is some specialization along regional and linguistic lines. All Cantonese hand laundries are run by people from Kwangtung, and most owners are from the county of Toysan in Kwangtung Province. Shanghainese, Szechuan, and Peking restaurants are run by Mandarin-speaking people, which means northerners. Real estate companies and garment factories tend to be controlled by, and give preference in hiring to, Cantonese-speaking immigrants from Hong Kong.

In addition to using traditional kinship, friendship, and family relationships, new immigrants sometimes secure employment through social networks in various Chinatown associations (Wong 1977), especially the Consolidated Chinese Benevolent Association (CCBA). New immigrants also use alumni groups and regional and dialect associations to obtain jobs. Increasingly, new immigrants turn to employment agencies in the community, which have played a more important role in the past twenty years with the expansion of Chinatown and the growing number of Chinese businesses. These agencies principally place job seekers with Chinatown establishments. Since the agency owner and staff are bilingual immigrants, they can also negotiate with American employment brokers in mid-Manhattan. They refer suitable Chinese applicants to the mid-Manhattan brokers and, in return, receive a commission fee for the referrals. Social workers in Chinatown social agencies such as the Chinese Development Council and Chinatown Planning Council are also instrumental in helping new immigrants obtain jobs outside of Chinatown. Thus, these social workers are not simply employment brokers, but culture brokers linking the Chinese community with the outside world. Traditionally, this function was performed mainly by the CCBA. Today, due to funding available from the federal and state government, many bilingual social workers have established social agencies that not only serve the Chinese community but make the community more open to the larger society.

A major change, then, from the pre-1965 era is that there are new avenues for gaining employment—social agencies, for example, new associations, and commercial employment organizations. Moreover, in the pre-1965 era most Chinese worked within the community. Today, more jobs are available to Chinese outside the Chinatown area because of reduced discrimination. Given their educational backgrounds, many new immigrants have been able to obtain such positions.

NEW IMMIGRANTS AND THEIR
IMPACT ON NEW YORK CITY

The new immigrants have not simply adapted to life in New York City. They have influenced the city as well: in housing, banking, labor unions, travel businesses, and the real estate market. Indeed, they have changed Chinatown itself in many crucial ways.

Gentrification of Chinatown

The recent influx of new immigrants as well as capital from Hong Kong have led to dramatic transformations in the Chinatown community. Not only have the borders of Chinatown expanded but there are growing pressures for gentrification.

Since 1965, Chinatown has experienced a marked housing shortage. Most recently, Chinatown has spread into nearby neighborhoods of Manhattan's Lower East Side. Some real estate developers have called this expansion the "modernization" of the community. This term is used because expansion also involves the upgrading of buildings, the construction of new high-rises, and the replacement of small business firms by high-rent office facilities. Meanwhile, longtime Chinatown residents face rising rents, and many traditionally family-run restaurants and garment factories have had to move to sections of Brooklyn or Queens.

This process of upgrading, or gentrification, has split the community. Some residents are determined to fight gentrification for practical, economic, or philosophical reasons. Practically, older residents are used to the convenience of shopping and to the warmth of the old culture which the community engenders. One can stroll through Chinatown's streets, speaking a familiar dialect and addressing others with traditional kinship terms, something that is especially important for older Chinese who cannot speak English. Economically, some believe that building new offices at the expense of traditional Chinese businesses will ruin the livelihood of many people. It is said that new offices will provide few jobs for community residents, since not many have training in English. Many small garment factories and restaurants, which have been important economic bases for the community, also face increased rent. Their absence would deprive many people of jobs and change the nature of the community. Philosophically, the argument is that expansion is a case of the "haves" expelling the "have-nots"—big businesses driving out small businesses. In fact, modernization appears to be favored by wealthy Chinese rather than by economically disadvantaged newcomers. Community groups such as Asian Americans for Equality and the Asian-American Legal Defense Fund have launched great efforts to fight gentrification, and among their concerns is the fate of new immigrants who are still to come. Manhattan's Chinatown is not just an economic center, but also an ethnic and enculturation center for new immigrants, who use Chinatown as an entrepôt—a transitional place, a stepping-stone to American society.

The plans for the modernization of Chinatown typify two common phenomena in the United States: the disappearance of traditional ethnic neighborhoods that preserved many Old World features, and emerging conflicts between old and new immigrants (Wong 1976). Early arrivals who have established themselves see no problems with the modernization or gentrification of Chinatown. They believe Chinatown should have more office spaces for professionals, for instance, and better housing for middle-class Chinese. Real estate brokers, condominium developers, landlords, speculators, and bankers are also in favor of modernization. Most new immigrants prefer to have a modernized appearance for Chinatown. On the other hand, they oppose modernization projects for they cannot afford the exorbitant rents for their residential or business facilities that modernization will bring.

What factors are responsible for the trend toward modernization or gentrification in the community? As I have emphasized, Chinatown needs more living space given the tremendous influx of new immigrants since 1965, and there is a pressing demand for better housing from the general Chinese population. Other Asians, and some non-Asians, also want to live in the community for convenience and local color. People who work in the Wall Street area find that Chinatown is not only close to their offices but peaceful and full of excellent and inexpensive restaurants. In addition to the demand for housing, two other forces have contributed to gentrification: the city government's encouragement of high-rise housing construction in the area and the influx of capital from Hong Kong.[3] Part of the capital influx is a result of the deliberate movement of cash by some wealthy Hong Kong Chinese who are worried about the future of Hong Kong, and part appears to be attributable to a "natural inflow" since the United States is the British colony's primary trading partner. Among the rich in Hong Kong there is a saying that Hong Kong Chinese already own Vancouver, half of San Francisco, half of Toronto, and what is left is part of New York City. The availability of Hong Kong capital has driven up Chinatown's real estate values, and the demand for real estate now far exceeds the supply. As a result, the value of land per square foot is on a par with that in the fashionable areas of Manhattan's Fifth Avenue. So far, real estate purchases by Chinese and Chinese-American investors have been estimated at $150 million in 1983 and most of the transactions have been in Manhattan (*New York Times*, September 21, 1984).

Manhattan's Chinatown may be the main area for real estate investment by Chinese and Chinese-Americans, but parts of Brooklyn and the Flushing section of Queens are also prime areas. Real estate developers and the New York Chinese press have been spreading rumors about the establishment of a "second Chinatown" in Flushing, and newcomers from Hong Kong have purchased property there with "flight capital."[4] Indeed, people and businesses have moved to Flushing, although these movements have not been as great as expected. The craze for real estate in Manhattan's Chinatown and in Flushing may well be an artificial phenomenon, directly related to, and therefore subject to, changing political and economic arrangements between China and Great Britain.

Other Changes

In addition to influencing the real estate market, the new Chinese immigration has had other effects—both within and outside of the Chinatown community.

The presence of so many new immigrants has stimulated the growth of the banking industry in Chinatown. Immigrants, as many economists note, tend to work hard and are eager to accumulate savings, and the Chinese are no exception. They are frugal and save money for such major expenditures as houses, appliances, and automobiles. As a result, many major banks in New York have opened branch offices in Chinatown. Realizing the lucrative nature of banking in Chinatown, some affluent Chinese businessmen from Hong Kong and Taiwan have also organized banks to cater to new immigrants. By 1985, in an area of less than two square miles, there were already fifteen banks and, according to one informant's estimate, they employed more than 400 people, mainly non-Chinese New Yorkers. This is in marked contrast to the pre-1965 era when there were only a handful of banks in the community, employing not more than 100 people.

Various labor unions will soon have to deal with the increasing number of Chinese union members in their ranks. In 1985, there were more than 20,000 Chinese factory workers, most union members, in the 500 Chinese garment factories. So far, the higher echelons of the International Ladies Garment Workers' Union (ILGWU) have been white Americans. To serve members better, the ILGWU needs more Chinese professionals (such as lawyers, accountants, and managers) who can speak both English and Chinese. In the restaurant trade, Chinese workers fear that the existing labor union will discriminate against Chinese because of traditional prejudice and racism and because no union officials speak Chinese. As a result, Chinese restaurant workers have talked about organizing their own labor union without affiliation to any unions of the larger society. Whether this possibility will lead the existing restaurant workers union to organize its locals to cater to the needs of Chinese restaurant workers is unclear.

In the entertainment field, especially in restaurant and travel businesses, new immigrants have been important culture brokers for New Yorkers. New Yorkers' interest in regional Chinese foods other than Cantonese has been stimulated by the culinary talents of new immigrant chefs from different parts of China and also by improved U.S.-China relations since President Nixon's 1972 China visit.

In the field of travel, a number of new immigrants have used their expertise in Chinese culture and their ability to speak Chinese to organize special tours for Americans to visit China. Many Chinese travel agents have considerable contact with Chinese consulates and the Chinese government's travel organizations, and help customers obtain visas and arrange trips for handsome fees. While these travel agents serve as "culture brokers" for American tourists, they also, in the process, learn more about the workings of American society.

The recent U.S.-China normalization has also opened up entrepreneurial opportunities in the import-export sector for new immigrants. In turn, this new business activity has had an impact on the city at large, not only making Chinese goods widely available but also making the Chinese a more visible presence outside the Chinatown community.

New immigrants are particularly suited for import-export trades since these businesses require knowledge of Chinese as well as American and Chinese cultures. In fact, these new immigrant entrepreneurs must improve their facility in English to be able to deal with American businessmen. Such business interaction leads to social interaction, and many new immigrant entrepreneurs—in the import-export trade as well as in other businesses—have considerable contact with people outside of Chinatown. A number of Chinese businessmen have moved out of Chinatown to live among white business associates. Some of these associates have identified pleasant residential areas or have recommended their realtors to help Chinese immigrants find better housing in Queens, Brooklyn, or even on Long Island.

CONCLUSION

The examination of new immigrants' adaptation to New York City in this essay shows that new Chinese immigrants differ significantly from the old settlers. The social and economic resources the new immigrants brought with them are simply not comparable to those brought by the old settlers. The urban origins of new immigrants, coupled with the assistance of family members, have turned out to be important assets in their creation of a new life in the New World. Many new immigrants come from highly literate backgrounds and a good number have had higher education or specialized training. Unlike the old sojourners who arrived in this country years ago, the new immigrants are more committed to participate in the realization of the "American dream." They came here with business plans and, often, even with savings.

The social and economic backgrounds of the new immigrants, however, cannot alone explain why their adaptation patterns differ from those of old settlers. New immigrants have also benefited from the 1965 immigration law which permitted migration of family members and talented individuals, a change that helped immigrants in the financing, establishment, management, and stability of many new business firms. Moreover, changed attitudes in the larger society toward ethnic groups, the equal opportunity and affirmative action programs, and the general interest in "things Chinese" since normalization of U.S.-China relations in 1972 have also given new immigrants more scope in pursuing their goals. Although racist and discriminatory attitudes toward the Chinese still exist, they have diminished.

New immigrants have more contacts outside Chinatown than old settlers did, and the community has expanded geographically, penetrating surrounding areas in lower Manhattan. There is even indication that a second Chinatown will soon be established in Flushing, Queens. Socially, more successful new immigrants have begun interactions with the white middle class, and some live among and work with white Americans as colleagues. Politically, new immigrants are more interested than old settlers in their rights. They are committed to making the United States their permanent home, and, though still novices, they have gradually become involved in American political life. New immigrant activists in particular see the need to organize the Chinatown community as an ethnic "interest group" to participate in the resource distribution of the larger society. Furthermore, political candidates from the neighborhood have been testing the waters in their recent efforts to participate in the 1984 elections for various offices in city and state government.

Although the Chinese are increasingly accepted in New York City, certain barriers still limit economic opportunities. Most new immigrants still have to depend on the ethnic niche. Restaurants, garment factories, and grocery stores remain the lifeblood of new immigrants. However, the size, scale, management, and organization of present businesses differ substantially from those of the past. The old so-journers intended to stay briefly in America, make some quick money, and then return to China. New immigrants, intending to make America their permanent home, are more determined than old settlers to achieve economic success through business achievement and are more entrepreneurial in style. New immigrant businessmen are also more willing to venture into non-Chinatown areas, and they have been pioneers in developing the new Chinatown in Queens.

While carving out their ethnic niche in New York City, new Chinese immigrants also play an important role in the vitality of the host culture. They generate profits for New York garment manufac-turers and, by creating a demand for housing, have supported con-struction as well as real estate businesses in Chinatown. New immigrant businesses have multiplier effects on non-Chinese enter-prises in such fields as transportation, fashion, textiles, construction, and the grocery trade. With the influx of new immigrants, Chinatown has also become a more important neighborhood for non-Chinese Americans, and new immigrants' grocery stores, travel agencies, and laundries provide important services for cosmopolitan New Yorkers. Indeed, new immigrants help introduce New Yorkers to aspects of the otherwise "mysterious" Chinese culture: traditional Chinese fes-tivals, Chinese regional cuisine, the Chinese way of entertaining, and the language of China. These activities and customs enhance the cultural life of New Yorkers and facilitate intercultural communica-tion.

The Chinese community of New York's Lower East Side is no longer the "quiet" community it used to be. It has changed greatly. New immigrants in today's active community have to deal with prob-lems of family disorganization, union disputes, aging, housing short-ages, and gangs—some of these problems, perhaps, the social costs of rapid Americanization. On the positive side, new immigrants have established flourishing businesses and enriched the cultural, social, and economic life of Chinatown and New York City itself. New im-migrants, moreover, are gradually changing the conservative, apol-itical community into a dynamic urban enclave with political and economic power. New York's Chinatown is, in fact, changing from a "voluntary segregated community" (Yuan 1963) into a voluntary "ethnic interest group."

NOTES

1. The data on which the present paper is based were obtained by field work in New York's Chinatown in 1972, 1974, 1980, and 1984. A total of twenty-four months was spent doing field research, principally in participant observation and interviewing informants. Written sources were also consulted.

2. In 1985, nine major Chinese dailies, all written in Chinese, were published in New York City's Chinatown: *The World Journal, Sing Tao Jih Pao* (New York edition), *The United Journal, Sino Daily Express, China Daily Express, China Daily News, The China Post, China Voice Daily, The China Tribune,* and *The Peimei News.*

3. This observation was voiced by many realtors in Chinatown. Several newspapers made similar statements (e.g., *The Christian Science Monitor,* January 3, 1985; *New York Times,* September 21, 1984).

4. Since the agreement was signed between Great Britain and the PRC in December 1984, there is a slight indication of the return of "flight capital" to Hong Kong. However, the amount of this return flow cannot be determined at this time.

REFERENCES

Barth, Fredrik. 1969. *Ethnic Groups and Boundaries.* Oslo: Universitetesforlaget.

Barth, Gunther Paul. 1964. *Bitter Strength: A History of the Chinese in the United States, 1850–1870.* Cambridge: Harvard University Press.

Beck, L. 1898. *New York's Chinatown.* New York: Bohemia.

Benedict, Burton. 1968. "Family Firms and Economic Development." *Southwestern Journal of Anthropology* 24:1–19.

Bennett, John W. and Iwao Ishino. 1963. *Paternalism in the Japanese Economy.* Minneapolis: University of Minnesota Press.

Chinatown Study Group. 1969. *Chinatown Study Group Report.* Manuscript. New York.

Hsu, Francis L. K. 1971. *The Challenge of the American Dream.* Belmont, Calif.: Wadsworth.

Kung, S. W. 1962. *Chinese in American Life: Some Aspects of Their History, Status, Problems and Contributions.* Seattle: University of Washington Press.

Lee, James. 1972. "The Story of the New York Chinese Consolidated Benevolent Association." *Bridge Magazine* 1:15–18.

Lee, Rose Hum. 1960. *The Chinese in the United States of America.* Hong Kong: Hong Kong University Press.

Novak, Michael. 1972. *The Rise of the Unmeltable Ethnics.* New York: Macmillan.

Sung, Betty Lee. 1976. *A Survey of Chinese-American Manpower and Employment.* New York: Praeger.

—— 1979. *Transplanted Chinese Children*. New York: Department of Asian Studies, City College of New York.

U.S. Bureau of the Census. 1982. *1980 Census of Population and Housing. General Population Characteristics, New York*. Washington, D.C.: U.S. Government Printing Office.

Wong, Bernard. 1976. "Social Stratification, Adaptive Strategies and the Chinese Community of New York." *Urban Life* 5:33–52.

—— 1977. "Elites and Ethnic Boundary Maintenance: A Study of the Roles of Elites in Chinatown, New York City." *Urban Anthropology* 6:1–25.

—— 1982. *Chinatown: Economic Adaptation and Ethnic Identity of the Chinese*. New York: Holt, Rinehart and Winston.

—— 1984. *Patronage, Brokerage, Entrepreneurship and the Chinese Community of New York City*. New York: AMS Press.

—— 1985. "The Chinese Family in New York with Comparative Remarks on the Chinese Family in Manila and Lima, Peru." *Journal of Comparative Family Studies* 16:231–255.

Wun, Cang-tsu. 1958. "Chinese People and Chinatown in New York City." Ph.D. dissertation. Ann Arbor: University Microfilms.

—— 1972. *"Chink!" A Documentary History of Anti-Chinese Prejudice in America*. New York: World Publications.

Yuan, D. Y. 1963. "Voluntary Segregation: A Study of New York's Chinatown." *Phylon* 24:255–268.

10. The Soviet Jews: Life in Brighton Beach, Brooklyn

Annelise Orleck

In 1980, after five years of living far from Brighton Beach, I returned to my childhood home to find that it had changed dramatically. Knowledge of English and Yiddish was no longer sufficient to make my way in the community. I now needed to know Russian as well, if only to speak to my neighbors and to shop for necessities in neighborhood stores. In five years Brighton Beach had become the largest Soviet immigrant community in the world. Dubbed "Little Odessa" by journalists, to differentiate it from smaller, predominantly Muscovite and Central Asian settlements in other parts of New York City, the Soviet Jewish community in Brighton was, by 1980, more than 20,000 strong. (Since then the number has risen to more than 25,000). About three-quarters of Brighton's new immigrants had come from the Ukraine, most from Odessa and surrounding towns in the Black Sea region. The remainder, including about 6 percent each from Moscow and Leningrad, came from towns and cities across the western USSR.[1]

This essay, based on field research in Brighton Beach from June 1980 through the present time, explores some of the many changes that the community has experienced since Soviet Jews have become a dominant presence there.[2] Just as the influx of Soviet immigrants has changed the face of Brighton Beach, so living in Brighton has had an impact on the new immigrants. The pages that follow offer a glimpse of what living in Brighton has meant to them.[3] In particular this essay looks at the processes of adjustment for Soviet Jews of different ages. It also examines the way that conflicts over Jewish identity and attempts to build a Soviet immigrant community life in Brighton have shaped the relationship of Soviet Jews to their new home.

BACKGROUND OF THE IMMIGRATION

Agitation by Soviet Jews for the right to emigrate from the USSR began, during the early 1960s, as part of a larger movement by Eastern bloc intellectuals for an end to human rights violations in the Soviet Union. Among the leaders of this movement were many Jews. In the aftermath of the Arab-Israeli war in 1967, an event that had a great emotional impact on Jews in the Communist world, a number of these Jewish intellectuals began to call for acknowledgment of the right of Jews to emigrate and settle in Israel. The movement gathered force as Jews began to hold demonstrations around the USSR, and the number of Jews allowed to emigrate rose sharply.

Between 1968 and 1970 more than 4,000 Jews left the Soviet Union, ten times the number of émigrés for 1962–64. Then, with the beginning of detente, and, according to Soviet authorities, because of U.S. promises to improve trade agreements between the two countries, the doors were opened wide. In 1971, more than 13,000 exit visas were issued to Soviet Jews, all of whom expressed their intention of settling in Israel. Between 1972 and 1974, 87,000 Jews emigrated to Israel. During the next three years the number of émigrés dropped to about 15,000 a year. It is not clear why this happened. Igor Birman, an émigré analyst, believes that the drop in numbers reflected a growing sense of disillusionment among Soviet Jews with conditions of life in Israel. By the mid-1970s, he notes, the most ardent Zionists had already gone. Few of those who now wished to leave were moved to do so for ideological reasons. Jews in the USSR began to think twice about undergoing the long, dangerous process of applying for an exit visa only to exchange the hardships of Soviet life for the hardships of life in Israel (see Birman 1979 and Dinstein 1979).

While this process of reevaluation was going on, an important shift occurred in settlement opportunities available to Soviet émigrés. From 1976 on, HIAS, the Hebrew Immigrant Aid Society, an organization that has facilitated Russian Jewish emigration since the late nineteenth century, began to routinely offer Soviet Jewish emigrants the chance to settle in the United States. This change in policy then caused and continues to cause controversy among Zionists who argue that Soviet Jews should be channeled into Israel, where their labor power and skills are needed. Nevertheless HIAS persisted and the result, many recent emigrants claim, was the subsequent resurgence of Jewish emigration.

Once the possibility of Soviet Jewish settlement in the United States was opened up, the number of Jews applying for exit visas rose again. In discussions with Soviets now living in Brighton, two issues emerged as the primary factors behind the decision to leave. The first concern of parents and young adults was with the ever-tightening quotas restricting the number of Jews allowed into Soviet universities and technical training institutes. The second concern, voiced by people of all ages, was with the shortage of food, clothing, and household necessities which had existed in the Soviet Union since World War II and has gotten worse in recent years. To many of these people, whose only exposure to American life had been through the popular media, immigration to the United States seemed the perfect solution to their problems. Hoping for access to the career opportunities and material abundance that America represented to them, 101,655 Jews left the Soviet Union between 1978 and 1980.

It is hard to verify exactly how many of these emigrants ended up in the United States—or the New York area. U.S. government figures are far lower than the estimates of New York City-based Jewish organizations. According to the 1980 census, there were about 35,000 Soviet-born living in the New York metropolitan area who had arrived since 1970 (see Kraly, this volume). The Jewish Union of Russian Immigrants estimated that in 1981 there were between 90,000 and 100,000 Soviet Jews living in New York City.

After a peak departure of about 51,000 Jews in 1979, the Soviet Union began to cut back on the number of exit visas being issued. Publicly, authorities said that the initial agreement to let Jews out had been based on the assumption that they planned to settle in Israel. Privately, Soviet officials cited a breakdown of detente between the United States and the USSR. Whatever the reason, the number of exit visas awarded to Jews has continued to drop since 1981, with the exception of a slight rise in 1984. In 1985, only 920

Jews were granted the right to leave (*New York Times*, November 3, 1985). Although Jewish organizations continue to agitate for free emigration, it seems that, at least for now, the massive recent wave of Jewish emigration from the Soviet Union has been virtually halted.

SETTLING IN BRIGHTON BEACH

The first stop for Jewish emigrants from the Soviet Union was Vienna. There they were met by HIAS agents who offered them the choice of going to Israel or the United States. Those who chose the United States were then flown to Rome, where they were housed, sheltered, and offered classes in English while their applications to immigrate were processed. "In Rome," one middle-aged immigrant recalls, "we got our first taste of the West. It was beautiful. Not only the history, which was, of course, interesting to us, but the clothes, the food. We went crazy. For three months we celebrated." Such remembrances notwithstanding, the processing time in Rome was not all spent dining and shopping. For many it was a time of confusion, disorientation, and wondering about the future, hoping that the decision to leave had been the right one. Particularly for elderly people, on whom the traveling was hard, and for parents of school-aged children, whose daily routines had been shattered, this in-between period took its toll. They were anxious to get to the United States, to begin the process of settling into their new lives.

Once the immigrants landed in New York, the vast majority of those who planned to stay in the city were aided by NYANA, the New York Association for New Americans. After studying the city carefully the agency came up with several areas that seemed promising for Soviet settlement: Washington Heights in Manhattan, Rego Park in Queens, Williamsburg and Brighton Beach in Brooklyn. These neighborhoods all had relatively cheap, available housing, easy access to transportation, and an established East European Jewish community which the agency hoped would ease the newcomers' transition to life in a strange new country.

Although Queens became the favored area of settlement for many of the best-established intellectuals and professional Soviet immigrants, Brighton Beach quickly became the most popular choice of the majority. It fit NYANA's criteria perfectly. There was an abundance of cheap, solid housing available, as well as cheap commercial space. An organized senior citizen community offered important services to the large numbers of Soviet immigrants who were over sixty. Almost everyone already living in Brighton had themselves emigrated from Eastern Europe. And finally, for those from the Black Sea area, Brighton offered the lure of proximity to the Atlantic Ocean.

Out on the edge of Brooklyn, close to the sea and also to public transportation, Brighton has been a popular settlement area for Eastern European Jews since the end of World War I. Set in the center of a narrow finger of land, the neighborhood is just fifteen blocks long and three avenues wide, fronted by the Atlantic and cut off from the rest of Brooklyn by the Belt Parkway running along its back side. Although it is shadowed by the elevated subway track, which runs above its only commercial street, and though it is one of the most densely populated areas of Brooklyn, still Brighton has an open feel because of its closeness to the sea and to the three-mile stretch of beach that connects it to Coney Island.

Brighton was originally developed in the 1880s as a middle-class summer resort. For almost three decades the Brighton Beach Hotel, Music Hall, and the racetrack attracted tens of thousands of visitors each summer. When New York State banned horse racing in 1909, Brighton's fortunes as a resort began to decline. By the outbreak of the First World War the racetrack had been razed and the hotel was on its last legs. However, a group of developers, whose bungalow colonies attracted Jewish immigrant families seeking to escape the swelter of summer in the inner city, decided to publicize Brighton as an ideal spot for year-round settlement. When New York City was gripped by a housing shortage at the end of the war, a number of summer renters decided to settle in Brighton permanently.

A real estate boom in 1925 radically transformed this little seaside village. Within five years, thirty six-story apartment houses were built in Brighton and their developers had little trouble filling them. Brighton became a thriving and diverse Jewish immigrant community. It supported several synagogues, a ritual bathhouse, a variety of Yiddish afternoon schools with competing ideologies, and a myriad of charitable and political organizations, including branches of the Jewish Labor Bund and the Socialist and Communist parties. With the onset of the Depression, thousands more immigrant Jews flooded into Brighton to board with relatives, to share apartments with friends who could not afford their rents, and to take advantage of a tenants' rights movement so well organized that its leaders could boast that, whatever happened elsewhere in America, nobody would ever be evicted in Brighton for inability to pay their rent.

By the end of World War II, Brighton Beach was seriously over-crowded. An exodus of American-born children of immigrants began at this time and continued through the mid-1960s. But, as this American-born group left Brighton for more affluent areas, a new group of immigrants was arriving—the second wave of Eastern European Jews to come to Brighton, refugees of the Holocaust. These new arrivals, mostly from Warsaw and other large Polish cities, added a new layer of Jewish immigrant culture to Brighton Beach.

Then, during the late 1960s and early '70s there was yet another influx of immigrant Jews to Brighton—this time an internal migration of the elderly from their homes in older immigrant neighborhoods, including Brownsville and East Flatbush in Brooklyn and the Grand Concourse in the Bronx, where they no longer felt safe. The completion of the Warbasse Housing Project (funded by the Amalgamated Clothing and Textile Workers' Union) opened up thousands of new apartments. Brighton Beach became the second-largest senior citizen community in the United States. It is also one of the best organized. The newcomers, mostly union retirees, joined with Brighton's old-time radicals to deal with issues like medical care, transportation, and Social Security benefits. As well, they organized regular cultural activities including a series of free concerts held in Brighton's Seaside Park, which feature performers as varied as the Workmen's Circle Choir and the New York Philharmonic.

Still, however unified it may be, a community composed primarily of senior citizens cannot regenerate itself. As elderly residents died off or moved to Florida, their apartments became vacant and no one arrived to fill them. By 1975 Brighton had an almost 30 percent vacancy rate; stores as well as apartments stood empty. On several Brighton streets, old summer houses were turned into SROs (single room occupancy buildings). These were soon filled by psychologically marginal people, a large group of whom descended on Brighton in the late '70s when financial troubles forced New York City and State mental hospitals to release thousands of nonviolent patients.

The community was gripped by fear as the elderly worried that Brighton Beach was finally dying.

Hoping to solve two problems at once, case workers at NYANA began settling Soviet immigrants in Brighton in 1976. Their plan proved to be a smashing success. The first few Soviet immigrants came to Brighton simply because they were offered cheap, decent housing there. But word spread fast. Brighton Beach was a nice place to live. The apartments were large and well taken care of. There were empty stores just waiting to be transformed and reopened. And, best of all, it was on the sea. Said one elderly Odessan, "The first time I saw the Boardwalk and the beach, I decided I wanted to live here. It reminds me a little of home." Far enough away from the center of the city that the Soviet Jews could feel at ease as they began to form their own community, Brighton was also within easy access of Manhattan. Jews from the Ukraine, from Moscow and Leningrad, and even a small number from Central Asia, moved into Brighton. Within five years the neighborhood, which had had a vacancy problem, was overcrowded again. Soviet immigrants living in other parts of the city put their names on two-year waiting lists for an apartment in Brighton Beach. Brighton became the largest Soviet émigré community in the world.

In a few years the Soviet immigrants radically changed the face of the old community. All along the fifteen blocks that Brighton Beach Avenue runs, signs written in Cyrillic letters have replaced old English and Yiddish signs. Luncheonettes and newsstands along the Avenue now sell more copies of *Novye Amerikanets* (the New American) and *Novaya Russkaya Slova* (the New Russian Word) than they do of the Yiddish-language *Forward* or the *New York Times*. One by one Brighton's old-time kosher bakeries have been replaced by fancy new Russian pastry shops. Next to kosher "appetizing stores," home cooking take-out stands, and The Brighton Dairy Restaurant, long-time purveyors of Brighton cuisine, have sprung up half a dozen new "international-style" groceries, with European packaged goods lining the shelves, smoked whole fish piled high on the counters, and ten different kinds of sausage hanging from the ceilings. One can read the history of Jewish immigration to Brighton from the storefronts along the Avenue. Beside the stores that have been there for half a century—shoemakers', glaziers', tailors', and dusty charity shops selling donated clothing to support a variety of causes—are the shiny new stores recently opened by Soviet immigrants. Gino Venucci shoes, with its silver and neon decor and its handmade Italian shoes, and Romano Video, offering both American and Soviet movies on tape, cater to a clientele with very different tastes than those served by Brighton's older stores.

About a dozen new restaurants and nightclubs have been opened in the last five years by recently arrived Soviet immigrants and new ones are being opened every few months. Brighton's only record store sells nothing but Russian recordings and the Black Sea Bookstore offers everything from the classics of Russian literature to contemporary *samizdat* (opposition) writing. Well-dressed Soviet immigrants of all ages fill the streets, greet each other, enjoy the freedom and variety of the American marketplace. On the surface everything seems to be going extremely well for Brighton's newest residents. Beneath the surface the processes of change and adjustment are more complex.

ISSUES OF IDENTITY AND RELATIONSHIP TO OTHER JEWS

The question of Jewish identity is a thorny one for Soviet immigrants, filled with conflicts and contradictions, but it is a key to understanding their adjustment to life in Brighton and their relations with first- and second-wave Jewish immigrants. The reality of being Jewish and the shared experience of having been persecuted for it ties Soviet immigrants into Brighton's larger Jewish immigrant community. Yet the fact that the Soviets have a very different sense of Jewish identity than other sectors of the Brighton population has also created divisions and misunderstandings.

When Soviet immigrants began to land on Brighton's shores, looking not like the huddled masses of seventy-five years ago but like the well-dressed, well-educated, big city people that most of them are, the old Jews of Brighton reacted with confusion. Many of these old immigrants had participated in the American movement to free Soviet Jewry, but they had a conception of Soviet Jewry that was bound to a past that no longer exists. Having left Eastern Europe thirty-five to seventy years earlier, most had little idea of what life is

like for modern Soviet Jews. The elderly Brightonites, moreover, expected the newcomers to actively participate in Jewish community
activities. When the Soviet immigrants (two-thirds of whom grew up
in the deeply antireligious atmosphere of post-World War II Soviet
society), responded with suspicion and ambivalence to repeated invitations to become part of Brighton's Jewish community life, old-
time Brightonites reacted angrily. "We fought for them so that they
could be free to live as Jews," said one first-wave immigrant. "And
here they are, they don't want to be Jews." Every synagogue in the
neighborhood issued invitations to the Soviets to special holiday celebrations being conducted in Russian for their benefit. Yet few of the
newcomers responded. Of the eleven synagogues in Brighton only
five were able to lure new Soviet members, and, almost without
exception, these were people over sixty, much closer in age and upbringing to the majority of Brighton's religious Jews than their children and grandchildren.

As the Moscow-born actor/writer Alexander Sirotin (n.d.) explains,
the cultural gap between Soviet Jews and earlier Jewish immigrants
is very wide. "American Jews try to teach the Russian immigrant
about Jewishness using a strange language, and then wonder why
he does not understand." Sirotin, who has been trying to help his
fellow immigrants come to terms with their Jewish identity in a positive way, through his work for the Jewish Union of Russian Immigrants and his radio show *Gorizont*, compares these immigrants to
concentration camp survivors. "They were starving for food," he
writes. "We are not starving physically but we are starving for Jewishness. You can't shove food down a starving man's throat. It is the
same with these Jews. They must be fed *Yidishkayt* [Jewishness] with
a teaspoon."

Despite initial resistance, life in Brighton is having an effect on the
Jewish identity of Soviet immigrants. This can be seen most clearly
in their changing attitudes toward public religious observance. First
consider their responses in 1980, when most of them were new to
Brighton. At that time there had been a rash of firebombing attacks
against poor synagogues in the neighborhood. When the oldest of
these synagogues lost its nine Torah scrolls to arson, the community
came together to raise money for a new scroll. In keeping with tradition, first a funeral ceremony was held for the damaged Torahs,

then a march through the streets with the new Torah, accompanied by dancing, singing, and *klezmer* (Yiddish jazz) music. As the march wound its way up and down the side streets of Brighton I noticed a crowd of silent, nervous-looking bystanders. With open mouths and tensed brows newly arrived Soviet Jews watched but would not join in. For the elderly among them it had been fifty years since they had seen a Jewish religious ritual performed so openly. For the younger generations this was something completely new.

Within a few years Soviet immigrant reticence about public displays of Jewishness had begun to change. Increasing numbers of them come every year to the annual community commemoration of the Warsaw Ghetto Uprising; on the fortieth anniversary of the massacre of Jews at Babi-Yar (in the Ukraine in 1941), the Soviets organized a huge and moving commemoration, adding a new memorial to the calendar of annual community days of mourning. A similar change marked the attitudes of Soviet shopkeepers. Initially Soviet shops remained open even on the holiest of Jewish holidays, as they would have had to back home. Within a year or two, stores began to close on religious holidays. Citing both pride in their Jewishness and a desire to respect the sensibilities of their religious customers, Soviet shopkeepers began to post signs wishing their customers *mazl* (good luck), peace, and prosperity for the Jewish New Year. Slowly Yiddish phrases began to creep into the Russian of these shopkeepers. I asked one where she had learned these words. She said, "Many years ago I used to hear my grandparents speak them. But I forgot it all until I moved here."

A final but significant example of this trend is that the Soviet immigrants have begun to celebrate Jewish rites of passage publicly and with some attention to Jewish traditions. Though the details of many of these observances seem shockingly irreligious, even mocking, to some orthodox Jews, any public expression of Jewishness is an extremely important step for the Soviets. It is unquestionably a sign of change that weddings and Bar Mitzvahs (the traditional Jewish initiation of thirteen-year-old boys into full status in the religious community) have become occasions for celebration, for inviting friends and family to join in communal acknowledgment of their Jewishness. Despite the importance of these events in heightening the sense of community and Jewishness among the immigrants, these public ceremonies often hold different meanings for Soviet Jews of different ages—and, in fact, age-related differences are crucial for understanding the general immigrant experience.

IMMIGRANTS OF DIFFERENT AGES

Members of each age group among the Soviet immigrants in Brighton—the elderly, working-age adults, and children—relate to their Jewishness and their Soviet background in distinctive ways. In general, their adjustment to life in America differs. These age-based differences stem partly from the fact that individuals in each group were born and raised during very different periods of Soviet history. Also, their emigration and subsequent attempts to adjust came at different stages in their lives.

The Elderly

Of all the newcomers to Brighton none have made the transition quite so well as the elderly, those over sixty who comprise about one-third of the total Soviet settlement in Brighton. For them Brighton is comfortable physically and culturally. For the first time in their lives many are able to afford the luxury of living alone. Yet at the same time Brighton offers a community of well-organized peers to socialize with. This is facilitated by the fact that the Soviet Jews share with other Brighton elderly a common *mamaloshn*, or mother tongue, Yiddish. All those born before the 1917 Revolution, or at least before the 1930s when Stalin began his campaign to wipe out all remaining vestiges of Jewish community life, were raised with Yiddish as their first language. After World War II, Stalin climaxed his anti-Jewish campaigns by arresting and executing the nation's twenty-four leading Yiddish writers, and Yiddish is now a dying language in the Soviet Union. Although most of the Soviet elderly have spoken little Yiddish for thirty years, they still remember it from their youth. Thus, from their first days in Brighton they were able to communicate with neighbors, shopkeepers, even strangers on the street. Brighton was not so forbidding to them as it was to their children and grandchildren.

For some, like Fanya from Odessa, who moved to the United States in 1978 with her daughter and two young granddaughters, landing in Brighton felt like coming home. "The first time I heard Yiddish spoken on the street here, I couldn't believe my ears. Then I saw little boys wearing *yarmulkes*, walking down the street, unafraid, and I cried." Although Fanya's daughter, who owns a small grocery in Brighton, speaks no Yiddish, her granddaughters are learning Yiddish in addition to Hebrew at the religious school they attend. "In the First World War," Fanya recalls, "I lost my father, in the Second World War my husband. Since then I have had a bad heart. I could not cry at all. Here, for the first time, I cried. Here, when my own little ones speak to me in Yiddish, my heart feels better."

Fanya is typical of the Soviet elderly in that she came here with her children and grandchildren. Like the earlier great waves of Jewish immigration to the United States, this third wave has been a family migration, at least to the extent that the arbitrariness of Soviet emigration policy will allow. (One of the more tragic aspects of Soviet immigrant life is the seemingly endless waiting some must do for relatives still unable to secure permission to leave the Soviet Union.) Those lucky enough to have arrived here with their whole family intact make use of relatives of all ages in their attempts to build a new life in America.

Like other grandparents in Brighton's Soviet community, Fanya has played an important part in bringing up her grandchildren. This system of child care brought over from home encourages both grandmothers and grandfathers to care for youngsters, thus freeing the parents to work. Like most Soviet elderly in Brighton Fanya has her own apartment, a big change from Soviet cities where a severe housing shortage forces three, sometimes four, generations to share one apartment. In Brighton, the elderly rise each morning to walk to their children's homes in time to take charge of their grandchildren before their parents leave for work. During the day grandparents shop for working children, do laundry and a variety of household chores, including walking their youngest grandchildren to and from school. For both older men and women this system works well. It satisfies their need to be close to their families, fills their days with useful work, and provides a necessary service for their children.

Grandparents often play another important role in easing the process of adjustment for their families, that of cultural liaison between their Soviet-educated children and the Old World Jewish community in which they now live. This is particularly useful when young children in the family attend Jewish religious schools. When the Soviets first arrived in Brooklyn, several religious academies offered them free tuition, hoping, in that way, to attract these mostly irreligious Jews back to the path of Orthodoxy. Most parents who chose this option did so because they liked the idea of sending their children to private schools. Years of reading horror stories in the Soviet press left them with a deeply ingrained fear of the New York City public school system. Although only about a third of the Soviet youngsters have chosen to remain in *yeshiva* after their first year, the children that do continue their religious education face the problem of returning each day from a religious school to areligious or even antireligious parents. The result, in some cases, has been tension and division in the family between these children and parents who received their education in a militantly atheistic school system. Most often, in these cases, it has been the grandparents who have mediated, explaining Jewish culture to their children while providing their grandchildren with some continuity between their home and school experiences.

Although not all Soviet elderly are religious, a good many retain a strong sense of secular Jewish identity. Indeed, through Yiddish culture, attendance at synagogues and joining in secular Jewish celebrations, Soviet elders are increasingly becoming part of the larger senior citizen community. Some, in addition, socialize with elderly members of first- and second-wave groups in a variety of cultural organizations and at the Shorefront Y Senior Center.

Still, despite their considerable contact with elderly members of the larger Brighton community, the most important relations for elderly Soviet Jews, outside of the family, continue to be forged among members of their own group. These ties develop and are nurtured in informal contexts. Like many other of Brighton's elders, the Soviet old people come out to sit on the boardwalk, in parks, and on chairs in front of their buildings. One vest-pocket park, recently renamed Babi-Yar Triangle, in memory of the 1941 massacre, has become community space for one large group of Soviet elderly. The men gather around stone checkerboard tables to engage in or to watch intense battles at chess. Dressed in long coats, wool berets or fur hats, they meet each day to argue or chat in Yiddish. Nearby the women line long wooden benches, wearing angora berets and colorful head-scarves, talking of family and friends, of who has gotten married, died, just been denied or granted permission to leave the Soviet Union.

The elderly, of course, do face difficulties in adjusting to life in a new country. And for a minority the transition has been hard. Some miss relatives they had to leave back home. Others just miss the familiarity of places they used to know. It is especially difficult for the few who made the move alone, and for those whose children, soon after arrival here, move somewhere else and rarely call or visit. All Soviet seniors are given minimum Social Security benefits to live on and access to reduced-cost senior citizen housing. The Shorefront Jewish Community Council, an arm of the Metropolitan Council on Jewish Poverty, also provides companions to help the Soviet elderly clean and shop if they need that kind of assistance. Still, it is not easy to get used to American ways after a lifetime in the USSR.

One serious problem faced by many Soviet elderly has been their confusion about how to make use of available medical services in the community. Sophie, a former Odessan who now teaches English to Soviet senior citizens, held a special class to explain to her students that they need not be afraid if, when they call for an ambulance, a police car comes first. "This is normal here," she told them. Even then, some of her students, who remembered too many stories of people leaving for hospitals and never returning, were uncertain. Deep-seated fears do not disappear quickly.

Despite problems such as these, the transition to Brighton life has been relatively smooth for most of the Soviet elderly. Living in their own apartments, free from the burden of having to work for a living, supported by local senior citizen services and a large network of peers, most have adjusted fairly quickly. Settled into a community that offers familiar foods and a familiar language, few of the older immigrants wish to move again. The transition has not been as easy for their children, many of whom had to give up successful careers to come to the United States where they must take whatever jobs they can find to support themselves and their families. For this middle group, especially those between forty and sixty, the process of adjustment to life in New York City has been most difficult and complex.

Working-Age Adults

The working-age adults among the Soviet immigrants in Brighton are, on the whole, a well-educated group. According to data gathered by a local immigrant aid agency, more than one-third of the working-age adults who have come to Brighton from the Soviet Union are trained professionals. Among these are doctors, lawyers, teachers, and a variety of engineers—a term used in the Soviet Union to describe a wide range of professions, from electronics to agriculture. Many of the remaining two-thirds, though they have not attended colleges or professional institutes, have a secondary school education and often some kind of specific technical training. In other words, most working-age Soviet immigrants came to this country with skills to offer, and the belief that, in a wealthy country like the United States, there would be no problem finding jobs suited to their skills. Educated in a society that guarantees placement to all trained workers, the shock of having to compete for jobs in a tight American marketplace has been a sobering experience for many Soviet immigrants.

"We never dreamed it would be hard to find work in America," said Shura, fifty-seven, formerly a teacher and translator in Kiev. Like many other middle-aged professionals, Shura left the Soviet Union to ensure that her children would have better opportunities for occupational advancement and material success. "We thought in such a rich country as America, everyone works. I still don't really understand why this is not so." Shura, who works only at freelance translating jobs, is representative of a large number of well-educated, middle-aged Soviet immigrants in Brighton, who, despite their training, have had little success finding satisfying work in New York. In Shura's case, qualifying for a teaching job here would have meant going back to school to meet teaching certification requirements. Her translation skills have been hard to market, especially because her primary fluency after Russian is French. Lack of fluency in English is a problem for many older Soviet professionals seeking work in this country, particularly doctors. The medical training of Soviet doctors is not recognized as sufficient by the American Medical Association, and their English is not good enough to pass muster in the medical courses open to them. NYANA has offered several different classes in technical English for Soviet trained professionals, but only a small number have been able to learn enough to pass licensing exams.

Sonya, fifty-one, formerly a doctor in Leningrad, now works as a companion for an elderly Soviet woman, at minimum wage. Though hers is an extreme case, many Soviet doctors, especially middle-aged female pediatricians, have experienced downward mobility in New York. Some Soviet women doctors, to be sure, have fulfilled licensing requirements in New York State. The same is true of a larger percentage of male doctors, particularly specialists. Their shingles have appeared around Brighton, where they provide essential services to the Soviet community. As for other professionals, some journalists have been able to tap into the booming trade in Russian-language newspapers. Some teachers, especially those who are fluent in English, have found work either in positions of service to the Soviet community or in private schools. However, for most middle-aged professionals among the immigrants the change of locale, social system, and language as well as licensing requirements have proven to be insurmountable obstacles. They have had to take less satisfying and less prestigious work, and some professional women have ended up not working at all.

Many, like Sonya, are gratified by the fact that their children have been successful in this country. As Sonya commented, she would only have worked as a doctor for another ten or fifteen years at best, while her son, now an electronics engineer in Texas, has a lifetime ahead of him. Despite her happiness for her son, Sonya finds that she is often bored and lonely in Brighton. As she sums it up, "I could be more fulfilled."

Max, forty-nine, formerly a lawyer in Moscow, now makes his living driving a cab. Language barriers and too many differences between the American and Soviet legal systems prevented him from taking the bar in New York. "It's not what I would call an intellectually challenging existence," he says, "but I support my family very well. That's what America is about," he smiles, "isn't it?" Cab driving has become one of the financial mainstays of the Soviet immigrant community. Faced with the need to support their families, many former professionals and technical workers have decided in America to learn to become entrepreneurs. For middle-aged men, used to making a living but too old to start again from the bottom, cab driving has proven to be one of the best routes to economic stability. Compared to other kinds of businesses, it is cheap to get into, pays off well, and offers a work environment free from the supervision of bosses. Typically, a group of men get together to rent cabs, agreeing to pool their savings toward the purchase of a medallion. Once they buy the medallion, they split shifts so that the cab is in use twenty-four hours a day.

Entrepreneurship of all kinds has worked well for many members of Brighton's Soviet community. Enough people have been able to open small businesses of one kind or another—groceries, restaurants, clothing stores, car services, travel agencies, import/export companies—that they can employ a good number of their fellow immigrants. They obtain the capital necessary to set up these businesses in a variety of ways. Pooling savings to start a business is one method commonly used, with one partner often branching out to open a separate business if things go well. Some small-time entrepreneurs have been able to get loans from Jewish philanthropic agencies, whose support of Soviet Jews has aroused resentment among older first- and second-wave immigrants who complain that they did not get as much help when they first settled in Brighton. However, the most important means of acquiring capital has come, in a complex fashion, from the sale of belongings before leaving the Soviet Union.

Although Soviet Jews are forbidden to take anything of value with them when they leave the USSR, they have worked out a rather ingenious way of helping both those who must stay behind and those immigrating to the United States. Once a visa has been approved, those about to leave give their valuables to people who have not applied to emigrate but who have relatives already established in Brighton. An agreement is drawn up stating the value of the items exchanged. This agreement is sent or carried to the Brighton branch of the family that received the goods. Once the newcomers are in the United States they are paid, in installments, for the goods they left behind, by the family of the people to whom those goods were sold. Remarkably, this complicated system has worked smoothly for much of the last decade.

The first of the Soviet-owned stores to appear on Brighton Beach Avenue were the groceries. They were clean, bright and quite modern-looking compared to the old-fashioned corner stores that had served the neighborhood since the 1920s. These stores occupy a special place in the Soviet community, for they offer daily reminders of the difference between the Soviet Union and the United States, where the "miracle" of abundance is a fact of everyday life. For Soviet shoppers, keeping a family fed has meant standing on lines for hours each day just to purchase essential foodstuffs, bribing grocery store workers, and keeping abreast of news about special black market shipments. In Brighton immigrants can now choose between eight groceries offering Polish, Hungarian, German, Russian, and American meats, cheeses, juices, chocolates. They may also choose between a variety of well-stocked bakeries, fish stores, butchers, and fruit stands.

These stores, along with the tailoring, leather working, and shoe repair establishments that Soviet immigrants have recently taken over from long-time first- and second-wave immigrant owners, serve as informal community centers for the third-wave immigrants. They are places where news is exchanged and congratulations or condolences are offered. They also serve as bridges between the Soviet newcomers and older Brighton immigrants. As these stores have become part of the daily shopping routines of many long-time Brightonites—where old and new immigrants greet each other and chat—barriers have broken down. As the owners of one small luncheonette put it, "With time we're all beginning to see that we're not so different after all. We're just Jews who left Russia at different times."

While the small stores and groceries have helped to deemphasize differences between the various immigrant groups in Brighton, another kind of Soviet business accentuates these differences. "Flash and glass" establishments have added a touch of disco glitter to dirty Brighton Beach Avenue in the last few years, but have been a shock to many old-time Brighton residents because of their style and their emphasis on youthful glamour. Long a senior citizen community, Brighton has again become an age-integrated neighborhood with the arrival of the Soviet immigrants. Many of the neighborhood's newest stores—like Gino Venucci Shoes, the Marquis Gift Shop, Alta Moda, and New Deal Furs—cater to Soviet teenagers and young adults who want to dress and live well, in keeping with their conceptions of "the American good life."

Although most of the old timers know that these new stores have revived an area that was dying commercially, some are hostile toward both the owners of the stores and their clientele. "They're taking the neighborhood away from us," I've heard more than one elderly Brightonite complain. These newcomers do not have the religious ideals or the radical political vision that sustained many first- and second-wave immigrants. "Look at the makeup, the clothes, the hair!" the offended say. "Feh! These are not Jews."

They are unquestionably Jews. However, many Soviet immigrants, particularly among the teenagers and adults twenty-five to thirty-five, came to the United States with visions and ideas quite distinct from those of earlier generations of Russian Jewish immigrants. For many Soviet Jews, born since 1941, buying Western clothing, wearing unusual makeup, listening to American music and imitating what they knew of American styles was a way of rebelling and of expressing individuality in the USSR. Since adopting these fashions was, as my Russian teacher Marya commented, the only form of rebellion allowed in Soviet society, it was done consciously by many Soviet young people. In this way they could express their desire for a freer life, a life with more individual expression and material comfort. Indeed, for many Soviet Jews, their only understanding of American life was derived from rock music, movies, and sensational literature. Marya recalls how a dog-eared copy of Jaqueline Susann's *Once Is Not Enough* was passed from hand to hand in Leningrad. "Inside ourselves," she remembers, "we knew it was a distorted picture of American life. But it offered up everything forbidden by Soviet censors—drugs, homosexuality, rich living. In a way we wanted to believe that was America—pure abandon."

As for Jewish identification, it must be remembered that few people under fifty in the Soviet Union had the chance to know anything positive about their Jewishness. In fact, since 1952, the teaching of Jewish religion or culture has been radically restricted. Yet, at the same time, Jews are never allowed to forget that they are Jews. In the Soviet Union, Jews are officially considered an ethnic minority or, in Soviet terms, a nationality. Every Soviet citizen must carry an internal passport; to travel anywhere, to apply for jobs or to attend school, they must present it. On line 5 of these passports a person's nationality is recorded—Russian, Ukrainian, or Jew, for example. The letter J on their internal passports makes otherwise assimilated Jews liable to petty harassment from government officials, keeps all but a few out of universities, and restricts their freedom to travel—even within the USSR. For many, if not most, assimilated Jews, the longing for America embodied a longing to escape the stigma of their Jewish parentage, not to become more Jewish in either cultural or religious terms. After their arrival in Brighton and their first positive exposure to Jewishness, many began to express a desire to learn more about Jewish heritage and culture, and to incorporate positive elements into their sense of Jewish identity. But, like most assimilated American Jews, they have wanted to do this in their own way and on their own time.

While middle-aged Soviet immigrants in Brighton often have difficulty adjusting to New York, younger adults, ages twenty-five to thirty-five, step easily into a New York City life-style. Those who already had professional training or had begun practicing their professions before leaving the USSR often work toward qualifying to practice their professions in the United States. A good number who came here in their teens have been able to take advantage of the fine training given in math and the sciences in Soviet schools. They have done quite well in New York schools and colleges, many obtaining degrees in engineering or other professional fields. Others, after a couple of years of schooling or technical training in New York, have been able to find work in Manhattan as secretaries, electronics technicians, word processors, hair dressers, department store buyers and a variety of other jobs. They climb the stairs to the elevated train each morning in Brighton, dressed in finely tailored business clothes, carrying folded copies of *Novaya Russkaya Slova* or *Novye Amerikanets* under their arms. Their English is accented, and Russian is still the language they speak to each other, but these largely big-city born and bred people are comfortable in New York.

Some young immigrant adults have already left Brighton, and many others would like to move. To many of the younger generation of Soviet immigrants, Brighton represents only a temporary stop on the way to higher-status American communities. They have little interest in becoming part of an old-time Jewish community like Brighton—and they are ambitious. They have a lifetime of work and moneymaking ahead of them and they are determined to achieve some version of the American "good life" which they dreamed of while still in the USSR.

Children and Teenagers

The youngest children of these young adults have made the transition to American life as easily as their parents, perhaps even more easily. Children who left the Soviet Union between the ages of three and ten have tended to pick up English very quickly and without a trace of an accent. Often, in fact, it is these children who teach their parents English. In families where parents have had difficulty learning to read English, these children act as translators, reading official communications from the city, the schools, and the U.S. Immigration and Naturalization Service.

When asked if they consider themselves American or Russian, almost all of the young children will answer American without a moment's hesitation. Few remember much about the country of their birth; Brighton is the only home they know. Although they speak Russian at home, most speak English to each other, replete with all the latest Brooklyn slang. And, like American-born youngsters, they dress in jeans, T-shirts, baseball jackets, and stylishly cut sweaters and sneakers.

The majority of these Soviet children now attend one of Brighton's two public elementary schools. As I mentioned earlier, almost two-thirds of Soviet youngsters end up attending New York City public schools. However, most, if not all, start out, for at least a year, in a *yeshiva*, or religious academy. Why do they leave these schools? "There's too much praying," remarks Misha, a boy of eleven. His parents agreed. "I came to learn, not to pray," says Natalya, a girl in the seventh grade. Unhappy with the religious atmosphere and the rigid discipline of many religious schools, they find that they are more comfortable in public schools, despite the larger classes and lack of personal attention.

The teenage brothers and sisters of these children have had a harder time adjusting to American life. Neither religious nor public schools are easy settings for Soviet immigrant teens, after seven to ten years of Soviet schooling. "Like most teenagers," a counselor on the staff of one of Brighton's teen programs comments, "these Russian kids are concerned primarily with looking good, feeling good and fitting in. That's hard enough anywhere when you're sixteen. It's a lot harder when you come from a radically different country, when your first language, your upbringing, your way of thinking about the world are different from those of your classmates."

The problems of forging a distinct identity and asserting independence faced by all teenagers are compounded, for Soviet teens, by the problems involved in adjusting to a foreign culture. Added to this, they experience the emotional changes of adolescence while their parents, too, are going through the changes of immigration and rerooting. The result has been that some Soviet teenagers have changed their names, their styles, and the image they seek to project several times in the course of a year. As confused about their parents' identities as they are about their own, many Soviet teens have a very difficult time figuring out what place they want to occupy in American society.

The inevitable generation gap between parents and teenagers is exacerbated by the fact that immigrant parents experienced their adolescence in the Soviet Union while their children are growing up as immigrants in the United States. Both the reality and conception of adolescence in those two societies are very different. As a result the teens feel that their parents do not understand what is required of them every day in school and in their social lives. Forced into a situation where they must learn English quickly, both in order to do well in school and to fit in socially, they feel a tremendous amount of pressure. As one junior high school guidance counselor explained, "They do very well in math and science. Their training in those areas is far superior to what we offer. However, they are lacking in any real humanities training. So, not only must they struggle with English, they have to try and learn to think in a new way, to broaden their understanding of what schooling is about."

Thrown into deep waters immediately, some Soviet teenagers manage; others drop out of school as soon as they are of age, hoping to feel more at ease in a job than they do in school. In either case teenagers feel that whatever success they achieve has been done without their parents' help. Teenagers in the Soviet community are staunchly independent. With the access to the larger American culture that their facility with English affords them, they believe should come freedom to live their lives as they see fit.

Parents are panicked by this attitude. Schooled in the Soviet system, immigrant parents are shocked by the relative laxness and freedom of the New York City schools, and of American teen culture in general. "There is no respect for authority here," one parent told me, echoing the complaint most commonly voiced by Soviet immigrants. There is too much freedom in the United States, they say. "In Russia," remarks one father, "they put innocent people in jail. In America they let criminals run free in the streets. It's not safe either way." The greatest fear of Soviet immigrant parents, fueled by years of reading highly colored reports in the Soviet press about New York public schools, is that their children will become involved with drugs unless they are carefully watched. Although there is some experimentation with drugs, teen counselors say, it is not a serious problem with this group of young people.

Their most serious problems are in the area of identity confusion. "It is even hard to know what we are supposed to be becoming," one Russian teen commented. "Everybody here is from someplace else." The ethnic diversity of local public schools and the high percentage of students whose first language is not English means that Soviet teens do not stand out as much as they might elsewhere. However, this diversity confuses many Soviet teens who cannot figure out who they are supposed to emulate to become "more American." Few Soviet teenagers had any sense of the ethnic diversity of New York City before they arrived here. Many had never seen a black person, except perhaps an African student or diplomat. They were also unprepared for the strong ethnic identifications with which American born Jews, Italians, Puerto Ricans, and Irish distinguish themselves in Brooklyn. "Where are the Americans is all I want to know?" asked one Russian teenager. "I haven't met any yet."

Some teenagers solve this identity problem by emulating the group of students in their school that seems to be the "coolest," the best dressed and the least vulnerable. An extreme case is that of Igor, a fifteen-year-old who changed his name to Nicky. He refused to answer his parents when they called him by his given name, told new friends that he was Italian, and took to wearing the same clothing he saw on his Italian-American schoolmates. The major problem was that he had no Italian friends. His friends and family were all Soviet immigrants with whom he refused to speak in Russian. It was only through long attendance at the local RAP (Russian Adolescent Program) groups that he began to feel comfortable with a mixture of elements in his identity.

As Soviet immigrant teenagers become more accustomed to New

York life and as they enter young adulthood, most come to a surer sense of themselves and they develop identities with a mixture of Soviet, Jewish, New York, and American elements. An increasing number of dropouts are returning to graduate from public or Jewish high schools, and some even continue their education and go to college. Indeed, now that the immigration has slowed almost to a halt, the particular problems faced by first-generation Soviet immigrant teenagers are fading away.

COMMUNITY LIFE

Despite the fact that Soviet immigrants of different ages have distinct experiences of adjustment and daily life, most feel a strong sense of belonging to a larger Soviet immigrant community. Among earlier waves of Jewish immigrants to Brighton, social, political, and cultural organizations nurtured a sense of community. The Soviet Jews, accustomed by years of Soviet socialization to being discreet about their public meetings, have created few communal organizations. The many small Soviet businesses now open in Brighton reinforce a sense of collectivity among the new immigrants, providing them with an informal context where friends and neighbors can meet and converse. But it is the neighborhood's dozen Soviet-style restaurants that provide them with public space for the larger, formal gatherings that have come to be extremely popular among Brighton's Soviet Jews.

Brighton's Soviet-style restaurants vary in size from small luncheonettes, with counters and fast-cooked meals, to the sleek, cavernous National Restaurant, which caters affairs of up to 500 people. These restaurants serve many of the same functions that *landsmanshaftn* (village societies), workers' organizations, and benevolent associations served for earlier generations of Jewish immigrants. Not intended for casual clientele but for habitués, they are almost like private clubs where Soviet immigrants may go at the end of a hard day to share their frustrations and successes with others who can understand. Also they are the places where community members gather to celebrate special days—birthdays, anniversaries, weddings, and Bar Mitzvahs. Because these restaurants seek to cater to the Soviet community alone, not to the largely elderly community of first- and second-wave immigrants, nearly all are open only at night. During the day, then, Brighton Beach Avenue still has something of its old Yiddish flavor. It is crowded with shoppers and vendors and thick with the smell of Jewish cooking. Yiddish is still spoken in the knisheries and appetizing stores, in the dairy restaurants and in the home cooking stands where Brighton's older immigrants come to eat each day. But after dark, when the old stores close and the restaurants open, the Yiddish sounds and smells of the day give way to a flashy night life that is entirely Russian. Of all the changes the Soviet immigrants have wrought in Brighton Beach, this is the most dramatic—the transformation that occurs each night from Brighton Beach to "Little Odessa."

Russian Nights in Brighton Beach

Ten years ago Brighton Beach Avenue was completely quiet after dark. Now, from 8 P.M. until well after midnight the avenue is filled with little knots of people heading to or from Russian restaurants. Everyone is dressed in the flashiest clothes they can afford. They speak animatedly in Russian, stopping every block or so to greet the friends and neighbors they inevitably meet on the only main street in this crowded little community. On weekends Soviet immigrants from Rego Park and Washington Heights make the trip for a night out in Brighton Beach. It is the center of Soviet immigrant nightlife.

Like the communal societies set up by earlier immigrants, the Soviet-style restaurants are modeled on the gathering places Soviet Jews patronized in their home cities and towns. Because the Brighton Soviet community comes from all over the western USSR, the new neighborhood restaurants reflect that diversity. One reason why the community can support so many restaurants on one street is that each caters to a different regional taste. Kavkas serves Caucasian food, for example. The Zodiac serves Odessan-style Continental. The Uzbek, naturally enough, serves Uzbeki food. The music (and almost all offer nightly live performances) also varies according to the regional affiliation of the restaurant management. While the music in all the restaurants is a hybrid of contemporary Russian, American disco, and traditional Jewish rhythms and melodies, each mixture is distinctive to the region of the band members.

These immigrant restaurants have their roots in Soviet Jewish culture, where it was not only difficult but dangerous for Jews to gather in groups. Hidden behind carefully camouflaged facades, these restaurants were among the only places where Soviet Jews could come together in a relaxed atmosphere. These gatherings provided vital psychological release, especially during the long, anxious period of waiting for official permission to emigrate (Sirotin n.d.). In Brighton these restaurants still offer a vital release from the daily pressures faced by newly arrived immigrants.

"The spirit of Soviet Jewry really came to life in restaurants," Alexander Sirotin (n.d.) has written. "There, ordinary workers, by day forced to comply with Soviet officials, to submit to constant harassment, could finally become people of character, of unique identity. This was the only place where they could remove all masks, to reveal openly a Jewish face. In the absence of other possibilities, the restaurant became the center of life for many Jews in Soviet cities. This custom was carried here. That is certainly one of the reasons why Russian restaurants are so popular in Brighton now."

The custom of camouflaging the facades of their restaurants is also one that Soviets in Brighton brought with them from the USSR. This custom, which reflects both a lingering distrust of strangers and a desire to discourage tourists from entering, distinguishes these restaurants from most other ethnic eating places in New York City. Brighton's Russian restaurants advertise almost exclusively by word of mouth, and they waste little money on exterior decoration. None are open to the street. Those that have windows at street level block them with opaque curtains. The National has only a wooden door opening into a blank, black wall. The Sadko, a two-floor black and silver discotheque, has recently put up a new wooden facade, with portholes high above the heads of passersby. But for five years after it opened only an abandoned pizzeria faced the street, left exactly as it was on the day it closed, complete with white counter and pizza ovens. The only change that had been made was on the sign that had originally said "Mama Mia Pizzeria" and now said "Sadko Pizzeria." The entrance to this disco was a plain door hidden away on a side street; from Brighton Beach Avenue there was no way in. Though confusing to outsiders this kind of secrecy made the Soviet immigrants more comfortable. As a result of these precautions strangers rarely venture into these places and, when they do, they are often left feeling that they have intruded on a family celebration.

A Bar Mitzvah at the Odessa

Of all these community restaurants, one of the largest and friendliest is the Odessa. I have returned to the Odessa many times over the years to observe and take part in a variety of community celebrations. One of the most interesting was a Bar Mitzvah which took place on a Friday night in the fall of 1983. This event embodied all of the elements that make places like the Odessa important to the Soviet community. It was a celebration of the abundance of American life, a public expression of Jewishness, and finally, a chance for immigrants to eat together, dance and drink together, and give thanks for mutual support.

The Odessa occupies a long, low-ceilinged room above a bakery and tailor shop on Brighton Beach Avenue. The style of the restaurant is European, with long tables creating a family-style atmosphere even for those who come to dine alone or in couples. The price-fixed menu has only recently been supplemented by a selection of à la carte entrees which, according to the restaurant's newest owner, was a step toward Americanization. Though some people come to the Odessa for a night out, it is really a place for large parties, for celebrations not only of individual passage from one stage of life to another, but of an immigrant community's passage from old country to new. And to the people gathered here America means two things: the good life and freedom. The glittering decor, the extravagant spreads of food, the elaborate service, and expensive clothing are tributes to the good life for which they came. The gathering itself, open and Jewish, is a celebration of freedom.

At the time of the Bar Mitzvah described below the Odessa was done in blue and silver, with crystal chandeliers, gold-speckled ceilings, and a plaster Cupid fountain spouting multicolored water. At the fountain stood Semyon Kommissar, a poet friend. "You don't know what it means that we can just get together like this, in public, to celebrate a Bar Mitzvah," he told me. Kommissar had been involved in organizing Jewish protest gatherings in Minsk during his last decade in the Soviet Union. But these gatherings had to be carefully timed and planned, he recalled, to minimize the possibility of individual arrests. Most often they were held on days when Soviet authorities were busy with official government-sponsored celebrations. Though Kommissar recognizes that positive Jewish identification is hard for many of his fellow immigrants, he maintains that the spark of Jewishness, of pride in tradition, is there in most Soviet Jews. Once the fear is removed it is possible for Soviet immigrants to become more open about their Jewish feelings.

Kommissar looked around. "Now I know I am in America," he said. "In Minsk I had to circumcise my grandson secretly, hiding, afraid all the time that someone would report me and I would be arrested. In Minsk, if this many Jews were gathered together for any reason the KGB would already be knocking at the windows." Kommissar recalls the fear of the small group of Jews who gathered in Minsk in 1971 to mourn publicly for the Jewish victims of the Nazis. But this was a conscious act of protest, not a celebration. No one had celebrated Bar Mitzvah there. He laughed. "It couldn't happen."

I had come to dinner with several American-born Jews, two Polish Jewish immigrants, and a non-Jew knowledgeable about Jewish religious culture. "But this is Friday night," one of them said, "after sundown. It's already Sabbath. How can they hold a party on Friday night?"

"And there's a band," said another, who gasped audibly when the electric guitars accompanied the Bar Mitzvah boy's singing of the blessings over food and wine. As the father of the boy blessed his son, praying through the microphone that he become a source of pride to the Jewish people and to his new country, someone at my table noticed that shrimp, strictly forbidden by Jewish dietary laws, was being served to the Bar Mitzvah guests. "Amazing," he whispered. A hundred flashbulbs popped. The guests heartily applauded the boy and sat down to eat their shrimp.

Between the shrimp and the main course the guests got up to dance. Crowding onto the tiny dance floor they formed three circles, one inside the other, and with arms across each other's shoulders, they proceeded to twirl to the electrified Russian and Yiddish disco numbers that the Odessa band specializes in.

"It is possible," Kommissar said, explaining the unusual ceremony, "that we have forgotten everything about the Jewish religion. But we have not forgotten that we are Jews. Can you understand what it is to these parents, and even more to the grandparents, to hear their boy recite Hebrew prayers in front of the community, their friends and neighbors? This is a wonderful thing for everyone here, not just for the family. This is something we did not even dream of. This is something we are only just learning here in America."

Dinner was served—brisket of beef, stuffed derma, and chicken, then fruit and pastries and coffee. Afterward the guests rose to dance again. The band launched into a medley of Yiddish show tunes that had somehow made their way from New York's Lower East Side to Odessa and now back to Little Odessa—Brighton Beach. At midnight the band struck up its theme song—"Oy Odess." Everyone kicked off their shoes and began to sing. Even the outsiders at my table were drawn into the party, invited by the guests first to drink to the boy, then to his grandparents, then to Odessa and finally to America. Soon nearly everyone was on the dance floor, with arms around each other dancing in concentric circles. The dancing lasted until 2 A.M.

Since that evening, the Odessa has changed its colors several times, reflecting the speed with which Brighton's Soviet immigrants seem to be adapting to American life. The mirrors on the wall are gone; so are the crystal chandeliers, the gold sparkles, and the plaster Cupid fountain. Now the main room of the Odessa is red and silver. Downstairs, a street-level storefront has been fixed up as The Odessa Lobster and Crêpe House. The Odessa, in its new form, is as popular as ever. The clientele is the same, but their styles of dress have changed, as if to go along with the toned-down decor. There is less purple chiffon and pink satin, less makeup on the women these days. Fewer men are wearing their shirts opened to the chest. Black and white evening clothes have made their way onto the new, still tiny dance floor. Circle dancing seems to have almost entirely disappeared, giving way to couple dancing. And, on my most recent excursion to the restaurant, the behavior seemed more reserved, perhaps more consciously "American." No toasts were exchanged between tables, no invitations to dance extended by strangers.

Yet despite the quick changes in decor, etiquette, and clothing styles the Odessa remains much the same. It is still a safe place for immigrants to try out newly acquired American styles and to show off newly acquired American wealth. The language of the management, customers, and performers is still Russian. For this nonreligious people, still uncomfortable forming open political and cultural associations, restaurants like the Odessa remain the most important communal centers they have, the only places of their own making where they can go to feel a sense of solidarity with others like them, to celebrate themselves and their accomplishments.

CONCLUSION

Each in their own way, Soviet Jews of all ages have been adjusting to New York life. For teens and many working-age adults this experience has meant not only adapting to the Jewish immigrant milieu of Brighton Beach but also to the cosmopolitan business world of Manhattan or the mixed ethnic and American youth culture of New York City public schools. For those too old or too young to work, and for those who make their living in Brighton Beach, this adjustment has involved negotiating between the Soviet urban culture from which they came and the culture of the immigrant community of Russian and Polish Jews into which they have moved. In the process, Soviet Jews have had to come to terms with the Ashkenazic Jewish heritage they share with older immigrants in Brighton. Initial hostilities between the Soviet immigrants and other Brighton Jews have begun to fade and a sense of community has begun to develop.

The presence of 25,000 Soviet Jews has transformed both the face and the community life of Brighton Beach. From a dying strip of old stores, Brighton Beach Avenue has turned into a thriving commercial center. In a few years this almost exclusively elderly community again has become a multigenerational community with children, young and middle-aged adults as well as a large population of elderly. Long a neighborhood with a Yiddish flavor, Brighton Beach lately sounds, smells, and tastes increasingly Russian. And yet, with all these changes, the Soviet influx has, in a very important way, preserved something essential about Brighton—its Jewish immigrant culture. Of all the old-time Jewish immigrant neighborhoods in New York, Brighton is the only one which houses vital communities of first-, second- and third-wave Eastern European Jewish immigrants. Their interaction within the narrow confines of one crowded urban neighborhood—their linguistic, cultural, and political cross-fertilizations—have produced a unique type of Jewish community life.

As for the future of Brighton's Soviet immigrants, many of the youngest generation are likely to leave Brighton for more affluent areas, just as the children of first- and second-wave immigrants did in the 1950s and 1960s. Most of the older Soviet immigrants, however, will probably remain in Brighton. The third who are over sixty have already become part of Brighton's larger senior citizen community. As for those between forty and sixty, most will probably stay in Brighton, ensuring the neighborhood's future as an elderly Jewish immigrant enclave. And yet, as much as they are growing accustomed to Brighton life, much as it has rekindled in them a sense of pride in Jewishness and in the Eastern European Jewish tradition, they continue to transform the old neighborhood and to give it a decidedly Soviet flavor.

NOTES

1. These figures were supplied by Project ARI: Action for Russian Immigrants. The figures of 20,000 and 25,000 for Brighton include children of Soviet Jews born in the United States.
2. My field research among Soviet Jews in Brighton—part of a larger project on the community as a whole—was conducted full-time during the summer and fall of 1980 through the winter of 1981 and has continued on and off since that time through the present. During these years I interviewed over fifty Soviet immigrants of different ages and generations. I also observed the immigrants in informal settings—in their homes and stores—as well as in more formal contexts such as restaurants, synagogues, Brighton community centers, and schools. I especially wish to thank my Russian teacher Marya (a pseudonym), the actor/writer Alexander Sirotin, and the poet Semyon Kommissar, who served as inside cultural interpreters, helping me to understand the inner workings of Soviet community life in ways I never could have without them. Marya's name, like the names of most persons mentioned in this essay, has been changed. In a few cases, however, real names have been used at the request of the speaker.
3. Unfortunately, little has been written on Soviet Jews in New York. Kessner and Caroli (1981) have a chapter on Soviet Jews in their book on new immigrants in New York and an article by Simon, Shelley, and Schneiderman (1986) compares the socioeconomic adjustment of Soviet Jewish men and women based on a survey of 900 Soviet immigrants in fourteen U.S. cities, including New York. Most of what has been published, however, is journalistic, focusing on isolated crimes, or, less sensationally, on tourist attractions, places to shop and eat in Brighton Beach. More detailed information about the Soviet immigrant community in Brighton can be obtained from Project ARI, 3300 Coney Island Avenue, Brooklyn, N.Y. 11235. The magazine *Insight* (Euro Jewish Publications, London),

covers a wide range of issues concerning Soviet Jews and emigration. See also the journal *Soviet Jewish Affairs* for articles on Jewish life in the Soviet Union. Literature on Soviet Jewry that has been particularly helpful in preparing this article includes writings by Aksenov (1979); Birman (1979); Dinstein (1979); Hirszowicz (1977); Lamm (1967); Sirotin (n.d.); and Struve (1967).

REFERENCES

Aksenov, Michael Meerson. 1979. "The Influence of the Jewish Exodus on the Democratization of Soviet Society." In David Sidorsky, ed., *Essays on Human Rights*. Philadelphia: Jewish Publication Society of America.

Birman, Igor. 1979. "Soviet Jews and Emigration." *Soviet Jewish Affairs* 9:46–63.

Dinstein, Yoram. 1979. "Soviet Jewry and International Human Rights." In David Sidorsky, ed., *Essays on Human Rights*. Philadelphia: Jewish Publication Society of America.

Hirszowicz, Lukasz. 1977. "The Soviet-Jewish Problem: Internal and International Developments." In Lionel Kochan, ed., *The Jews in Soviet Russia Since 1917*. London: Oxford University Press.

Kessner, Thomas and Betty Caroli. 1981. *Today's Immigrants, Their Stories*. New York: Oxford University Press.

Lamm, Hans. 1967. "Jews and Judaism in the Soviet Union." In William C. Fletcher and Anthony J. Strover, eds., *Religion and the Search for New Ideals in the USSR*. New York: Praeger.

Simon, Rita, Louise Shelley, and Paul Schneiderman. 1986. "The Social and Economic Adjustment of Soviet Jewish Women in the United States." In Rita Simon and Caroline Brettell, eds., *International Migration: The Female Experience*. Totowa, N.J.: Rowman and Allanheld.

Sirotin, Alexander. N.d. "The Wandering Jew." Unpublished essay translated from Russian to English by Annelise Orleck (1981).

Struve, Nikita. 1967. "Pseudo-Religious Rites Introduced by the Party Authorities." In William C. Fletcher and Anthony J. Strover, eds., *Religion and the Search for New Ideals in the USSR*. New York: Praeger.

Index